Alexander Johnston

Connecticut

A Study of a Commenwealth-Democracy

Alexander Johnston

Connecticut

A Study of a Commenwealth-Democracy

ISBN/EAN: 9783742811837

Manufactured in Europe, USA, Canada, Australia, Japa

Cover: Foto ©ninafisch / pixelio.de

Manufactured and distributed by brebook publishing software
(www.brebook.com)

Alexander Johnston

Connecticut

American Commonwealths

CONNECTICUT

A STUDY OF A COMMONWEALTH-DEMOCRACY

BY

ALEXANDER JOHNSTON

PROFESSOR OF JURISPRUDENCE AND POLITICAL ECONOMY IN
PRINCETON COLLEGE

BOSTON AND NEW YORK
HOUGHTON, MIFFLIN AND COMPANY
The Riverside Press, Cambridge
1887

Copyright, 1887,
By ALEXANDER JOHNSTON.

All rights reserved.

The Riverside Press, Cambridge:
Electrotyped and Printed by H. O. Houghton & Co.

To
TIMOTHY DWIGHT,
PRESIDENT OF YALE UNIVERSITY.

THEIRS is a pure republic, wild, yet strong,
   A " fierce democracie," where all are true
To what themselves have voted — right or wrong —
   And to their laws denominated " blue ; "
If red, they might to Draco's code belong.
   A vestal State, which power could not subdue,
Nor promise win, — like her own eagle's nest,
Sacred, — the San Marino of the West.

A justice of the peace, for the time being,
   They bow to, but may turn him out next year;
They reverence their priest, but, disagreeing
   In price or creed, dismiss him without fear :
They have a natural talent for foreseeing
   And knowing all things; and, should Park appear
From his long tour in Africa, to show
The Niger's source, they 'd meet him with — We know.

They love their land because it is their own,
   And scorn to give aught other reason why;
Would shake hands with a king upon his throne,
   And think it kindness to his majesty;
A stubborn race, fearing and flattering none.
   Such are they nurtured, such they live and die.

      ·   ·   ·   ·   ·   ·   ·   ·

                                FITZ-GREENE HALLECK.

PREFACE.

THIS volume is not meant to deal mainly with the antiquarian history of Connecticut, with the achievements of Connecticut men and women, or with those biographical details which so often throw the most instructive side-lights on local history. These fields have been explored so thoroughly by abler hands that it would be presumption for the writer to enter them, unless to take advantage of the materials thus stored up. The volume is one of a "Commonwealth Series," and it aims to take the history of Connecticut from another side. Its purpose is to present certain features in the development of Connecticut which have influenced the general development of the State system in this country, and of the United States, and may be grouped as follows: —

I. Connecticut's town system was, by a fortunate concurrence of circumstances, even more independent of outside control than that of Massachusetts; the principle of local government had here a more complete recognition; and, in the form in which it has done best service, its beginning was in Connecticut.

II. The first conscious and deliberate effort on this continent to establish the democratic principle in control of government was the settlement of Connecticut; and her constitution of 1639, the first written and democratic constitution on record, was the starting-point for the democratic development which has since gained control of all our commonwealths, and now makes the essential feature of our commonwealth government.

III. Democratic institutions enabled the people of Connecticut to maintain throughout their colonial history a form of government so free from crown control that it became really the exemplar of the rights at which all the colonies finally aimed.

IV. Connecticut, being mainly a federation of towns, with neither so much of the centrifugal force as in Rhode Island, nor so much of the centripetal force as in other colonies, maintained for a century and a half that union of the democratic and federative ideas which has at last come to mark the whole United States.

V. The Connecticut delegates in the convention of 1787, by another happy concurrence of circumstances, held a position of unusual influence; the frame of their commonwealth government, with its equal representation of towns in one branch and its general popular representation in the other, had given them a training which enabled them to bend the form of our national constitution into a corresponding shape; and the peculiar constitution of our congress, in the different bases of the senate and house of representatives, was thus the result of Connecticut's long maintenance of a federative democracy.

VI. The first great effort at westward colonization, in the Wyoming country, was managed by Connecticut through her traditional system of free towns; and the example is enough to account for the subsequent power of this principle in the organization of the great Northwest.

VII. Individual capacity and energy, the natural fruit of a democratic system, have enabled the people of Connecticut to survive and prosper under the industrial revolution of later times, and to show that a commonwealth almost without natural advantages, and forced to rely almost entirely on the conversion of foreign products into other forms, may reach the highest degree of prosperity through the individual mechanical genius of her people.

For these reasons, the writer thinks that Connecticut has a claim to a high place among characteristic commonwealths; and that the antiquarian, biographical, and other features which usually abound in State histories, should in this instance be made subordinate to the study of her democracy and its influences. So far as the usual details can be given, and as they illustrate the controlling features of the volume, they have been used; but the volume is not bound to them.

Connecticut migration has been so great that it has been necessary to resist an almost constant temptation to diverge to the influence of Connecticut men and ideas in Vermont, New York, New Jersey, Ohio, Michigan, and other commonwealths. How large that influence has been is not widely known. Hollister states that in 1857 a single county (Litchfield) had been the birthplace of thirteen United States senators, twenty-two representatives from New York, fifteen supreme court judges in other States, nine presidents of colleges and eighteen other professors, and eleven governors and lieutenant-governors of States. The remark is attributed to Calhoun that he had seen the time when the members of congress born or educated in Connecticut lacked but five of being a majority. This must be taken with allowance, even if it were exact; for by no means all those educated in Connecticut have done much to carry Connecticut characteristics elsewhere. But, with all allowance, the foreign influence of Connecticut has been extraordinary. One must sympathize with the astonishment of the Frenchman who, hearing that this and that distinguished man, though a resident of another State, was born in Connecticut, went to the library to find the location of the State, and found that it was "nothing but a little yellow spot on the map." If there be anything in the claims for the work of the Connecticut commonwealth, they must be still further strengthened by the influence which the children of the commonwealth have carried into all sorts of channels.

The original scheme of the Series did not include the feature of foot-notes for authorities, and the writer followed the plan of putting his authorities into a bibliography. It has not seemed necessary to alter the arrangement, and it has been retained as an essay toward a bibliography of the commonwealth for the further use of students.[1] It is not meant to be implied that all, or nearly all, the books there named have been used exhaustively; very many of them have merely been referred to in order to keep the writer from going astray in matters on which their authors are authority and he is not. If he has, nevertheless, erred in these respects, he will feel under great obligations to those who will call his attention to the errors. The whole list is inserted in the hope that it may be of some preliminary service to those who shall further and more effectively prosecute the study of this commonwealth's great and honest work.

The approaching year 1889 is the 250th anniversary (or, to adopt the modern phrase, the quarter-millennial) of the Constitution of 1639, which seems to the writer the most far-reaching political work of modern times, and from which he conceives there are direct lines of communication running down to all the great events which followed,

[1] See Appendix, p. 397.

— to commonwealth organization and colonial resistance, to national independence and federation, to national union and organization, and even to national self-preservation and reconstruction. During the same year the nation will celebrate the one hundredth anniversary of the inauguration of its Constitution, to whose essence and expression Connecticut contributed so largely. This volume has been written in the hope that it may aid in widening the appreciation of Connecticut's first constitution, so that its birthday shall not pass without its fair share of remembrance.

PRINCETON, N. J., *May* 1, 1887.

CONTENTS.

CHAPTER I.
The Physical Geography of Connecticut 1

CHAPTER II.
Jurisdiction of the Connecticut Territory 7

CHAPTER III.
The First Settlements of Connecticut 14

CHAPTER IV.
The Indians of Connecticut 26

CHAPTER V.
The Pequot War 34

CHAPTER VI.
The Connecticut Colony 56

CHAPTER VII.
The New Haven Colony 83

CHAPTER VIII.
The Saybrook Attempt and its Failure 108

CHAPTER IX.
Connecticut until the Union 120

CHAPTER X.
The Two Colonies until the Union 143

CHAPTER XI.
The Charter and the Union 163

CHAPTER XII.
THE COMMONWEALTH. 1662-1763 192

CHAPTER XIII.
ECCLESIASTICAL AFFAIRS. 1636-1791 220

CHAPTER XIV.
FINANCIAL AFFAIRS. 1640-1763 248

CHAPTER XV.
COMMONWEALTH DEVELOPMENT. — WYOMING AND THE WESTERN RESERVE 265

CHAPTER XVI.
THE STAMP ACT AND THE REVOLUTION 285

CHAPTER XVII.
THE ADOPTION OF THE FEDERAL CONSTITUTION 315

CHAPTER XVIII.
INDUSTRIAL DEVELOPMENT 328

CHAPTER XIX.
CONNECTICUT IN THE WAR FOR THE UNION 374

CHAPTER XX.
CONCLUSION 385

APPENDIX. THE CONSTITUTION OF 1639 389
    BIBLIOGRAPHY 397
    THE GOVERNORS OF CONNECTICUT 401
    INDEX 403

NOTE. — The seal on the title-page is a fac-simile of that which appears on the title-page of the first revision of the laws of Connecticut, made in 1672 and published at Cambridge, Massachusetts, by S. Green in 1673. A discussion of the seals of Connecticut will be found in the Collections of the Connecticut Historical Society, I. 251.

CONNECTICUT.

CHAPTER I.

THE PHYSICAL GEOGRAPHY OF CONNECTICUT.

THE story of the commonwealth of Connecticut is one which is not strongly marked by the romantic element. Here are no witchcraft delusions or persecuted Quakers, no doughty paladins or high-souled Indian maidens, no drowsy burghers or wooden-legged governors, — only laborious and single-minded men building a new state on a new soil, exemplifying in the process the tendency of their race, when placed in a wilderness, to revert to the ancestral type of civil government, ignoring the excrescences which centuries have bred upon it. The record of their work need not lose value from its simplicity.

Connecticut is the furthest southwest of the little group of six American commonwealths to which the popular name of New England has been attached. It is of oblong shape, its northern and southern boundaries being about eighty-eight and one hundred miles long respectively, and its eastern and western boundaries forty-five and seventy-two miles. The northern and eastern boundaries are nearly straight lines east and west, and north and south, respectively. The western boundary is irregular at the southern extremity. The irregularities will be considered more fully hereafter, as they are the embodied mementos of certain steps by which the material form of the commonwealth was built up. The irregular southern coast is washed by the waters of Long Island Sound, beyond which lies the island which nature, confirmed by law, assigned to Connecticut, though the greed of the house of Stuart, superior to both law and nature, transferred it permanently to New York. The area of Connecticut is 4,990 square miles, about one third that of Denmark and not quite one half that of the Netherlands.

The trend of the rivers will indicate the general nature of the surface of the commonwealth, which is a succession of north and south hill ranges, separated by river valleys. The great central valley, about twenty miles in width, is drained by the river Connecticut as far south as Middletown, where the stream, forcing an outlet between two encroaching cliffs, pursues its way to the Sound at Saybrook, while the valley extends southwest to New Haven. This central valley, the seat of the early colonization, has an ideal agricultural soil, a deep, rich loam, as far south as the point where the river leaves it; thence to New Haven it is more sandy and less profitable. The smaller and more broken valleys of the eastern part of the commonwealth, the former "Pequot Country," where the hill summits are not of great elevation, attracted the early settlers through their advantages for grazing: their water power has since proved a greater source of wealth from manufactures. The western part of Connecticut is even more broken than the eastern, and the sharp and ragged character of the hill-range summits make them a somewhat greater obstacle to east and west travel. Rough as is the general surface of the State, its highest point is less than 1,000 feet above sea-level.

Agriculture, in its various forms, was the first inducement to settlement; but the settlers soon found that the soil contained metals. Of these, iron alone was profitable; the manufacture of nails of all sizes was for a long time the principal home industry for the colonists in their leisure hours. Much of the iron used for the weapons of the Revolution came from Connecticut; and its hematite ore still furnishes the best iron of its class in the country. Copper and lead exist in sufficient amount to lure a never-ending stream of adventurers into financial difficulties. The copper mines of Simsbury (now in East Granby) were discovered about 1705, ruined a number of successive proprietors, and were finally made the state prison. They furnished the material for the "Granby coppers," coined in 1737, and for other coins, including the first United States coinage. There is even an *ignis fatuus* of gold and silver. The rocks of Connecticut have proved richer than a gold mine to those who have developed them. Lime-stone, marble, brown-stone, and flagging-stone are found in excellent quality and unlimited amount, and a large portion of the State leaves its borders annually in this form of export. The supply of feldspar and other minerals has been developed as sharper demand for them has arisen.

The beautiful southern shore of Connecticut, which holds countless pictures in every mile of its extent, has many harbors, and one, that of New London, has advantages beyond the others. There was not, however, in early years, sufficient agricultural wealth or other material support behind these harbors to build up any great foreign trade, beyond a moderate export of mules, live stock, and some food products to the West Indies; and, in later years, the railroad has been a channel sufficiently capacious to provide for the outflow and inflow of the wealth in whose production it has been so essential a factor in Connecticut. The time will come when the harbors of Connecticut will be a necessary vent for foreign trade, but it has not yet come.

To an intending English colonist in 1630, considering this oblong as an unbroken wilderness, there would have been in it two points of great material advantage. One was the upper valley of the Connecticut, with its rich soil, its broad meadows, and its capacity for luxuriant vegetation; and this garden spot was the breach to which the first assaulting party naturally directed its course. The other was the inviting haven at the mouth of the Thames River, apparently designed by nature for the site of a great commercial city; and this was seized during the first decade. There were other minor advantages in other parts of the territory, such as the trade with the Indians for skins, or the pursuit of the fish with which Connecticut's waters and shore have always been stocked; but these two spots, the upper Connecticut Valley and the site of the present city of New London, were those to which material interests most strongly turned the first immigration. Succeeding companies, finding these spots occupied, were filtered through them into the surrounding portions of the territory.

Material interests, however, were far from being the only or controlling incentives to settlement. The New Haven company deliberately passed by the Thames River and sacrificed its preëminent commercial advantages, which must have been sufficiently evident to the shrewd merchant who was at the head of the enterprise; and it is at least not an improbable notion that the sacrifice was grounded in the desire to give religion a place of recognized and permanent superiority to commerce in the new settlement. The first break from Massachusetts into the Connecticut Valley was governed by religious, as it was actuated by material, motives. To the Connecticut settler, religion was an essential part of daily life and politics, and logic was an essential part of religion. Town and church were but two sides of the same thing. Differences of opinion there must be, in church as well as in town matters; and, when the respective straight lines had diverged sufficiently, a rupture became inevitable. The minority, unwilling to resist the majority or to continue in illogical union with it, preferred to begin a new plantation, even in a less hospitable location. Thus, every religious dispute usually gave rise to a new town, until the faintest lines of theological divergence were satisfied; while the original disputants, finding that a distance of even a few miles was enough to soften down differences which once seemed intolerable, were able to live together in congregational unity and harmony.

These three — Hartford, New Haven, and New London, and mainly the two former — were thus the openings through which immigration flowed in, and, under natural pressure, was distributed over the whole territory, even those less inviting portions of it which would have waited longer for settlement but that the pressure from behind made distribution easier than return.

CHAPTER II.

JURISDICTION OF THE CONNECTICUT TERRITORY.

THE claim of England to the jurisdiction of the territory included in Connecticut rested on the discoveries of the Cabots in 1497, and more especially in 1498. This claim, however, was allowed to lie dormant until the organization of the London and Plymouth companies in 1606, when the territory now in Connecticut was included in the grant to the Plymouth Company. No effort was made to reduce this territory to possession. The Dutch were allowed to plant a colony at New Amsterdam, and the only white men who adventured on Long Island Sound were occasional Dutch skippers. The first of these was Adrian Blok, who in 1614 found the mouth of the Connecticut River, and explored the river as far north as the present site of Hartford. As the tides affect the Connecticut much less than they do the Hudson, the Dutch naturally gave the former the name of Varsche (or Fresh) River. Blok was merely a discoverer, and he sailed on to Narragansett Bay, leaving but a geographical impress on the territory, whose importance to the Dutch lay only in its trade in peltries.

In 1620, and without the original permission of the Plymouth Company, English immigration fixed its first grip on the New England territory. The Plymouth Company itself did none of the work of colonization. It gave or sold patents for colonies, and, after a reorganization, gave up its imbecile existence in 1635, and returned its charter to the king, having first carefully divided up the soil among its own members. The allotments which are of interest in our subject were those of the Duke of Richmond and the Earl of Carlisle, between the Hudson and Connecticut rivers; and those of Sir Ferdinando Gorges and the Marquis of Hamilton, between the Connecticut River and Narragansett Bay. None of these grants was ever asserted or made troublesome to the colonists, with the exception of the Hamilton grant.

The common story in our histories is that the Council of Plymouth in 1630 granted the territory now in Connecticut to the Earl of Warwick, and that he, in 1631, transferred it to Viscount Say and Sele, Lord Brooke, and others, who were disposed to establish another Puritan colony in New England. They were detained in England by the approach of civil war; but their agents, Winthrop at Boston and Fenwick at the mouth of the Connecticut River, maintained their claims, and gave the settlers in the upper Connecticut Valley either a private or a tacit permission to enter their domain. In 1662, with the consent of the surviving patentees, the jurisdiction was transferred to the Connecticut colony, which could thus claim unbroken continuity of title from the beginning of English colonization in America.

The insistence of Connecticut authorities on this chain of evidence was undoubtedly due in great measure to the desire to make out a title paramount to anything which the rival New Haven colony could offer, and to put the New Haven colonists into the legal position of original trespassers, whose defect of title could never be cured after the grant of the charter in 1662. Even after this result had been attained, and New Haven had submitted to incorporation with Connecticut, another motive to continue the old claim was found in the claims of the Hamilton family and the colony's desire to antedate them with its own. The story above given made out an admirably harmonious title from beginning to end; and it was natural that it should become the official Connecticut account.

The foundation of the whole account, the grant to Warwick, is altogether mythical; no one has ever seen it, or has heard of any one who claims to have seen it. It is not mentioned even in the grant from Warwick to the Say and Sele patentees in 1631. In that document, "Robert, Earl of Warwick, sendeth greeting in our Lord God everlasting to all people unto whom this present writing shall come." He "gives, grants, bargains, sells, enfeoffs, aliens, and confirms" to the Viscount Say and Sele, Lord Brooke, John Pym, John Hampden, and others, the soil from the Narragansett River to the Pacific Ocean, and all jurisdiction " which the said Robert, Earl of Warwick, now hath or had or might use, exercise, or enjoy." What jurisdiction he had, or whence he had acquired it, he is careful not to say; the deed is a mere quitclaim, which warrants nothing, and does not even assert title to the soil transferred. In the Hamilton grant, on the contrary, the claim of title is carefully and fully stated. Why the Warwick transaction took this peculiar shape, why Warwick transferred, without showing title, a territory which the original owners granted anew to other patentees in 1635, are questions which are beyond conjecture. It is evident, however, that the New Haven colonists were until 1662 on an absolute equality with their brethren of Connecticut; that all were legally trespassers; and that the charter of 1662 could have no retroactive effect in validating the Say and Sele title, for that was a nullity. The charter of 1662 is the only legal title of Connecticut; the only legal titles prior to it, the grants of 1635, were barred by prescription before the Hamilton heirs undertook to prosecute their claim. In yielding to the final junction, New Haven yielded to royal power, not to a better title enforced by law.

The jurisdiction of Connecticut had a far better

title than could have been conferred by any charter; and the titles of both Connecticut and New Haven stood on exactly the same footing. In 1630 the territory was a wilderness. The king of England had laid claim to it by virtue of the undisputed fact that Sebastian Cabot might possibly have caught a distant glimpse of it as he passed by the coast more than a century before. The king granted it to a company which had not yet either settled or granted it. Just before the outbreak of the Civil War in England, the territory was reduced to possession by immigrants, who quieted the claims of the Indians by contract, and enforced the contract by public force. The Civil War and its consequences upon royal authority lasted long enough to cover the time which human law takes as a title by prescription. When Charles II. returned, who could show a better title to the soil of Connecticut than the colonists themselves?

This could cover, at the best, only the title to the soil; the civil jurisdiction is of more importance. The first settlements, at Hartford, Windsor and Wethersfield, were an irruption of subjects of the king of England into an unorganized and unoccupied territory, very much like the first settlements in the territory of Iowa, more than two centuries later. But there was one very great difference between the two cases: the Iowa settlement was an irruption of individuals; the Connecticut settlement was an irruption of organized towns. In Massachusetts, the original towns, or "plantations," were hardly to be taken as organized governments; and the advent of the charter government reduced them, and subsequent towns as well, to a condition of subordination. In Connecticut, three fully organized Massachusetts towns passed out of the jurisdiction of any commonwealth, and proceeded to build up a commonwealth of their own; while in New Haven the original town and its successive allies entered their new locations without ever having owned connection with any commonwealth since leaving England. The commonwealth jurisdiction of Connecticut is peculiar in that it was the product, instead of the source, of its town system.

As a commonwealth, Connecticut has never lost the characteristics due to its origin. Although the commonwealth, by the royal charter of 1662, obtained a legal basis independent of the towns and superior to them in law, the towns have retained a marked individuality, and the commonwealth a narrowness of function, which indicate the original relations of both. When Connecticut undertook to push her claims in Wyoming and in Ohio, the instrument to which she instinctively turned was the town system, rather than the commonwealth. And she still is, in many respects, a congeries of towns, though the commonwealth spirit has grown stronger with the years. Curious and worthy of study as is the New England town system, there are few phases of it more worthy of study than the manner in which, in Connecticut, it succeeded in creating a commonwealth body for itself; in pushing back the asserted boundaries of its neighbors; and at last, when the royal power could no longer be evaded, in using the royal power to round out and complete its own form, as it could not have done itself without a fratricidal struggle with a sister colony.

CHAPTER III.

THE FIRST SETTLEMENTS OF CONNECTICUT.

DURING the ten years after 1620, the twin colonies of Plymouth and Massachusetts Bay had been fairly shaken down into their places, and had even begun to look around them for opportunities of extension. It was not possible that the fertile and inviting territory to the southwest should long escape their notice. In 1629, De Rasières, an envoy from New Amsterdam, was at Plymouth. He found the Plymouth people building a shallop for the purpose of obtaining a share in the wampum trade of Narragansett Bay; and he very shrewdly sold them at a bargain enough wampum to supply their needs, for fear they should discover at Narragansett the more profitable peltry trade beyond. This artifice only put off the evil day. Within the next three years, several Plymouth men, including Winslow, visited the Connecticut River, "not without profit." In April, 1631, a Connecticut Indian visited Governor Winthrop at Boston, asking for settlers, and offering to find them corn and furnish eighty beaver skins a year. Winthrop declined even to send an exploring party. In the midsummer of 1633, Winslow went to Boston to propose a joint occupation of the new territory by Plymouth and Massachusetts Bay; but the latter still refused, doubting the profit and the safety of the venture.

Three months later, Plymouth undertook the work alone. A small vessel, under command of William Holmes, was sent around by sea to the mouth of the Connecticut River, with the frame of a trading house and workmen to put it up. When Holmes had sailed up the river as far as the place where Hartford was afterward built, he found the Dutch already in possession. For ten years they had been talking of erecting a fort on the Varsche River; but the ominous and repeated appearance of New Englanders in the territory had roused them to action at last. John Van Corlear, with a few men, had been commissioned by Governor Van Twiller, and had put up a rude earthwork, with two guns, within the present jurisdiction of Hartford. His summons to Holmes to stop under penalty of being fired into met with no more respect than was shown by the commandant of Rensselaerswyck to his challengers, according to the veracious Knickerbocker. Holmes declared that he had been sent up the river, and was going up the river, and furthermore he went up the river. His little vessel passed on to the present site of Windsor. Here the crew disembarked, put up and garrisoned their trading house, and then returned home. Plymouth had at least planted the flag far within the coveted and disputed territory.

In December of the following year, a Dutch force of seventy men from New Amsterdam appeared before the trading house to drive out the intruders. He must be strong who drives a Yankee away from a profitable trade; and the attitude of the little garrison was so determined that the Dutchmen, after a few hostile demonstrations, decided that the nut was too hard to crack, and withdrew. For about twenty years thereafter, the Dutch held post at Hartford, isolated from Dutch support by a continually deepening mass of New Englanders, who refrained from hostilities, and waited until the apple was ripe enough to drop.

With respect to the claims of the Indians, the attitudes of the two parties to the struggle were directly opposite. The Dutch came on the strength of purchase from the Pequots, the conquerors and lords paramount of the local Indians. Holmes brought to the Connecticut River in his vessel the local sachems, who had been driven away by the Pequots, and made his purchases from them. The English policy will account for the unfriendly disposition of the Pequots, and, when followed up by the tremendous overthrow of the Pequots, for Connecticut's permanent exemption from Indian difficulties. The Connecticut settlers followed a straight road, buying lands fairly from the Indians found in possession, ignoring those who claimed a supremacy based on violence, and, in case of resistance by the latter, asserting and maintaining for Connecticut an exactly similar title, — the right of the stronger. Those who claimed right received it; those who preferred force were accommodated.

One route to the new territory, by Long Island Sound and the Connecticut River, had thus been appropriated. The other, the overland route through Massachusetts, was explored during the same year, 1633, by one John Oldham, who was murdered by the Pequots two years afterward. He found his way westward to the Connecticut River, and brought back most appetizing accounts of the upper Connecticut Valley; and his reports seem to have suggested a way out of a serious difficulty which had come to a head in Massachusetts Bay.

The colony of Massachusetts Bay was at this time limited to a district covering not more than twenty or thirty miles from the sea, and its greatest poverty, as Cotton stated, was a poverty of men. And yet the colony was to lose part of its scanty store of men. Three of the eight Massachusetts towns, Dorchester, Watertown, and Newtown (now Cambridge), had been at odds with the other five towns on several occasions; and the assigned reasons are apparently so frivolous as to lead to the suspicion that some fundamental difference was at the bottom of them. The three towns named had been part of the great Puritan influx of 1630. Their inhabitants were "new-comers," and this slight division may have been increased by the arrival and settlement, in 1633, of a number of strong men at these three towns, notably Hooker, Stone, and Haynes at Newtown. Dorchester, Watertown, and Newtown showed many symptoms of an increase of local feeling: the two former led the way, in October, 1633, in establishing town governments under "selectmen;" and all three neglected or evaded, more or less, the fundamental feature of Massachusetts policy, — the limitation of office-holding and the elective franchise to church-members. The three towns fell into the position of the commonwealth's opposition, a position not particularly desirable at the time and under all the circumstances.

The ecclesiastical leaders of Dorchester were Warham and Maverick; of Newtown, Hooker and Stone; of Watertown, Phillips. Haynes of Newtown, Ludlow of Dorchester, and Pynchon of Roxbury, were the principal lay leaders of the half-formed opposition. Some have thought that Haynes was jealous of Governor Winthrop, Hooker of Cotton, and Ludlow of everybody. But the opposition, if it can be fairly called an opposition, was not so definite as to be traceable to any such personal source. The strength which marked the divergence was due neither to ambition nor to jealousy, but to the strength of mind and character which marked the leaders of the minority.

Thomas Hooker and Samuel Stone were of Emmanuel College, Cambridge. Hooker began to preach at Chelmsford in 1626, and was silenced for non-conformity in 1629. He then taught school, his assistant being John Eliot, afterward the apostle to the Indians; but the chase after him became warmer, and in 1630 he retired to Holland and resumed his preaching. In 1632, he and Stone came to New England as pastor and teacher of the church at Newtown; and the two took part in the migration to Hartford. Here Hooker became the undisputed ecclesiastical leader of Connecticut until his death in 1647. John Warham and John Maverick, both of Exeter in England, came to New England in 1630, as pastor and teacher of Dorchester. Maverick died while preparing to follow his church, but Warham settled with his parishioners at Windsor, and died there in 1670. George Phillips, also a Cambridge man, came to New England in 1630, as pastor of the church at Watertown. He took no part in the migration, but lived and died at Watertown. Fate seems to have determined that Wendell Phillips should belong to Massachusetts.

Roger Ludlow was Endicott's brother-in-law. He came to New England in 1630, and settled at Dorchester. He was deputy governor in 1634, and seems to have been "slated," to use the modern term, for the governorship in the following year. But this private agreement among the deputies was broken, for some unknown reason, by the voters, who chose Haynes, perhaps as a less objectionable representative of the opposition. Ludlow complained so openly and angrily of the failure to carry out the agreement that he was dropped from the magistracy at the next election. He went at once to Connecticut, and was deputy governor there in alternate years until 1654. Incensed at the interference of New Haven to prevent his county, Fairfield, from waging an independent warfare against the Dutch, he went to Virginia in 1654, taking the records of the county with him. It is not known when or where he died. Pynchon, the third lay leader of the opposition, took part in the migration, but remained within the jurisdiction of Massachusetts, founding the town of Springfield.

At the May session of the Massachusetts General Court in 1634, an application for "liberty to remove" was received from Newtown. It was granted. At the September session, the request was changed into one for removal to Connecticut. This was a very different matter, and, after long debate, was defeated by the vote of the Assistants, though the Deputies passed it. Various reasons were assigned for the request to remove to Connecticut, — lack of room in their present locations, the desire to save Connecticut from the Dutch, and "the strong bent of their spirits to remove thither;" but the last looks like the strongest reason. In like manner, while the arguments to the contrary were those which would naturally suggest themselves, the weakening of Massachusetts, and the peril of the emigrants, the concluding argument, that "the removing of a candlestick" would be "a great judgment," seems to show the feeling of all parties that the secession was the result of discord between two parties.

Haynes was made governor at the next General Court. Successful inducements were offered to some of the Newtown people to remove to Boston, and some few concessions were made. But the migration which had been denied to the corporate towns had probably been begun by individuals. There is a tradition that some of the Watertown people passed this winter of 1634-5 at the place where Wethersfield now stands. In May, 1685, the Massachusetts General Court voted that liberty be granted to the people of Watertown and Roxbury to remove themselves to any place within the jurisdiction of Massachusetts. In March, 1636, the secession having already been accomplished, the General Court issued a "Commission to Several Persons to govern the people at Connecticut." Its preamble reads: "Whereas, upon some reasons and grounds, there are to remove from this our Commonwealth and body of the

Massachusetts in America divers of our loving friends and neighbors, freemen and members of Newtown, Dorchester, Watertown, and other places, who are resolved to transport themselves and their estates unto the river of Connecticut, there to reside and inhabit; and to that end divers are there already, and divers others shortly to go." This tacit permission was the only authorization given by Massachusetts; but it should be noted that the unwilling permission was made more gracious by a kindly loan of cannon and ammunition for the protection of the new settlements.

If it be true that some of the Watertown people had wintered at Wethersfield in 1634–5, this was the first civil settlement in Connecticut; and it is certain that, all through the following spring, summer, and autumn, detached parties of Watertown people were settling at Wethersfield. During the summer of 1635, a Dorchester party appeared near the Plymouth factory, and laid the foundations of the town of Windsor. In October of the same year, a party of sixty persons, including women and children, largely from Newtown, made the overland march and settled where Hartford now stands. Their journey was begun so late that the winter overtook them before they reached the river, and, as they had brought their cattle with them, they found great difficulty in getting everything across the river by means of rafts.

It may have been that the echoes of all these preparations had reached England, and stirred the tardy patentees to action. During the autumn of 1635, John Winthrop, Jr., agent of the Say and Sele associates, reached Boston, with authority to build a large fort at the mouth of the Connecticut River. He was to be " Governor of the River Connecticut " for one year, and he at once issued a proclamation to the Massachusetts emigrants, asking "under what right and preference they had lately taken up their plantation." It is said that they agreed to give up any lands demanded by him, or to return on having their expenses repaid. A more dangerous influence, however, soon claimed Winthrop's attention. Before the winter set in, he had sent a party to seize the designated spot for a fort at the mouth of the Connecticut River. His promptness was needed. Just as his men had thrown up a work sufficient for defense and had mounted a few guns, a Dutch ship from New Amsterdam appeared, bringing a force intended to appropriate the same place. Again the Dutch found themselves a trifle late ; and their post at Hartford was thus finally cut off from effective support.

This was a horrible winter to the advanced guard of English settlers on the upper Connecticut. The navigation of the river was completely blocked by ice before the middle of November ; and the vessels which were to have brought their winter supplies by way of Long Island Sound and the river were forced to return to Boston, leaving the wretched settlers unprovided for. For a little while, some scanty supplies of corn were obtained from the neighboring Indians, but this resource soon failed. About seventy persons straggled down the river to the fort at its mouth. There they found and dug out of the ice a sixty-ton vessel, and made their way back to Boston. Others turned back on the way they had come, and struggled through the snow and ice to "the Bay." But a few held their grip on the new territory. Subsisting first on a little corn bought from more distant Indians, then by hunting, and finally on ground-nuts and acorns dug from under the snow, they fought through the winter and held their ground. But it was a narrow escape. Spring found them almost exhausted, their unsheltered cattle dead, and just time enough to bring necessary supplies from home. The Dorchester people alone lost cattle to the value of two thousand pounds.

The Newtown congregation, in October, 1635, found customers for their old homes in a new party from England; and in the following June Hooker and Stone led their people overland to Connecticut. They numbered one hundred, with one hundred and sixty head of cattle. Women and children were of the party. Mrs. Hooker, who was ill, was carried on a litter; and the journey, of "about one hundred miles," occupied two weeks. Its termination was well calculated to dissipate the evil auguries of the previous winter. The Connecticut Valley in early June! Its green meadows, flanked by wooded hills, lay before them. Its oaks, whose patriarch was to shelter their charter, its great elms and tulip-trees, were broken by the silver ribbon of the river; here and there were the wigwams of the Indians, or the cabins of the survivors of the winter; and, over and through all, the light of a day in June welcomed the new-comers. The thought of abandoning Connecticut disappeared forever.

During the summer of 1636, the body of the church at Dorchester settled at Windsor, having Warham as its pastor. Maverick had died before the removal was completed. The Watertown people also completed their removal, having Henry Smith as pastor, Phillips remaining behind. Pynchon, with eight companions, settled at Springfield, just north of the boundary between Massachusetts and Connecticut. When the spring of 1637 had fairly opened, there were about eight hundred persons within the present limits of Connecticut, two hundred and fifty of whom were adult males and fighting men. Perhaps the "strong bent of spirit" to remove to a commonwealth where individuality was not to be sacrificed to "steady habits" was not entirely confined to Newtown, Watertown, and Dorchester.

CHAPTER IV.

THE INDIANS OF CONNECTICUT.

The aborigines of Connecticut did not differ from other New England Indians so much as to demand any extended notice. They were not numerous; the lowest and most probable estimate of their numbers is six or seven thousand, and the highest twenty thousand. The northeastern section of the territory was inhabited by the Nipmunks. The upper Connecticut separated the Tunxis Indians on its western banks from the Podunks on the eastern. To the south of both were the Wangunks. New Haven is now in the centre of the former territory of the Quinnipiacks. To the west of the Quinnipiacks were the Paugussetts, and to the west of them a great number of scattered tribes, known generally by the names of their respective sachems or of the English towns in which they dwelt.

All these tribes were alike unclean in their habits, shiftless in their mode of life, and much addicted to powowing, devil-worship, and darker immoralities, if we may trust the possibly hasty and prejudiced accounts of the early Puritan observers. The Indian rule, that all work is to be done by the women, was enforced in its full rigor; but the correlative virtue of prowess in war was not so prominent in the men, who were rather prone to shout at a distance than to expose their lives to the hazards of battle. They had, however, developed military science so far as to have become acquainted with the rudiments of fortification. It is not easy to say how far their constructions deserved the name of forts, but they were numerous, and were an advance on the ordinary Indian methods of fighting. The Connecticut Indians were indebted for the advance, not to natural genius, but to their chronic terror of their lords or enemies, the Mohawks.

The Five Nations of Iroquois in central New York had become the leading Indian power of eastern North America. Its original five members, the Mohawks, Oneidas, Onondagas, Cayugas, and Senecas, were increased by the addition of the Tuscaroras from North Carolina in 1712, and the confederacy was thereafter known as the Six Nations; but, at all periods of its history, the Mohawks were so emphatically the leading member that their name was regularly put by synecdoche for the whole. The Connecticut Indians, at any rate, never stopped to discriminate minutely between the various branches of the Six Nations, but, on the appearance of any of them, promptly fled with the panic-stricken cry, "The

Mohawks are coming!" There seems to have been hardly the thought of resistance, when, every year, two elders of the Mohawks appeared in Connecticut, passing from village to village, collecting tribute, and announcing the edicts of the great council at Onondaga. To this exercise of supremacy they seem to have made but one exception, the kindred tribe of the Pequots.

The Indians of Connecticut, Rhode Island, and probably Massachusetts, were originally of one blood, perhaps divided into a few strong tribes. A few years before the arrival of the English, according to tradition, a sept of the Mohegan blood from New York, crossing the Hudson and moving eastward to the Connecticut River, passed southward and conquered a permanent home for themselves on the shore of Long Island Sound, in the southeastern part of the present State. This irruption split the Indian population into two parts. To the east of the Pequots were the Narragansetts, the powerful tribe of Miantonomoh and Canonchet, dwelling in Rhode Island, but claiming still some portion of the soil of Connecticut. They were sufficiently intact to make head against the Pequots, and waged continual war with them; but, lacking the ferocity and fervor for war which was a Pequot characteristic, they had difficulty in maintaining their position. To the west of the Pequots, the pressure of the strangers on one side and the Mohawks on the other ground up the

Indians into that mass of petty tribes which has been referred to, none of which dared to offer resistance after the power of the Pequots had been once established, all being interested merely to escape the notice of their oppressors as far as possible. Thus the Pequots, with but seven hundred fighting men, were able to overawe all the western tribes, while maintaining equal warfare with the Narragansetts, whose warriors are variously estimated at from one to five thousand. There are no annals of Indian diplomacy from which we may learn how the Six Nations and the Pequots avoided collision in the matter of supremacy over their tributaries; but it is not probable that either power was intent on establishing a right of exclusive extortion. Both were satisfied by the payment of their respective tribute, and the Pequot irruption merely doubled the burden of the aboriginal inhabitants.

At the time of the English entrance to Connecticut, the grand sachem of the Pequots was Tatobam, or Sassacus. One of his sagamores was Uncas, whose grandmother was the sister of the grandfather of Sassacus. Uncas had connected himself still more closely with the sachem's house by taking the daughter of Sassacus in marriage. He was Sagamore of Mohegan, the most important Pequot district. His courage, strength, and cunning were remarkable even among the Pequots; and the relations between him and Sassacus soon became strained and finally broke. Unable to resist the grand sachem, Uncas fled to the Narragansetts, was allowed to return, rebelled again, and was again defeated and fled. It was inevitable that the coming of the English should act as a wedge on this rift in the conquering tribe, and should make its downfall the surer.

The Dutch had at first recognized the Pequots as lords paramount of the territory, and had made their purchases of land from them. But the Pequots, unable to restrain the savagery of their natures, had lain in wait for and killed some of their enemies at the Dutch trading-house, and had thus interfered very seriously with the course of trade. In retaliation, the Dutch had killed the father of Sassacus. Anxious to get rid of his troublesome neighbors, Sassacus had acquiesced in the invitation of Winthrop to furnish settlers for the Connecticut Valley. But when Holmes at last came, he brought back some of the old sachems, who had been expelled by the Pequots, and made his purchases of land from them. Furthermore, a certain lewd and drunken ship-captain named Stone, from Virginia, having brought his vessel into the Connecticut River during the summer of 1633, was taken for a Dutchman by the Pequots, who murdered him while he lay in a drunken sleep in his cabin. During the following year, Sassacus sent messengers who made a treaty with the government of Massachusetts Bay, by the

terms of which many of the difficulties between
his tribe and the English were put out of sight.
The Pequots were to allow the English to colonize
and trade within their borders; were to give up
the murderers of Stone; and were to pay a tribute
of wampum, a part of which was to be transferred
by the English to the Narragansetts, so as to bring
about a peace between these two ancient enemies
without subjecting the haughty Pequot chief to
the degradation of a personal appeal for cessation
of hostilities. The terms were largely nominal.
The English made no demand for those who had
murdered Stone, and Sassacus paid none of the
stipulated tribute and was asked for none.

The murder of John Oldham, in 1636, first
brought the English into collision with the Pequots. Oldham, with a crew of two boys and two
Narragansett Indians, had been trading with a
pinnace on the shore of the Pequot country, and
had passed on to Block Island. Here he was
killed by the Island Indians. The murder had
hardly taken place when John Gallop, who was
sailing from the Connecticut River to the east end
of Long Island, found Oldham's vessel in possession of Indians. He first fired duck-shot into the
naked Indian crew until he had driven them under
hatches, and then rammed Oldham's vessel until
all but four of the Indians had jumped overboard
and were drowned. Two surrendered, and he
made sure of one of them by throwing him over-

board. As the sea was rising he took Oldham's body into his vessel, and allowed the derelict to drift ashore with two of the Indians still in her hold.

It is difficult to see how the Pequots were concerned in all this. But Governor Vane and his council, of Massachusetts Bay, in sending Endicott with an expedition to punish the Block Islanders, assumed that the Pequots had harbored some of the murderers, and must be included in the punishment. No proof was offered to the indictment against the Pequots, who seem to have held the same place in the English mind that Habakkuk held in the Frenchman's, and to be "capable of anything." But Endicott gathered no laurels in his Pequot expedition. His ferocious antagonists did not wish to fight, and could hardly be persuaded to fight. A few of them, and none of the English, were killed and wounded; and the expedition, having satiated its wrath by burning the Indian wigwams and crops, returned to Boston.

Enough had been done to range the Pequots against the English. As a choice of evils, Sassacus proposed to the Narragansetts a treaty of alliance against the foreigners, but this was thwarted by the influence of Roger Williams, who induced the Narragansetts to send ambassadors to Boston and conclude a treaty with the English. The Pequots were thus left to maintain alone their ancient title, by courage, to their territory. They did not hesitate. The fort at Saybrook, whose commander, Lieutenant Gardiner, had strongly disapproved Endicott's expedition, was first attacked. A foraging party was cut off, and several men were captured and put to the torture. Other parties were similarly caught in ambuscades, and the fort was beleaguered through the whole winter. In the spring of 1637, the war was opened in the upper Connecticut Valley. The people of Wethersfield had agreed, in buying lands from Sequin, a friendly Indian, to allow him to remain within the town limits. The agreement was violated, and he was expelled. In revenge, he brought the Pequots down upon the little settlement. They almost took it by surprise, killed a number of the people, and inflicted considerable damage before they were driven off. Four days afterward, the successful Pequots sailed past the fort at Saybrook, waving the clothes of their victims and exhibiting two captive girls. The Pequot war had fairly begun, and, in the nature of things, it could be ended only by the extermination of one party or the other. For this severe strain upon an infant colony, the Connecticut colonists were indebted to the stupidity or willfulness of Governor Vane and his council. They must have appreciated Cromwell's subsequent estimate of the governor.

CHAPTER V.

THE PEQUOT WAR.

The Connecticut General Court met at Hartford May 1, 1637, the ninth meeting of that body which is on the records. It is not likely that it represented, as yet, more than eight hundred souls, though the proportion of fighting men in so young a colony must have been abnormally large. Its action was thorough-going. It resolved that there should be " an offensiue warr against the Pequoitt," and a draft of ninety men was ordered from the three towns, — forty-two from Hartford, thirty from Windsor, and eighteen from Wethersfield, — the whole to be under command of Captain John Mason, of Windsor. The minute distribution of the assessment of the requisition for stores upon the three towns, and the proviso that one half of the corn is to be baked into biscuit "if by any meanes they cann," are evidences of the poverty of the colony, and the resolution with which its rulers drove their demands upon its patriotism up to the highest possible point. It is certain that the people were nearly starving when they were thus called on for a full third of their able-bodied men.

Nine days after the call, May 10, the ninety men were ready, and, with seventy Mohegans under Uncas, who was thereafter the ally of the colonists, embarked on the river in three small vessels. Uncas and his men soon found the voyage uncomfortable, and begged to be allowed to make the trip to Saybrook by land. When Mason reached Saybrook, after five days of tedious sailing, he found Uncas there, exultant in the success of a battle with the Pequots, in which he had killed seven of his enemies and captured another, who had been living among the colonists as a spy. The spy could appeal to no law, civilized or savage, for safety; but it is a repulsive business to read the punishment which was allowed to be inflicted. He was handed over to the mercy of Uncas and his Mohegans, who tortured and roasted him, and finally ate him.

Lying wind-bound in front of the fort at Saybrook, Mason knew well that his motions were under the sharp eyes of Pequot scouts, and that his entry into the Thames River would find his enemies thoroughly prepared to meet him. Fortified by a council of war, and by an all-night prayer of the chaplain, Mr. Stone, he decided to disobey instructions, pass on to Narragansett Bay, and attack the Pequots from the eastward. The change of programme was no doubt watched carefully by the runners of Sassacus; and when the three vessels had passed the only available landing place in the Pequot country, the Thames or Pequot River, the doomed tribe abandoned itself to a sense of triumphant security : the white men had not dared attack them after all, but had chosen the less formidable Indians of Block Island or the Bay as the objects of their revenge. The danger had passed them by.

On Saturday, May 30, the little squadron came to anchor in Narragansett Bay, too late in the afternoon to effect anything that day. It is a witness of their conscientious exposition of the Puritan theory that the urgent need for prompt action in order to gain the advantage of a surprise could not induce them to devote Sunday to that purpose; and then an unfavorable wind kept them from landing until Tuesday night. Marching at once to the village of Miantonomoh, the Narragansett chief, Mason demanded his assistance against their common enemy. The chief considered their enterprise a most laudable one, but thought the English too few to deal with such " great captains " as the Pequots. All that could be obtained was permission to pass through the Narragansett country, but a number of individual volunteers from the surrounding Indians joined the troops on their march. A few days' waiting would have increased their force by a Massachusetts reinforcement under Captain Patrick, which had already reached Providence; but Mason balanced the advantage of surprise against this increase of force and pushed on. Thirteen men were sent back with the vessels to meet the main body at the Pequot River; and the army now consisted of seventy-seven Englishmen, Uncas's Mohegans, and about two hundred exceedingly doubtful Narragansett auxiliaries, who were present rather as spectators and critics than as fighting men.

One day's march carried the expedition nearly across the present State of Rhode Island, and on the next morning the eagerness of the Narragansett auxiliaries to act as a rear guard proved that the trail was becoming uncomfortably warm. Toward evening, when just north of the present town of Stonington, Mason called a halt, and was told by the Narragansetts that they were now close to one of the two great Pequot forts; the other, the chief residence of Sassacus, being several hours' journey further on. Camp was formed, and the men slept on their arms, their outposts having been pushed near enough to the fort to hear the revelry of the Indian garrison, which lasted until midnight. Before daybreak, June 5, the men were up and on the march. Two miles of an Indian trail brought them to the foot of a swelling hill, still known as Pequot Hill, near Groton. Here Uncas was called on for explanations, as there were no signs of the Pequots. He told Mason that the fort was at the top of the hill before him, and that the Narragansetts at the rear had now fallen into a condition of abject fright. "Tell them not to fly," said Mason, " but stand behind, at what distance they please, and see now whether Englishmen will fight."

Underhill with part of the men on the southern slope, and Mason with the rest on the opposite side, stole cautiously up the hill. There were no sentinels, and the garrison was still sound asleep. As the assailants came within a rod of the palisade, there was a bark from an Indian cur within it, and some Pequot warrior, perhaps starting up from a dream, called out " Owanux! Owanux!" (Englishmen.) Still there was no general alarm within the fort until the assaulting party fired a volley through the palisade, which was answered by a terrified yell from the awakened garrison. The piles of bushes which served for gates were torn down, and the English swarmed through into the fort, but still the Pequots remained within their wigwams. Mason, after entering, stood in the main street and saw not an Indian in it to the other side of the fort. Every wigwam which was entered, however, became the stage for a desperate hand-to-hand struggle. Some of the Pequots began to shoot from the wigwam doors; and Mason, shouting " We must burn them," touched a firebrand to the mats which covered a neighboring hut. The fire, fanned by a rising northeaster, spread through the fort; Underhill on the other side aided it with gunpowder; and soon the attacking party was forced to hurry out of the furnace heat. There was no such privilege for the hated Pequots. In an hour, from four to six hundred of them were roasted to death, seven being taken prisoners, and seven breaking through the line and escaping. From one hundred and fifty to two hundred of the Indians were warriors; the rest were old men, women and children.

It is true that two of Mason's party were killed, and about twenty wounded, in the whole struggle, but many of the recorded casualties bear strong testimony to the disadvantages under which the Indians fought. Some of the men were saved from arrow wounds by their neck-cloths: when so slight a buckler was sufficient, the force of the weapon could not have been very terrible. Similarly, a piece of cheese in the pocket of another was enough to intercept an arrow in its deadly flight. In recounting the subsequent attack upon the retreating party, Underhill contemptuously says that the Pequots fought with the Mohegans and Narragansetts in such a manner that neither would have killed seven men in seven years. The arrow was shot into the air at such an elevation as to drop on an adversary, if the adversary had not sufficient forethought to step out of the way; and each arrow was retained until the result of its predecessor was ascertained. The English regularly avoided the weapon, then picked it up and broke it, and thus gradually exhausted the ammunition of the enemy. Savages though they were, it is pitiful to think of human beings, locked up in a furnace by a circle of guns and keen-tempered swords, and forced to rely on such weapons as the fallacious Indian arrow. And yet to the last the Pequots crawled up to the palisade and shot their impotent bolts at their inaccessible foe.

Mason's thorough-going massacre of men, women and children has been compared to Arnold's butchery at New London, long afterward, to Mason's manifest disadvantage, since Arnold at least did not burn the village, drive the women and children back into the flames, and roast them in the ashes of their homes. The comparison is unfair. Arnold had not the slightest reason to apprehend from the women and children of New London such treatment as Mason knew that the Indian squaws and children would mete out to his men if they were defeated and captured. In the gray of the opening morning, while Indian men and women, hardly to be distinguished from one another by their dress and appearance, were vying with one another in the ferocity of their resistance, it was practically impossible for Mason's men to make distinction. To say this is not to assert that they were under a controlling desire to make such a distinction. On the contrary, probably not a man of them but was there under the religious confidence that the Pequots were acting the part of the Canaanites in resisting the children of Israel, and that a similar fate was their proper portion. In this they probably differed from Benedict Arnold. Much as we may regret that Endicott's unpardonable raid had decided that Sassacus was to be the enemy of the colonists, and the disreputable Uncas their friend and ally, this decision, when reached, had no possible result but the complete overthrow of the Pequots. It is easy to talk of sparing non-combatants, but not easy to apply it to a case in which the non-combatants insist on fighting to the death. Nevertheless, it is a truth that there is no feature in the history of the commonwealth which is more unpleasant reading than the conduct of the Pequot war from its causeless outbreak down to its conclusion.

Hiring some of his generous Narragansett allies to carry the wounded, Mason now began a retreat to his vessels, which were just sailing into what is now New London harbor, but half a dozen miles away. By this time, nearly the whole remaining power of the Pequot tribe had gathered at the ruins of the fort. The chroniclers calmly state the details of the ecstasy of rage into which the sight of their slaughtered comrades threw them; they note with a curious interest, as if speaking of the almost human affection of a she-bear robbed of her whelps, how the Pequots stamped, shrieked, tore their hair, and finally rushed down the hill to charge the rear of the retiring column. But — alas for all excuses for the expedition! — they also note that a rear guard of a dozen men was sufficient to repulse all the assaults of two thirds of the whole Pequot power. The English force reached the vessels without difficulty, finding there Captain Patrick and the Massachusetts contingent. Putting the wounded on the ships, the uninjured men returned in triumph by land to Saybrook.

The last council of the Pequot nation was held on the day following the capture of the fort. It is not difficult to imagine the feeling of the participants. They had proved, even to themselves, that it was impossible for them to resist the strangers in the field; and it seems to have been as impossible for them to conceive the notion of surrender. Having first put to death every relative of Uncas within their reach, they came to a Roman resolution. The route by which they had originally entered Connecticut was now blocked by the new English towns; but there was a possible road of return along the Sound, where there were as yet no settlements. Burning their villages and crops, they set out on their desperate venture. Thirty of the men, with many of the women and children, soon abandoned it and returned to their old home, where they took refuge in a swamp. Toward the end of June, a Massachusetts party of one hundred and twenty men under Stoughton was guided to their hiding place by the Narragansetts, who had not ventured to attack them, but said they were "holding them" for the English. The Pequots met their fate calmly and without resistance. All the men were put to death in cold blood with the exception of two, who promised to guide the party to the hiding place of Sassacus; and even these, proving unwilling to fulfill their bargain, were subsequently killed. Thirty-three of the eighty women were presented to the Indian allies; the remainder were sent to Massachusetts and sold as slaves.

The main body of the tribe pursued their march for the Hudson under Sassacus and Mononotto. While crossing the Connecticut, they came upon three white men in a canoe, killed them after a stout resistance, and hung their bodies on the trees upon the shore. After passing Saybrook, they were driven by lack of supplies to take a route close to the shore, in order to dig shell-fish. Such circumstances were not favorable for a forced march; the daily journeys grew shorter; and that keen-scented hound, Uncas, was on their track. Stoughton's men had joined Mason, and the combined force had taken ship at Saybrook to pursue by the Sound, while Uncas and his men searched the shore. Stragglers from the main body were occasionally met, and one incident will indicate their fate. Near Guilford, a Pequot chief with a few men was sighted. Escaping from view for a few minutes, the fugitives hid at the end of the cape which juts out from the eastern side of the harbor. Uncas searched the opposite side of the harbor, but sent part of his men to search the eastern cape. Driven from their refuge, the Pequots swam across the harbor and were shot as they landed by the Mohegans. Uncas cut off the head of the Pequot chief and lodged it in the branches of an oak, where it hung for years, giving the place the local name of Sachem's Head.

About the time when the pursuers had reached the place where the town of Fairfield was afterwards planted, a Pequot was captured who was found willing, in return for life, to engage to kill or betray Sassacus. He kept his agreement. He joined the main body, and, when suspected and forced to flee, brought back word that the main body of the Pequots had taken post in a swamp, the stronghold of a local sachem, near Greenfield Hill. The untiring pursuers set out at once for the place, some twenty-five miles away, found it, and undertook to surround the swamp. There were really two swamps, a larger and a smaller, separated by a neck of firm ground covered with bushes. After a hand-to-hand struggle, the besiegers succeeded in cutting down the bushes and reducing the coverts to one, which their numbers were sufficient to surround efficiently. A call for surrender was then sent in. It was accepted by the local tribe on whose hospitality the Pequots had forced themselves, and by the women and children of the Pequots, so that the number of the besieged was reduced from three hundred to one hundred. Those who were left were the picked men of the tribe. They saw, before them the strangers who had suddenly flung them from their supremacy to their present position, and they had a savage preference of death to surrender. They rushed so furiously on the messenger that the English found difficulty in rescuing him. All night long they crept up to the border of the swamp and shot their ineffectual arrows at the besiegers; and in the gray of the next morning they made their last burst for freedom. In a heavy fog they rushed on that part of the English line commanded by Patrick, and the fight at once became so furious that the rest of the English force had to be brought up to Patrick's assistance. In the confusion, about seventy of the hundred Pequots burst through and got off; but many of them were found dead in the pursuit. The subsequent course of the survivors is not known. There is a tradition that they made their way to the mountainous region of western North Carolina, and that, forty years afterward, the intelligence of King Philip's war brought them or their children as far north as Virginia, on their way back to strike another blow at the English, when they were stopped by hearing of Philip's death.

Sassacus and Mononotto had left their tribe before the swamp fight, either overwhelmed with unpopularity, or unable to spur the remainder of the tribe to the necessary celerity of movement. Their party of thirty or forty men escaped to the Mohawks; but their new hosts put them all to death, sending their scalps to the English to relieve them from further anxiety. Only Mononotto escaped, and it is not known what became of him. His wife, with her children, was among the captives at the swamp. It is pleasant to record that she had been very kind to the two captured English girls, and that Governor Winthrop gave directions that she should be treated with corresponding kindness. All the prisoners, even including the wife of Mononotto, were made slaves, some being kept in Connecticut, and others sent to Massachusetts or the West Indies. They proved, however, most unsatisfactory slaves, and their servitude was in almost every case soon terminated by death.

The downfall of the Pequots inured largely to the benefit of Uncas. Many of the original tribe took membership in the Mohegan branch, though some preferred to join the Narragansetts or the Long Island Indians. It was not long before the jealous Narragansetts called Uncas to account before the equally jealous colonists for harboring Pequots to such an extent as to make his own power a source of possible danger. An investigation showed that there were still at large some two hundred Pequots, half of which number were given to Uncas and the rest to the Narragansett chiefs. Late in 1638, the delicate negotiation was closed by a treaty between the Connecticut delegates, Miantonomoh for the Narragansetts, and Uncas. The two high contracting Indian parties were to retain their respective Pequots, paying an annual tribute for them and incorporating them into their tribes. Connecticut was to have all the territory formerly occupied by the Pequots, and was to act as umpire in any quarrel between Uncas and Miantonomoh. The former lords of the soil had disappeared, and the stranger had taken their place.

The tripartite treaty of 1638 settled the supremacy of the English for the future. Purchases of lands from the Indians went on with increasing frequency until prohibited by the general court in 1663. Even Uncas was unwary enough to make such transfers; and in one of them, in 1640, in return for "five and a half yards of trucking cloth, with stockings and other things," he is said to have transferred to the commonwealth his whole territory, covering the whole northern portion of New London County, with the southern portion of Tolland and Windham counties. The Mohegans, however, insisted that the transaction was only a covenant to sell their lands to no white men without first giving the commonwealth an opportunity to buy, and their claims were a longstanding source of difficulty.

Miantonomoh was not satisfied with the treaty

of 1638. It is not probable that he would have been permanently satisfied with any treaty which left the parvenu Uncas in the position of a great chief. An attack made by Uncas upon a chief related to Miantonomoh furnished an opportune *casus belli*. With a discretion worthy of a more highly civilized monarch, Miantonomoh postponed the declaration of war to the more urgent necessity of making war. The whole power of the Narragansetts was secretly set in motion for the Mohegan country. Uncas was not asleep. His runners saw the host of the enemy crossing a ford, and carried the intelligence to their chief at his fort near the present city of Norwich. When the Narragansetts found the lair of the Mohegan chief, they found that they had to deal with the whole strength of his tribe, which he had had time to call in.

Uncas had felt himself strong enough to advance a few miles, though he had but half the force of his enemy, for he relied with confidence on the mingling of unscrupulous treachery and headlong courage which had been the Pequot title to the soil from the beginning. He signaled for a parley as soon as the Narragansetts came within hearing, and, meeting the Narragansett chief between the lines, appealed to him to prevent a needless effusion of blood by a single combat of the leaders. Miantonomoh rejected the proposal, perhaps with some contempt, and Uncas at once gave the signal for which his men had been waiting, by dropping prone upon the ground. His men instantly poured a flight of arrows upon the Narragansetts, and followed it by a charge, which Uncas rose and headed. The battle lasted but a moment; the Narragansetts fled, almost without striking a blow; and Miantonomoh, deserted by his people and over-weighted by an English corselet, was caught, after a long chase, by Uncas and one of his sachems. The captive kept a stolid silence, refusing to beg for mercy, even by gesture.

The tender mercies of Uncas would doubtless have been swift to visit Miantonomoh but for one circumstance. The Rhode Island settlers were not forgetful of the benefits which they had received at the hands of the Narragansetts; and one of them, Gorton, of Warwick, sent Uncas a violent message, threatening him with English vengeance if he injured Miantonomoh. Uncas, unable to discriminate clearly between English sectaries or to balance the respective power of white faces, carried his prisoner to Hartford for trial. The governor and magistrates referred him to the commissioners of the united colonies, who were to meet at Boston in the following September. Until then, Miantonomoh remained at Hartford.

The commissioners, much as they dreaded Miantonomoh, did not see their way clear to condemning him to death. In the emergency they summoned into council five of the delegates to a synod then sitting at Boston. These counselors rode roughshod over the scruples which had given pause to the lay mind. To them the Narragansett was a Philistine, an Amalekite, who was of necessity guilty. They decided that he must die, and the commissioners acquiesced in the decision. They directed the Connecticut authorities to give him up to Uncas for execution outside of the commonwealth's jurisdiction, to detail witnesses to see that all should be done in order, and to defend Uncas against any threatened vengeance for the act. The most shocking attendant circumstance is the fact that the announcement of the sentence was postponed until the Connecticut commissioners had safely reached Hartford, for the reason that Miantonomoh himself had given notice that his people intended to capture them on the way and hold them as hostages for his safety. It is no wonder that so dangerous a chieftain should find no mercy.

The Narragansett chief was delivered to the custody of Uncas, two Englishmen joining the party to be witnesses to the execution. When the Mohegans had reached the scene of the battle near Norwich, Uncas gave a signal to his brother, Wawequa, whose place was just behind the captive. He at once sunk his hatchet into Miantonomoh's brain, and death followed instantly. Uncas devoured a piece of flesh cut from the dead man's shoulder, declaring it the sweetest meat he had ever eaten.

The only serious difficulties with Indians thereafter were in the southwest, and were really offshoots from the continual troubles between the Dutch and the Indians. There were several murders and savage assaults, the most notable victim being Mrs. Anne Hutchinson, of Massachusetts, who had settled near Stamford, and was killed, with some seventeen others, in a night attack by the Indians. The Narragansetts seem to have taken no concerted part in this border warfare. They had come to despair of making head against the whites; and their hopes of revenge were concentrated on Uncas and his tribe, upon whom they made repeated attacks. Their only results were renewed and increased fines and tribute imposed by the white supporters of Uncas. About 1658 these attacks ceased, and the Narragansetts resigned themselves to their fate.

The chiefs to whom Pequots had been assigned, and especially Uncas, were so greedy and tyrannical in their rule that the conquered people began to drift away from them and form scattered and illegal communities. One or two of their new chiefs showed themselves good friends of the English; and in 1655 the New England commissioners, to Uncas's unconcealed disgust, consented to a reorganization of the Pequots into two tribes under chieftains of their own blood, Hermon Garret and Cassasinamon. In 1667 the colony established a reservation for Cassasinamon's tribe in the present township of Ledyard, near Groton; and in 1683 a settlement was assigned to the other tribe in North Stonington. The original force of the Pequot has been persistent enough to carry their descendants, after a fashion, through the intervening years in which the subject tribes have disappeared. In 1850 the Ledyard settlement held 989 acres, and the North Stonington settlement 240, with a mongrel population of twenty-eight and fifteen persons respectively. In 1880 the county of New London still held the largest proportion of the Connecticut "Indians," 147 out of a total of 255 in the State.

As the record of Indian difficulties ends with the death of Miantonomoh, the record of Indian decadence begins. Individuals, under the tacit or express authorization of the general court, bought lands of the Indian proprietors; and the early town records begin with deeds given by a number of sachems, whose unutterable names are only a little less awe-inspiring than the hieroglyphics by which they are indicated, transferring their lands to whites for the pettiest considerations. Real property titles in the State are traced back to these Indian deeds. When a tribe had entirely gotten rid of the inheritance, its few remaining members drifted off to other parts of the country, or became a town charge as paupers. But the general court was careful so to limit these transfers as not to drive the few dangerous tribes to desperation, and the good results were seen in the outbreak of King Philip's war in 1675. The Connecticut Indians left the colony free to bend all its energies to the assistance of the sister colonies. Even the Pequots and Mohegans were faithful allies and soldiers, and enjoyed the Indian luxuries of seeing the final overthrow of the Narragansetts, and of executing Canonchet, the son of Miantonomoh.

Uncas died about 1683. Two of his alleged descendants were living in 1800. His tribe and its successive chiefs seem to have found a fatal fascination in the process of land transfer, which they never could master. Drunken sachems made transfers of land which was really the common property of the tribe; or the tribe, having a well-founded apprehension of the sachem's weakness for strong drink, made clumsy attempts to make trust deeds of their lands to white men in whom they confided, while the trustees considered these instruments as transfers of the fee simple. The result was abundant litigation; and some of the commonwealth difficulties arising from it will be considered hereafter. In 1721 a committee of the general court examined and decided on these transfers, reserving some 5,000 acres to the Mohegans, and making the tract inalienable so long as a single Mohegan should survive. This arrangement was practically confirmed by royal commissions in 1737 and 1743, on appeal by the Indians. The tribe sent many of its number into the American army during the Revolution, and some eighteen of them were killed. In 1786 a few of the survivors, with other Connecticut Indians, went to the Oneida country, in New York, and there established the Brothertown tribe. There remained to the tribe in 1850 some 2,300 acres of its reservation at Montville, with some sixty persons living on it, and about the same number scattered in other parts of the country.

However we may discredit the accounts given by the first settlers of Indian immorality, it is impossible to exaggerate their subsequent degradation. Ignorant, poverty-stricken, unclean, drunken, and licentious to the lowest degree, the smaller Indian tribes disappeared with startling rapidity. In 1680 there were but five hundred warriors left in the whole colony. In 1774 there were only eight left in Greenwich, nine in Norwalk, and none in Stamford. There is not now a drop of pure Indian blood in the State. The so-called Indians are the progeny of two centuries of irregular intercourse between Indians, negroes, mulattoes, and whites.

Efforts have not been wanting to civilize or evangelize the race, but they have been of little avail. Pierson, Fitch, and Barber preached to them with hardly any perceptible result; Gookin and John Eliot entered the colony for the same purpose, but withdrew defeated; and the only effort which ever came to anything like success met it outside of Connecticut. Eleazar Wheelock began preaching at Lebanon in 1735. In 1762 his Indian school numbered twenty, and he went to England to raise funds for it, developing it into what became Dartmouth College. Among his Connecticut pupils he had received in 1743 a Mohegan aged twenty, who took the name of Samson Occom. After an irregular education and service as teacher on Long Island and elsewhere, Occom was ordained in 1759 by the presbytery of Suffolk, L. I., and became a successful preacher. He stands out as about the only civilized product of Connecticut Indian origin ; and even he occasionally relapsed into intoxication, to his own bitter repentance. He made a part of the Brothertown tribe, and died among its members in 1792.

There is little room or excuse for romance in the Indian history of the commonwealth; and it has seemed best to bring it down to its conclusion at once, in order to confine the subsequent story of the commonwealth to the history of the dominant race.

CHAPTER VI.

THE CONNECTICUT COLONY.

WHEN the Pequot war broke out, there were but three English settlements within the present area of Connecticut. Leaving Massachusetts, the Connecticut River flows to the southwest and then to the southeast, forming two sides of a very obtuse and irregular angle. At the apex of this angle, and on the western side of the river, was planted the town of Newtown (the present capital city of Hartford). On the same side of the river were Dorchester (Windsor), a few miles above Hartford, and Watertown (Wethersfield), a few miles below Hartford. To the north, and just beyond the Massachusetts boundary line, was Agawam (Springfield), Pynchon's settlement; but it was not known for some years whether it was in or beyond the jurisdiction of the mother colony. Until this was ascertained, this town was taken and deemed to be a part of Connecticut. The first settlers had no notion of leaving government behind them when they left Massachusetts. The migration took place under direction of eight persons, headed by Roger Ludlow and William

Pynchon, acting under the commission from the Massachusetts General Court, which was to be in force for only óne year. By the time it expired, the new colony had begun its own system of government.

The meeting of the first legislative body, the "Corte," was held at Newtown, April 26, 1636. The three migrating towns at first retained even their Massachusetts names, and this inchoate commonwealth government was little more than a consequence of the Massachusetts commission. It was not until February 21 of the next year that the name of Hartford was substituted for that of Newtown, that of Wethersfield for Watertown, and that of Windsor for Dorchester. The name of Hartford was probably meant to commemorate the birthplace of Mr. Stone, Hertford, near London. Windsor was taken from its English namesake; and Wethersfield was named from Wethersfield in Essex, England, the birthplace of one of the leading men of the settlement, John Talcott, commonly called "Tailcoat" in the records. For a year the court met at the three towns in turn, two magistrates from each town making up its number, except when Pynchon was present and raised the number to seven. Like all the commonwealth legislatures of New England, this, one exercised both legislative and judicial functions, taking from the latter its title of the "Corte," afterwards the "General Court," as in the Massachusetts charter. For the first year its proceedings were confined to the prevention of the trade in muskets with the Indians, the enforcement of military drill, the regulation of swine and other animals, the appointment of constables, some probate business, and one suit at law, that of a land claimant against the people of Wethersfield.

On May 1, 1637, the legislature, now first called the General Court, met at Hartford in a form more fitting for a separate commonwealth. In addition to the six magistrates there were now present nine " committees," or deputies, three from each town. Hooker, in his letter to Winthrop, states that the " committees " were chosen by the towns; that they met at Hartford, elected the six magistrates, and gave them an oath of office. The migratory commission from Massachusetts was thus supplanted by a new government, deriving its authority directly from the towns. In the distinction between deputies and magistrates, slight at first, there was the germ of the commonwealth's subsequent bi-cameral system. Springfield was represented occasionally during 1637–38, and her affairs were considered to be under the jurisdiction of the new colony. For the next two years Springfield is neither represented nor referred to, the general court confining its attention to the other three towns. On June 2, 1641, the Massachusetts General Court recognized Springfield, on petition therefrom, as one of its towns, and appointed commissioners to define the boundary line between the two colonies.

The General Court, under its new constitution, at once assumed a wider range of action. Its first meeting declared war against the Pequots; its second, June 2, 1637, ordered a draft of thirty men "to sett downe in the Pequoitt Countrey and River in place convenient to mayntaine o^r right y^t God by Conquest hath given to vs." At the meeting June 26, it was decided that Haynes and Ludlow should "parle with the bay [Massachusetts] about o^r settinge downe in the Pequoitt Countrey." For Massachusetts had advanced a claim to the Pequot soil, based partly on the exceedingly hazy geography of the time, and partly on conquest; while Connecticut had a keen perception that this section was essential to her commonwealth's development, and meant to hold it. In the end her determination prevailed, and she still keeps the Pequot country.

It would hardly be too strong to say that the establishment of the town and of the church was coincident: the universal agreement in religion made town government and church government but two sides of the same medal, and the same persons took part in both. In fact, the three original settlements had entered the new territory not only as completely organized towns, but as completely organized churches, only one (Watertown) having left its minister behind. The original church of Watertown is therefore still in Massachusetts; the original churches of Cambridge (Newtown) and Dorchester are now in Hartford and Windsor. For nearly a century (until 1727) the same persons in each town discussed and decided ecclesiastical and civil affairs indifferently, acting as a town or a church meeting. The same body laid the taxes, called the minister, and provided for his salary. When the gradual recognition of other sects reduced the Congregational order from its exclusive to a merely predominant position in the commonwealth, a trace of the old system remained in the Congregational churches in the dual control of the "church and society" in each congregation, — the former, composed of church-members, having ecclesiastical jurisdiction; the latter, composed of pew-holders and contributors, having a financial and administrative control, and joint action of the two being usually necessary. The "society" represents the former town meeting. The Connecticut churches agreed with those of Massachusetts in their Congregational system; and their pastors and teachers were called upon again and again to make the journey through the wilderness to Boston, in order to take part in the synods made necessary by the vexed questions of Puritan belief and practice. Connecticut, however, did not agree with Massachusetts in making church-membership a prerequisite to voting and holding office. In this omission, it maintained the complete independence both of its churches and of its towns; but it gave rise to many of its subsequent ecclesiastical difficulties. It was largely a dispute on this point that had sent the first settlers into the wilderness, and the original three towns would undoubtedly have insisted on local freedom in this respect. When new towns were formed, offshoots from the first three, it was natural in the eyes of both town and colony that this freedom should be continued to them, and none of them desired any ecclesiastical restriction on the right of suffrage. Those who desired such an arrangement went into the New Haven jurisdiction, of which it was an essential part.

The independence of the town was a political fact which has colored the whole history of the commonwealth, and, through it, of the United States. Even in Massachusetts, after the real beginning of government, the town was subordinate to the colony; and, though the independence of the churches forced a considerable local freedom there, it was not so fundamental a fact as in Connecticut. Here the three original towns had in the beginning left commonwealth control behind them when they left the parent colony. They had gone into the wilderness, each the only organized political power within its jurisdiction. Since their prototypes, the little *tuns* of the primeval German forest, there had been no such examples of the perfect capacity of the political cell, the " town," for self-government. In Connecticut it was the towns that created the commonwealth; and the consequent federative idea has steadily influenced the colony and State alike. In Connecticut, the governing principle, due to the original constitution of things rather than to the policy of the commonwealth, has been that the town is the residuary legatee of political power; that it is the State which is called upon to make out a clear case for powers to which it lays claim; and that the towns have a *primâ facie* case in their favor wherever a doubt arises.

All this is so like the standard theory of the relations of the States to the federal government that it is necessary to notice the peculiar exactness with which the relations of Connecticut towns to the commonwealth are proportioned to the relations of the commonwealth to the United States. In other States, power runs from the State upwards and from the State downwards; in Connecticut, the towns have always been to the commonwealth as the commonwealth to the Union. It was to be the privilege of Connecticut to keep the notion of this federal relation alive until it could be made the fundamental law of all the commonwealths in 1787–89. In this respect, the life principle of the American Union may be traced straight back to the primitive union of the three little settlements on the bank of the Connecticut River. All this, however, may be left to the chapter on the Convention of 1787. The point in question here is the introduction of the *democratic* element into the American system, and the claims of Connecticut to the credit or responsibility for it.

The first constitution of Connecticut — the first written constitution, in the modern sense of the term, as a permanent limitation on governmental power, known in history, and certainly the first American constitution of government to embody the democratic idea — was adopted by a general assembly, or popular convention, of the planters of the three towns, held at Hartford, January 14, 1638 (9). The common opinion is that democracy came into the American system through the compact made in the cabin of the Mayflower, though that instrument was based on no political principle whatever, and began with a formal acknowledgment of the king as the source of all authority. It was the power of the crown "by virtue" of which "equal laws" were to be enacted, and the "covenant" was merely a makeshift to meet a temporary emergency: it had not a particle of political significance, nor was democracy an impelling force in it. It must be admitted that the Plymouth system was accidentally democratic, but it was from the absence of any great need for government, or for care to preserve homogeneity in religion, not from political purpose, as in Connecticut. It was a passive, not an active system; and it cannot be said to have influenced other American commonwealths. Another though less prevalent opinion is, that the first democratic commonwealth was the mother colony of Massachusetts Bay. The intensely democratic feeling subsequently developed in Massachusetts has been reflected on her early history, and has given it a light which never belonged to it. On the contrary, it is not difficult to show that the settlement of Connecticut was itself merely a secession of the democratic element from Massachusetts, and that the Massachusetts freemen owed their final emancipation from a theocracy to the example given them by the eldest daughter of the old commonwealth.

He who studies carefully the history of Massachusetts from 1629 until 1690 will see that there was a constant struggle in that colony between two conflicting forces, and that its earlier phases were coincident and complicated with the Connecticut secession. The better blood of the colony was determined to establish a privileged class of some sort; and the bulk of the freemen, instinctively inclined to democracy, found it difficult to resist the claims of blood, wealth, and influence, backed by the pronounced support of the church. For the ministers of the colony, in spite of their evidently conscientious wish to separate church and state, seem to have had no notion of the real boundaries between the two, and were constantly in favor of measures which tended straight to the establishment of an oligarchy. Whenever the dominant class desired to overcome the rising opposition of the commons, the readiest and surest means was to offer to submit the question to the decision of the "elders," or ministers. The commons never ventured to refuse; and the ministers never failed to decide in accordance with the wishes of the dominant class. The expressions of dissenting writers, as to the "spiritual tyranny" in early Massachusetts, must be taken always with very large allowance. Ecclesiastical punishments were not severe, according to the universal standard of the times; and the result of hostile research seems curiously inadequate to the indignation which has been spent in it. But one must admit that the early Massachusetts system, whatever else it may have been, was not even meant to be a democracy. "Democracy," said Cotton, the spokesman of the dominant class, "I do not conceive that ever God did ordain as a fit government either for church or commonwealth."

The question appeared with the transfer of the charter government from England to Massachusetts. The charter gave to the governor, eighteen assistants, and the freemen, assembled in a single chamber as the "great and general Court," the power of electing officers and making laws and ordinances. The dominant class of the colony was determined to restrict this general court;

which the superior numbers of the freemen could control, to the functions of a mere electing body, leaving to the assistants, what the charter did not give them, the duties of making and enforcing laws. The first meeting of the Court of Assistants in Massachusetts made the support of the clergy a commonwealth matter; the second assumed control of the admission of inhabitants to the towns; and, early in 1632, the settlement of town boundaries, and the control of town interests, were assumed by the assistants without any authority, either from the charter or from the towns. Secular and ecclesiastical influences were strong enough to induce the freemen, in 1630, to confirm the usurped powers of the Court of Assistants; and this was followed in the next year by the exclusion of all but church-members from "the liberties of the Commonwealth," that is, from voting. So wide was the effect that Hutchinson asserts, and Judge Story approves the estimate, that five-sixths of the people were still disfranchised as late as 1676. The whole system was upheld by Governor Winthrop of Massachusetts, in a letter to Hooker, on the ground that it was unwarrantable and unsafe to refer matters "of counsel or judicature" to the body of the people, because "the best part is always the least, and of that best part the wiser part is always the lesser." The people, or that better part of them who should be admitted to vote, were to choose the Court of Assistants; but that wiser body was to make the laws and enforce them.

Such a system was certain to arouse dissatisfaction; and a due regard to the fact will make it easier to understand why the Massachusetts charter was finally lost so tamely. Dissatisfaction, to the honor of the Massachusetts freemen, first took the shape of assertion of local liberty, of town freedom rather than of individual freedom. There were attempts at independent town action before 1634; but the curious and perhaps significant fact is that nearly all of them took place in the three towns which afterwards made up the Connecticut secession. The towns in 1634 informally sent two deputies each to Boston to get a sight of the patent. The sight was enough to expose the usurpation of the assistants; and at the general court in May the freemen would make no elections until their deputies had been recognized as a factor in the government. Nevertheless, influence, and particularly that of the ministers, was still strong enough to secure the passage of an act, the very next year, constituting a council for life, consisting at first of three members, but meant to be larger in future. There is every indication of an organized design to establish an hereditary order, or at least a life privilege for certain classes, in order to attract influential and wealthy immigrants from the mother country; but luckily Massachusetts freemen knew how to cut the knot. When it was proposed in 1639 to give the governor a life tenure, the freemen answered by taking all "magistratical" powers from the council, and that body died the death soon after. Time would fail in telling the further details of the struggle, — the success of the deputies in maintaining that share in the government which the charter had not given them; the efforts of the assistants to secure the "negative voice," by which they were to have a veto on the deputies; the famous "sow business," which convulsed the colony, and brought the "negative voice" into common disrepute; and the final compromise in 1644, by which the introduction of a bi-cameral system gave both the assistants and the deputies a negative voice. All these belong to Massachusetts history, and were the efforts of democracy to get its head out of water.

In every point, the ministers had been on the side of the assistants. The latter had always been willing to refer every disputed question to the elders, and had always been supported. The standing grievance had been that the assistants would not admit the right of the general court (which really meant the deputies, or the freemen whom they represented) to adopt a body of laws as a permanent limitation on the judicial powers of the assistants; they wished to decide every case "on its own merits." Winthrop himself acknowledged, in 1639, that the people "had long desired a body of laws, and thought their condition very unsafe while so much power rested in the discretion of magistrates;" and he adds the very credible note that the magistrates and some of the ministers were "not very forward in this matter." In December, 1641, a brief code of laws was extorted by the freemen; but it left great blanks, which the assistants still persisted in filling as they saw fit. In 1645 the elders formally declared that the freemen were to choose the assistants, but that the authority of the latter was not derived from the freemen or to be limited by them, and that they were to decide according to the word of God in the absence of express law. The deputies yielded; and it was not until 1649 that they at last secured a complete code of laws.

Reference has already been made to the patent differences between the three migrating towns and the five which they left behind them, and to the probability that there was some political difference to account for them. A regard to the coincident struggle against class power in Massachusetts will make it still more probable that the migrating towns were simply those which did not choose to continue the struggle longer at home, but preferred to establish a more democratic system for themselves in the wilderness, and without any charter. Hooker was undoubtedly the strength of the migration; and he had been so notoriously opposed to Cotton in the old colony that it would be reasonable to presume that he differed *toto cœlo* from Cotton's views as to democracy. In answering the letter of Winthrop mentioned above, he is evidently cautious, and unwilling to provoke an argument; but he dissents from Winthrop's entire position, and says: "In matters of greater consequence, which concern the common good, a general council, chosen by all, to transact businesses which concern all, I conceive, under favor, most suitable to rule and most safe for relief of the whole." The difference between him and Winthrop is marked; and it would not be difficult to say, from these two letters, which of them held the seed from which sprang the modern American commonwealth. Again, the first step of the Connecticut settlers was to secure what their Massachusetts brethren were still struggling for — popular control of legislation. Codes of laws were merely the symbol: democracy wanted the recognition of the deputies, the direct representatives of the towns, as a factor in the government; and this was secured by the constitution of 1639. It even provided a way by which the deputies, if the governor and the "magistrates" (answering to the Massachusetts title of "assistants") refused to call them together, might meet and organize a supreme legislature *without their associates*, — a provision wholly inexplicable without a careful regard to the contemporary struggle in Massachusetts.

Here the evidence that government "of the people, by the people, for the people," first took shape in Connecticut, and that the American form of commonwealth originated here, and not in Massachusetts, Virginia, or any other colony, might well stop. The case in favor of Hooker, however, has now an impregnable basis, which was wanting when the standard histories of the commonwealth were written. His letter to Winthrop might be made the foundation of the claim that he had supplied the spirit of the Connecticut constitution; and yet the basis is an unsatisfactory one. It is evident enough that the complete popular control over government which was the characteristic of the new Connecticut system was neither familiar nor welcome at the time in the other Puritan commonwealth; but the letter alone is not enough to establish a connection of this fact with Hooker. All this time there has been in existence an abstract of a sermon of Hooker's, preached at Hartford, May 31, 1638, some seven months before the framing of the constitution. Henry Wolcott, Jr., of Windsor, had been in the excellent Puritan habit of taking notes of the sermons to which he listened, and he had left behind him a MS. volume of abstracts of Hooker's sermons. Among them was this sermon. Dr. J. H. Trumbull saw its importance and deciphered its short-hand characters.

Any one who will read this abstract, and try to imagine the way in which the writer of the letter to Winthrop must have clothed this skeleton with flesh and blood, and the effect on his hearers, will appreciate its importance in American history. If the germ is potentially the whole development, this is the most important profession of political faith in our history. It is as follows : —

DEUT. i. 13. — Take you wise men, and understanding, and known among your tribes, and I will make them rulers over you. Captains over thousands, and captains over hundreds, over fifties, over tens, etc.

Doctrine. I. That the choice of public magistrates belongs unto the people, by God's own allowance.

II. The privilege of election, which belongs to the people, therefore must not be exercised according to their humours, but according to the blessed will and law of God.

III. They who have power to appoint officers and magistrates, it is in their power, also, to set the bounds and limitations of the power and place unto which they call them.

Reasons. 1. Because the foundation of authority is laid, firstly, in the free consent of the people.

2. Because, by a free choice, the hearts of the people will be more inclined to the love of the persons chosen and more ready to yield obedience.

3. Because of that duty and engagement of the people.

Uses. The lesson taught is three-fold : —

1st. There is matter of thankful acknowledgment in the appreciation of God's faithfulness towards us, and the permission of these measures that God doth command and vouchsafe.

2dly. Of reproof — to dash the councils of all those that shall oppose it.

3dly. Of exhortation — to persuade us, as God hath given us liberty, to *take* it.

And, lastly, as God hath spared our lives, and given us them in liberty, so to seek the guidance of God, and to choose in God and for God.

Here is the first practical assertion of the right of the people not only to choose but to limit the powers of their rulers, an assertion which lies at the foundation of the American system. There is no reference to a "dread sovereign," no reservation of deference due to any class, not even to the class to which the speaker himself belonged. Each individual was to exercise his rights "according to the blessed will and law of God," but he was to be responsible to God alone for his fulfillment of the obligation. The whole contains the germ of the idea of the commonwealth, and it was developed by his hearers into the constitution of 1639. It is on the banks of the Connecticut, under the mighty preaching of Thomas Hooker and in the constitution to which he gave life, if not form, that we draw the first breath of that atmosphere which is now so familiar to us. The birthplace of American democracy is Hartford.

From early times, certainly since 1656, Connecticut has placed upon her common seal vines, to represent her towns, at first three for the original towns ; then one for each town ; then, as the towns became more numerous, the original three again. The stripes on the flag of the United

States, increased to fifteen until after the war of 1812, are a curious parallel. With the vines was the significant motto of the commonwealth, at first on a scroll held by a hand coming out of a cloud, afterwards on a scroll below the vines: QUI TRANSTULIT SUSTINET. The motto was not meant as the record of an historical fact alone, or as an exclusion of the agency of man from the attainment of liberty. The spirit, if not the translation, of it is in the third of Hooker's "Uses" of his lesson, his "exhortation — to persuade us, as God hath given us liberty, to *take* it." This his flock proceeded to do in their constitution.

In the preamble, the inhabitants and residents of Windsor, Hartford, and Wethersfield, desiring to establish an orderly and decent government according to God, associated and conjoined themselves to be as one public state or commonwealth, for the purposes of maintaining and preserving the liberty and purity of the gospel, the discipline of the churches, and the orderly conduct of civil affairs according to law. There is no mention or hint of royal, parliamentary, or proprietary authority in any part of the constitution, or in the forms of oaths for governor, magistrates, and constables which make an appendix to it. The ecclesiastical excrescence upon it, probably inevitable at the time, but absolutely contrary to the spirit of the whole instrument, was to remain and trouble the commonwealth until the political system came fully up to its own original standard in 1818.

The constitution gave the general court power to "admit of freemen;" but the right of suffrage was given unequivocally, by a subsequent addition to the first section, to admitted freemen who had taken the oath of fidelity to the commonwealth; and in 1643, to settle the matter, the court declared that it understood by "admitted inhabitants" those who had been admitted by a town. The towns, therefore, retained complete political control of their own affairs. No attempt was made to define the powers of the towns, for the reason that they, being preëxistent and theoretically independent bodies, had all powers not granted to the commonwealth. To avoid any possible question, the general court, at its meeting in the following October, passed a series of orders, securing to the towns the powers of selling their lands; of choosing their own officers; of passing local laws with penalties; of assessing, taxing, and distraining for nonpayment; of choosing a local court of three, five, or seven persons, with power to hear and determine causes arising between inhabitants of the town, and involving not more than forty shillings; of recording titles, bonds, sales and mortgages of lands within the town; and of managing all probate business arising within the town. The really new point introduced by the "orders" was the direction to the towns to choose certain of their chief inhabitants, not exceeding seven, to act as magistrates. Out of this grew rapidly the executive board of the towns known as "selectmen," who have ever since held almost a dictatorship in their towns during the intervals between meetings of their towns, limited by the force of public opinion, by commonwealth statutes, and by personal responsibility. These orders are often called an "incorporation" of the towns by the general court. The word can hardly be defended. All these privileges belonged to the towns already; and the orders of October 10, 1639, are much more like the first ten amendments to the Constitution of the United States, a Bill of Rights, originating in the jealousy of the political units. Indeed, there is hardly a step in the proceedings in Connecticut in 1639 which does not tempt one to digress into the evident parallels in the action on the national stage one hundred and fifty years later. Like causes produced curiously similar effects.

Each town was to choose annually, by vote of the freemen, four persons as deputies to the general court, unless the number of towns should increase so as to make a reduction necessary. Each year there was to be a court of election on the second Thursday of April (afterwards changed to May), to choose a governor and six magistrates. The choice of magistrates was limited to those nominated at some preceding session of the court, each town making not more than two nominations, and the general court adding as many as it chose. At the court of election, the freemen brought in paper ballots stating their choice for governor for the following year, a plurality vote electing. It seems to have been the intention to make this election a pure democracy, in which each voter gave in his ballot in person. As population spread further from Hartford, the custom of sending ballots by proxies must have grown up; for the court order of 1660, which proposed a change in the governor's term of office, suggested to the "remote Plantations, that use to send Proxies at the election, by their Deputies," that they should vote on their ballots for or against the proposed repeal. After 1670, the regulations adopted by the assembly, to govern the manner of taking these proxies, amounted practically to election laws, to be enforced by the town selectmen. The governor was to be a church-member, and originally no one was to be chosen to the office two years in succession. In 1660, the general court, desiring to retain John Winthrop, Jr., as governor, proposed to the freemen to abolish the restriction of reëlection, and the freemen did so.

The six magistrates were the germ of the future senate of the commonwealth, but at first they can hardly be considered a separate chamber. Their "magestraticall powers" were quite undefined, and, until the charter, may be taken to cover not only judicial functions, but such duties as the general court saw fit to add thereto from time to time. In general, they were district judges, meeting from time to time in bank, with legislative powers when joined by the governor and deputies. At the court of election, the secretary for the time being read the nominations for the office of magistrate in the order in which they had been given him. As each was read, the freemen handed in either blank ballots counting against the candidate, or ballots containing his name and counting for him. The balloting continued until six names had obtained a majority of the votes cast. If six magistrates were not thus obtained, the number was filled up by taking those names which had received the largest number of votes in their favor.

On the second Thursday of September, the governor, magistrates, and deputies were to meet as a general court, " for makeing of lawes," otherwise expressed by the phrase " to agitate the affaires of the commonwealth." This body was to pass laws of general interest, to dispose of unappropriated lands, to act as a court of last resort, to decide on the amount of taxation, and to apportion it among the towns on the report of an apportionment committee on which each town was to be equally represented.

In the little town republics, the ancient and honorable office of constable was the connecting link between commonwealth and town. The constable published the commonwealth laws to his town, kept the " publike peace " of the town and commonwealth, levied the town's share of the commonwealth taxation, and went " from howse to howse " to notify the freemen of meetings of the general court, and of the time and place of elections of deputies thereto. " The parish," says Selden, " makes the constable ; and, when the constable is made, he governs the parish." He might even become the instrument of a legal revolution, in case the governor and magistrates refused to call the regular meetings of the general court, or, on petition of the freemen, a special meeting. In that case, the constitution provided that the freemen were to instruct the constables to order elections of deputies, who were to constitute a general court themselves, excluding the governor and magistrates. This power never was exercised, but it is an extraordinary feature in constitutional law. It was the Connecticut mode of ensuring recognition of the direct representatives of the towns.

This constitution was the first conscious and deliberate attempt to found a commonwealth democracy on this continent, and it lasted in reality until 1818, for the charter changed it in no essential point. It was a system of complete popular control, of frequent elections by the people, and of minute local government. It remained, throughout confiscations, modifications, and refusals of charters in other colonies, the exemplar of the rights of self-government which all the English colonies gradually came to aim at more or less consciously. In later times the length of service of its officers was again and again cited by Jefferson to prove that, in a real democracy, annual elections were no bar to prolonged tenure of office. The first election of officers under the constitution was held April 11, 1639. John Haynes was chosen governor. Six magistrates were elected. One of the magistrates, Roger Ludlow, was chosen deputy governor; another, Edward Hopkins, secretary; and another, Thomas Wells, treasurer; and these and twelve deputies, or "committees," made up the general court. Until 1660, it was a tolerably steady rule that the governor of one year was the deputy governor of the next, and *vice versa*. In this period of about twenty years Haynes was governor eight times, and deputy governor five times; and Hopkins was governor seven times, and deputy governor six times. In 1657 John Winthrop began his term of service as governor, which lasted, through the removal of the provision against reëlection, for eighteen years, the longest term of service reached by any of Connecticut's chief magistrates. In the next century, Gurdon Saltonstall held the office for seventeen years, 1707–24, Nathan Gold holding the office of deputy governor during all but the first year of Saltonstall's term. Saltonstall was followed by Joseph Talcott, who also held the office of governor for seventeen years, 1724–

41; having the same deputy governor, Jonathan Law, throughout his entire term. Law succeeded Talcott; and thereafter, until 1818, the rule was that a governor held office until he died or refused to serve longer, when the deputy governor took his place for a like term. Jonathan Trumbull, senior, was governor, 1769-84; and his son, of the same name, held the office 1798-1809.

Reëlection to other offices was never prohibited, and long terms of service in them have been almost too numerous for special mention. John Allyn, for example, became secretary in 1664 and held the office for twenty-eight years, influencing the policy of the colony strongly during the whole period. A more remarkable case is that of the Whitings, who held the office of treasurer for seventy years, — Joseph Whiting 1679-1718, and his son and successor, John Whiting, 1718-49. Even this family record was outdone by the Wyllyses in the office of secretary. Hezekiah Wyllys held the office 1712-35; his son and successor, George Wyllys, 1735-96; and Samuel Wyllys, George's son and successor, 1796-1810, the office having remained in the family but two years short of a century. Length of tenure was the rule in local offices as well. In the first two hundred and fifty years of its history, Hartford has had but twenty town clerks. One of them, John Allyn, held the office, by annual elections, for thirty-seven years, and another, George Wyllys, for fifty years. Cases of this kind were exceedingly common throughout the commonwealth. William Hillhouse, of New London, served in the general court for fifty-eight years, so that, as elections to the lower house of that body were semi-annual, he was sent by his town to one hundred and sixteen successive sessions.

It must be admitted that much of this permanency in democracy was due to the nature of the people; but a large share ought to be credited to their institutions. The people, fully satisfied with the complete control over the government which their constitution had secured to them, were content to allow circumstances to develop the men best suited to government. At the same time, the intense personal interest felt by every citizen in the commonwealth gave all of them a common motive, sharpened their intelligence, united their force, and carried the commonwealth safely through storms which would otherwise have been fatal. So much, at least, Connecticut owes to the constitution of 1639.

CHAPTER VII.

THE NEW HAVEN COLONY.

THE settlements of New Haven, Milford, and Guilford probably had their origin in closely connected movements at home, though they took place at different times. Every indication to be drawn from the records shows common characteristics of persons, methods, beliefs, and purposes.

The two most prominent men in the New Haven party of settlers were John Davenport (otherwise Damport or Dampard) and Theophilus Eaton, both Londoners, at least by adoption. Davenport was a Coventry man, an Oxford student, curate of St. Lawrence Jewry, and vicar of St. Stephen's, Coleman Street, London. His inclinations seem to have been at first those of a moderately Low Church man, in the modern sense; but Laud's persecutions had converted him into a "dangerous" Puritan by 1633, when he resigned and went to Holland. His acquaintance among Londoners of the middle class and of his own way of thinking was extensive; and it was from this class that the material strength of the New Haven settlement was drawn. Its leading representative was

Theophilus Eaton, an Oxfordshire man by birth, and a London merchant of sufficient prominence to have served in some semi-diplomatic capacity at the Danish court. In some way now unknown, the tentacles of the movement had run out into Yorkshire, Hertfordshire, and Kent; and these counties furnished the bulk of the purely agricultural population. The Hertfordshire families seem to have tended to Milford, and the men of Kent to Guilford, while the Yorkshiremen found New Haven most congenial.

The first or New Haven party of settlers, mainly Londoners, with Davenport and Eaton as leaders, landed at Boston, July 26, 1637. The wealth, influence, and coherence of the party made it a desirable acquisition, and the Bay colony made every effort to settle it within the jurisdiction. Many reasons combined to make the efforts fruitless. Theological disputes, notably the Hutchinson controversy, had harassed Massachusetts; and there was no great promise, to the critical eyes of the new-comers, of healing them. The peculiarity of Massachusetts, as distinguished from Connecticut, was the supremacy of the commonwealth over the towns, of church-members over non-church-members, and of influential classes over the church-members. This constitution of affairs was not so objectionable to the Davenport and Eaton party, for they followed it closely in their own colony, as the fact that in Massachusetts they would form only one or two towns, and would be under the control of the commonwealth, whereas they desired to *be* the commonwealth and control the subordinate civil divisions. They had no desire to assume the place of the commonwealth's opposition, from which the Connecticut settlers had just escaped. Again, they came to Boston at a time when the newly opened Connecticut territory was a common topic of conversation; and a "fine opening" has always been an almost irresistible temptation to the race. Finally, the chase of the Pequots along the Connecticut coast toward New Netherland had taken place within a month of their arrival; and who could pass through the southern borders of Connecticut in June without sounding their praises to his friends at Hartford and the Bay? The newcomers seem to have decided very quickly that they would not remain in Massachusetts; that they would go to the new territory; and that their settlement should be placed somewhere on the coast.

In the autumn of 1637, Eaton, with some of his party, explored the northern shore of Long Island Sound, and pitched on Quinnipiack, an Indian district having a good harbor, as the best seat for a colony. A hut was built, and a few men were left to try the winter climate by personal experience. The rest of the party remained in various Massachusetts towns, and even increased their numbers by accessions from their neighbors. The venture had a commercial as well as a politico-religious aspect. Each of the "free planters" had invested stocks, varying from Eaton's £3,000 down to the ordinary £10 share. Some of these "free planters" never came to New Haven or New England, investing money only; and, on the other hand, some Massachusetts men entered their names, and even promised their personal presence to the venture.

The company set sail from Boston March 30, 1638. Quinnipiack was reached in about a fortnight; and the memorable first sermon was preached by Davenport, April 18, under an oak-tree, probably from Matt. iv. 1: "Then was Jesus led up of the Spirit into the wilderness to be tempted of the Devil." It is a pity that no note of the discourse has been preserved, for the obvious application of the text to the situation of the hearers, the constant temptation to consider every unpleasant incident, or even the consequences of their own errors, as the intervention of their personal enemy and antagonist, the Devil, would go very far to explain or palliate many otherwise inexplicable events in their history.

Such incidents were not slow in coming. The season was so bad that the crops failed and had to be replanted; and a violent earthquake, June 1, seemed sent to daunt their spirits and drive them out of the territory into which they had intruded.

If any of these things moved them, it was probably only to a more stubborn resolution against Satanic power and Indian powowings. Their determination to stand their ground was not relaxed. On the contrary, and as if to deal fairly even with their spiritual enemies, they went on to complete their title to the soil by purchase from the Indians. On November 24 and December 11, 1638, Davenport, Eaton, "and others" bought the title from Momaugin and Montowese respectively, with their subordinate chiefs. Subsequent neighboring purchases made up, roughly speaking, the present county of New Haven, excluding the narrow strip on its northern border. For all this the price paid was one dozen each of coats, spoons, hatchets, hoes and porringers, two dozen knives, and four cases of French knives and "sizers" to one, and a dozen coats to the other, with a vague promise to both of protection against their enemies, and a reservation of the Indian right to hunt and fish on the ceded territory. Some may think that this was driving a sharp bargain with the adversary; but, all things considered, it must be admitted that the Indians received all that the territory was worth to them.

The colony purchases did not stop here: purchase was the colony's consistent policy. The Indian district of Wapoweage (subsequently Milford) was bought February 12, 1638 (9); Menunkatuck (Guilford), September 29, 1639; Rippowams (Stamford), in July, 1640; and Yennicock (Southold, L. I.), some time in 1640. These four plantations, subsequently developed into towns, with Branford, made up mainly of the purchase of December 11, 1638, and the parent settlement of New Haven, finally constituted the New Haven commonwealth.

New parties entered the colony from England throughout the autumn and winter of 1638-39, so that there were three ministers present — Davenport, Rev. Henry Whitefield, and Rev. Peter Prudden, with congregations more or less organized; and another, Rev. Samuel Eaton, a brother of Theophilus, who seems to have had no following. Homogeneous as this settlement was, there were evidently interests which would impel segregation, and it was decided that the Whitefield party should take Guilford, the Prudden party Milford, and Samuel Eaton Branford, if he could obtain settlers. The latter enterprise was a failure, and Eaton was a resident of New Haven for four years after 1640, then returning to England and dying there in 1664. The Milford and Guilford ventures were successful during the summer; and they were from the beginning so definite in organization that, though they were in New Haven in June, and afterwards followed the ecclesiastical and civil constitution then adopted, they did not intrude upon the proceedings which led to it.

More is known of the early topography and appearance of New Haven than of Hartford.

Atwater and Lambert give maps of early New Haven and Milford. The houses of the early leaders, at least, are pretty accurately described, and something is known of their interiors. Contemporaries were struck with the unaccustomed luxury of the New Haven houses. Some of them had tapestry hangings; and Governor Eaton's had Turkey carpets, tapestry carpets and rugs. It is certain, at any rate, that the colony was spared many of the privations incident to most of the New England settlements; and that, until the unhappy issue of the Delaware Bay settlement, which brought poverty into the colony, its affairs were unusually prosperous.

Soon after their arrival at Quinnipiack, the Davenport and Eaton party had framed what was called a "plantation covenant." Nothing is known of its terms, except that it was short and simple, merely engaging that the Scriptures should govern their proceedings not only in the gathering and ordering of the church, but in the choice of magistrates and other officers, the making and repeal of laws, the allotment of inheritances, and all other civil affairs. This, to be sure, furnished the lines on which the future constitution was to be constructed. It had, also, peculiar effects which deserve notice, though they may not be apparent on the surface. It practically abolished the excrescences, such as entails and primogeniture, which had grown up on the English common law; it was almost, if not quite, a declaration of independence; and it made it certain that nothing short of direct and overmastering force could make the commonwealth anything but a republic. But it was yet without form or consistence; and in spite of its Scripture provisions, the real work of constitution-making by the settlers did not begin until

"They in Newman's barn laid down
Scripture foundations for the town."

The planters met June 4, 1639, in a large barn belonging to Mr. Robert Newman, to settle a constitution. Rev. Mr. Davenport opened the matter by preaching from Prov. ix. 1: "Wisdom hath builded her house; she hath hewn out her seven pillars." The application of the text to the business in hand was that, in a wise ordering of church or state, it was essential to rest on seven approved brethren, to whom the others were to be added. It is not difficult to see, on a general survey of the whole proceeding, what was the underlying purport of this proposition; for, if the constitution of Connecticut looked of necessity to a government by the many, that of New Haven had as strong a disposition to secure government by the chosen few.

After the service, Mr. Davenport submitted six "foundamentall orders" to the planters before him; and as each was adopted by a show of hands, the whole became the constitution of New Haven. The orders were as follows: —

1. That the Scriptures hold forth a perfect rule for men in their family, church and commonwealth affairs.

2. That the rules of Scripture were to govern the gathering and ordering of the church, the choice of magistrates and officers, the making and repeal of laws, the dividing of allotments of inheritance, and all things of like nature.

3. That all " free planters " were to become such with the resolution and intention to be admitted into church fellowship as soon as God should fit them thereunto.

4. That civil order was to be such as should conduce to securing the purity and peace of the ordinances to the free planters and their posterity.

5. That church-members only were to be " free burgesses," and were to choose *from their own number* magistrates and officers to make laws, divide inheritances, decide cases at law, and transact all public business. This alone seems to have met opposition. It called upon those free planters who were not church-members to surrender political as well as ecclesiastical power into the hands of the comparative minority who were church-members, and to make the surrender permanent and fundamental. One man, probably Rev. Samuel Eaton, agreed to the general principle that voters and magistrates should be men fearing God, and that the church was the likeliest place to find such; " only at this he stuck, that free planters ought

not to give this power out of their hands." The vote left the objector in a minority of one. The number thus disfranchised in New Haven was probably a majority; in Guilford, nearly half; in Milford, but ten out of forty-four, and six of these were admitted within a year or two.

6. That the free burgesses, or church-members, were to choose twelve of their number, and that these twelve were to choose the "seven pillars" to begin the church. The twelve selected were Eaton, Davenport, Robert Newman, Matthew Gilbert, Richard Malbon, Nathaniel Turner, Ezekiel Cheevers, Thomas Fugill, John Ponderson, William Andrews and Jeremiah Dixon, all noted names in early New Haven history. The names given number but eleven. The reason for the deficiency is unknown. It may perhaps be found in a note on the record that one of the twelve was accused of extortion, confessed it with grief, and made restitution. His name may have been left out and never supplied.

A provision was added to the "foundamentalls" that no one be admitted as a free planter until he had signed them. This was to make the peculiarities of the constitution permanent.

Eaton, Davenport, Newman, Gilbert, Fugill, Ponderson and Dixon were chosen as the "seven pillars." These then entered into covenant with one another (August 22), this step constituting the church, and proceeded to gather the other brethren to them and it. They were thus a church before they were a civil government, and the organized church organized the government. On the same day the church at Milford was gathered in the same way.

The seven pillars met for the first time as a general court October 16, 1639. They elected Eaton " magistrate: " he was not called governor until the full development of the commonwealth in 1643. Newman, Gilbert, Turner and Fugill were chosen deputy magistrates, and Fugill secretary and notary public. It was agreed that future elections should be held in the last week of October yearly, and that the word of God should be the only rule for the guidance of judges and public officers. Popular control, carefully limited as to the general court, was as nearly as possible excluded from the periodical meetings of the magistrates' court held by Eaton and his four deputies. Even after 1643, when it became the Particular Court of New Haven, it was rather a court of both civil and criminal equity than anything else.

The republic of New Haven, thus constituted, had very little official communication with dependent or associated towns for some four years. Milford with forty-four free planters, and Guilford with forty, were settled in 1639, in November and August respectively, under governments carefully modelled on that of New Haven. Most of the Milford settlers were dissatisfied Wethersfield people, who had left the Connecticut jurisdiction to reach just such a social and ecclesiastical system as that of New Haven ; while the Guilford people were absolutely in sympathy with Davenport even before their departure from England. Each had its church, gathered to its seven pillars, who also acted as a legislature and court, and held the town lands in trust for the town. The separate life of New Haven may therefore stand as a fair representative of the others.

The lands belonging to the towns seem to have been distributed by common agreement or by lot, and with entire impartiality. The minister was given a first choice; and it was very natural that a man so distinguished among his fellows as Eaton was honored with a choice next after the minister. The leading military man, Captain Turner, and the deacons, were given a similar privilege, so that they might choose places convenient for the fulfillment of their duties. Thereafter the division bears a curious resemblance to the distribution of lands under the village community system. The limited area which was meant to be the real town was divided into home lots, and the outlying lands of the township, as distinguished from the town, were divided into corresponding plots of arable and meadow lands. Home lots and outlying plots were of different sizes, corresponding to the various known gradations of contribution to the common stock. In each grade of contribution, the contributors received share and share alike, though the higher grades of contributors had to be first satisfied. But "grades of contribution" did not depend simply on money values. In the distribution of January, 1640, each settler received five acres of upland and meadow for each hundred pounds of his estate, and for each head in his family two and a half acres of upland and half an acre of meadow; "and in the necke an acre to every hundred pound, and half an acre to every head." In the distribution of September, 1640, twenty acres of out-land were assigned to every "hundred pounds of estate given in," and two and a half acres for "every head;" and it was decided that each of the small lots in the town should have four acres of planting ground to each lot, and one acre to every head. As a restriction on the eagerness for acquisition, taxes were imposed from the beginning,— fourpence an acre per annum for upland and meadow, and twopence for second-division lands. Finally, no sales to outsiders were to be made without the approval of the general court; and common lands, including clay-pits, were reserved to the commonwealth.

These "common lands" were held under much the same conditions in the New Haven and Connecticut towns as in those of Massachusetts, though the materials for study are not so abundant. There was no hasty scramble from ship to shore, no location wherever choice and opportunity might lead a family to settle without interfering with prior rights. On the contrary, every step was ordered and directed by the voice of the town, expressed in that assembly which has always been the mainspring of the New England system. The voice of the town either chose each man's location for him, or fixed the principles on which it was to be chosen. Here the parallel with any form of the village community must stop, for the New England settlers had come from England thoroughly imbued with the idea of individual property in land; and the land, when once allotted, became purely individual property, subject to alienation or devise, without return to the common stock. But there was necessarily a certain amount of land, larger or smaller, which was not needed for immediate allotment; and the rules of the community were pretty rigidly applied to this. It was the property of all, and was at first regulated by the town authorities. In New Haven, January 16, 1642 (3), it was decided that the common land known as "The Neck" should be a "stinted common" for cattle, and should be fenced and fitted with gates. The owner of twelve acres could put in a horse, of six acres an ox, of three acres a two-year-old steer, and of two acres a calf. As allotments had not depended on wealth alone, but on "heads" as well, this gave every man a share in the common. So a Norwalk town meeting of May 30, 1655, voted that "all dry cattle, excepting two year old heifers, shall be herded together on the other side of the Norwalk river, and there kept by the owners of the cattle; every man keeping according to his proportion of the cattle there herded." And all the town records of early years contain provisions allowing the inhabitants to fell timber in the town "commonage" at particular seasons, or to carry away windfalls.

As long as the town commonage was large and comparatively valueless, its affairs were managed by the town meeting. As its area became smaller and more valuable, and as new-comers crowded into the town, the management fell into the hands of an association of proprietors, composed of descendants of the original settlers, and interminable lawsuits often varied the monotony of the management. All through the eighteenth century, the efforts of the "new-comers" to get a share of the common lands made up a large part of local politics; and, during the Revolution period, the same question underlies much of the difference between "Sons of Liberty" and "Tories." Finally, the commonage being reduced by sales to a minimum of land poor enough to bankrupt any corporation which should undertake to manage it in earnest, the association of proprietors dies out and disappears, or becomes an hereditary social organization.

A pronounced distinction between New Haven

and Connecticut was the inquisitorial character assumed by the former from the beginning of its existence. It is true that much of what appears to be inquisitorial proceeding was due to the peculiar theory which governed the constitution of the legislative bodies of New England: the legislatures were also courts, and their proceedings were interspersed with a vast number of cases which would now be thought beneath the attention of a commonwealth government, — cases of lewdness, drunkenness in servants, impertinence, promiscuous kissing, etc. But the difference, which is plainly perceptible from any reading of the respective records, is that such matters were rather matters of business with the Connecticut authorities, to be dealt with and got rid of as rapidly as justice would permit; while to the New Haven magistracy they were matters of deep and serious import, to be probed to the bottom with scientific accuracy in every moral and psychological detail. Every New Haven sentence bristles at least with implications of the moral law. "Never elsewhere, I believe," says Dr. Bacon, " has the world seen magistrates who felt more deeply that they were God's ministers executing God's justice." All this may be admitted without impairing the belief that this attempted personification of Divine justice had its drawbacks. It would be unjust to say, as is generally assumed, that it resulted in Draconic severity of punishment: New Haven punishments, as a rule, were not at all severe. It would be unfaithful not to say that it resulted in a meddlesomeness which must have done more moral harm than good, and in the end did much to overthrow the government itself. " Goodman Hunt and his wife, for keeping the councils of the said William Harding, baking him a pasty and plum-cakes, and keeping company with him on the Lord's day, and she suffering Harding to kiss her," were ordered to be sent out of town " within one month after the date hereof [March 1, 1643], yea, in a shorter time if any miscarriage be found in them." While the New Haven magistracy was sitting in solemn labor to bring forth such a mouse as this, its Connecticut rival was actively engaged in real commonwealth business, every step of which made its ultimate supremacy more assured.

The peculiar cast of mind of the New Haven magistracy has done injustice to the good name of the early town. Its records of trials contain a mass of filth from which the Connecticut records are comparatively free. Some think that the missing records, covering the years 1649-53, were even worse, and were destroyed by the authorities to protect the town's reputation. But the trials which remain really speak highly for the morals of the town. The amount of real uncleanness brought to light is singularly small; the "evidence" on which other convictions were based would not be even admitted in a modern court of law; and the whole makes up a record rather of the diseased suspicions of the magistrates than of the criminality of their people. Most of the "criminals" better deserved a medical than a "magistratical" examination; and their cases are merely a demonstration of the necessity of the recognized rules of evidence, not of the immorality of the early Puritans, as dissenting authorities are so fond of representing them.

Sumptuary laws were attempted in New Haven, as in Connecticut, and with as little success in one as in the other. Codes were drawn up to regulate prices of labor and materials, but they were probably meant mainly to regulate the rates at which taxes should be paid to the commonwealth in kind, in materials or labor. So far as they were meant to regulate individual contracts, they were evidently a failure, and they were soon repealed. Rules against excess in drinking and in apparel were also attempted, with the usual want of success; and in their failure, as in the matter of "watching and warding," there are indications that kissing is not the only thing that goes by favor. John Jenner, accused, February 5, 1639 (40), of being drunk with strong waters, was acquitted, "itt appearing to be of infirmyty and occasioned by the extremyty of the colde."

It needed but a few years for the little settlement to show its consciousness of independent existence. As soon as the establishment of houses and streets had given it a corporate appearance and feeling, its name was changed, September 1, 1640, to New Haven (commonly then Newhaven). Another step, though abortive, shows the spirit of the people. It was ordered, December 25, 1641, " that a free school shall be set up in this town." Davenport was to ascertain the amount of money which would be needed for it, and to draw up rules for the institution. Contemporary expressions go to show that the intent was not to establish a mere school, in the modern sense of the word, but to lay a foundation which could develop easily into some such institution as the powerful university with which New Haven's name is now so closely linked. It should not be forgotten that, at least in spirit, the establishment of Harvard by the commonwealth of Massachusetts Bay had a contemporary rival in the straggling little settlement on the shores of Long Island Sound. But for the different circumstances of the two peoples, and a deference to Harvard's appeals for support, their two universities would have been born almost together, and the two hundred and fiftieth anniversaries of Harvard and Yale would have been almost coincident.

When the separate existence of New Haven had lasted some five years, her government developed into a confederation. Many reasons might be assigned for such a result. The towns which had been founded on the New Haven purchases had been separated from the parent stem long enough to make Mr. Davenport's opinion something less than all-sufficient, and to develop a higher regard for the opinion of their own ministers; for there was a strong ecclesiastical tap-root to town independence, even under the New Haven system. Again, it may well be imagined that men like Goodyear and Leete had not been blind to the growth and possibilities of the Connecticut colony. New Haven claimed only what she had bought: Connecticut claimed every square foot on which a Pequot had ever collected tribute. If New Haven was to maintain her solidarity against her rival's indefinite and penetrating claims, it must be by turning a nominal hegemony into a real commonwealth. Closely connected with this point was the proposed New England Union. If New Haven were left out of it, she was practically subordinated to her rival in the new territory. If she was to present her claim to admission, it must be with all the prestige derivable from a cluster of allied, not dependent, towns. It is significant, perhaps, that the first suggestion of the change comes in the appointment, April 6, 1643, of commissioners to the New England Union "for the jurisdiction of New Haven." It is quite probable that the leading men of the various towns had already agreed on the general form which the "jurisdiction" was to take, but it was not settled until October, owing to difficulties in the case of Milford.

During Milford's four years of nominal dependence, but real independence, it had gone so far as to admit six men as " free burgesses," or voters, although they were not church-members. With the rise of the commonwealth proposition, the admission of these six Milford burgesses became a great international question, which cost a whole summer of negotiation before it could be settled. It was finally agreed that the six should continue to vote in peace so long as they remained in Milford, but that they should not hold office, and that Milford should never again scandalize the other towns by thus violating their common law.

Harmony having thus been restored, a constitution for the commonwealth was agreed upon, October 27, 1643, by a general court, consisting of Governor Eaton, now first so called; Deputy-governor Goodyear; three magistrates; and eight deputies, two each from New Haven, Milford, Guilford, and Stamford. The features of the new constitution were not essentially different from that of 1639. Free burgesses, or voters, were to be church-members only, except the six Milford anomalies. Only church-members were to hold office. The rights of " free planters," not church-members, were limited to " their inheritance and to commerce." Each town was to have its particular court, elected by the burgesses, dealing with causes of not more than £20, or, in criminal cases, involving no greater punishment than "stocking and whipping" or a fine of £5, with right of appeal to the general court. In the election of governor and other commonwealth officers, voters need not go to New Haven, but might vote by proxy. The general court, consisting of governor, deputy governor, magistrates and two deputies from each town, was to meet at New Haven twice a year, on the first Wednesday in April and the last Wednesday in October, the latter being the court of election. The magistrates were to meet separately, as a court of magistrates, on the Monday preceding the stated general court meetings, to try weighty and capital cases or appeals from town courts, and to perform most of the functions of a grand jury. Ordinary trial by jury was not a part of the New Haven system.

The general court was to provide for the maintenance of the purity of religion, and "suppress the contrary;" to make and repeal laws, and require the execution of them; to call magistrates to account for misdemeanors; to impose upon the inhabitants an oath of fidelity and subjection to the laws; to settle and levy taxes; and to try causes on appeal from any of the other courts. Its proceedings were to be in accordance with the Scriptures, and no law was to pass but by a vote of a majority of the magistrates and a majority of the deputies.

At the next stated meeting in April, 1644, it was ordered that "the judicial laws of God, as they were delivered by Moses," should be considered binding on all offenders, and should be a rule to all the courts of the jurisdiction, "till they be branched out into particulars hereafter." These are probably the provisions which have done most to develop the current notions of the criminal code of New Haven. They have very probably reflected upon the sister colony as well, and, since the provisions of the Connecticut criminal code were like those of New Haven, though without their expressed basis, both have helped to give currency to Mr. Peters's absurd code of "Blue Laws." A general reference to "the Mosaic code of New Haven" has usually been held sufficient rebutter to any attempt to argue against the Blue Law myth. Nor is the reason far to seek. It is not a violent assumption that the phrase, "the judicial laws of God, as they were delivered by Moses," has not, to the average reader or hearer of the present time, that clear-cut significance which it had to those who first used it, or which the death statutes of a modern state have to the criminal lawyer. It is true that the New Haven general statute, agreeing generally with those of Connecticut and Massachusetts, made some fifteen offenses capital crimes, — murder, treason, perjury aimed at life, kidnapping, bestiality, sodomy, adultery, incest, rape, blasphemy in its highest form, idolatry, witchcraft, "presumptuous" Sabbath-breaking, the third conviction for burglary committed on the Lord's day, and rebellion against parents. A formidable catalogue truly. But why is it the only one to be brought to the bar? Mackintosh, speaking in the English House of Commons so late as March 2, 1819, said: "I hold in my hand a list of those offenses which at this moment are capital, in number *two hundred and twenty-three.*" The New Haven and Connecticut colonists, by a single stroke of legislation more than a century and a half before, had reduced their list of capital offenses to fifteen. If such a reduction, with hardly an execution for any of them, be not considered a long step in the history of law reform, law reformers are hard to satisfy.

The government established in 1643 continued without essential change until its final absorption by Connecticut. Two towns, however, were added to the four already named. Southold, L. I., bought in 1640, was admitted as a town in 1649. It was at first called by its Indian name, Yennicott or Yennicock; and its English name, Southold or Southhold, perhaps signified the place of strength to the south of New Haven. It extended some forty miles west of Orient Point. Totoket, or Branford, was a part of the second purchase of 1638. Samuel Eaton having failed to settle it, it was granted in 1640 to another dissatisfied Wethersfield company, headed by William Swayne, and Branford was admitted as a town in 1651. In 1644 it had been reinforced by Rev. Abraham Pierson's church from Southampton, L. I., which sought a more congenial home under the New Haven jurisdiction when its town joined Connecticut. But Pierson's church was not to escape thus. Within twenty years, the union was consummated, and the church again broke away from Connecticut and founded Newark, N. J., a settlement which has given to New Jersey the mass of the Connecticut family names which have appeared in her history. Huntington, L. I., also applied to be admitted in 1656 and 1659, but was refused because of her demand that her local court should try all her civil cases and all criminal cases not capital.

Six towns, therefore, — New Haven, Milford, Guilford, Stamford, Southold and Branford, — made up the New Haven jurisdiction during its short history. With the exception of Stamford and Southold, the commonwealth lay immediately around New Haven. Its smaller members are now villages which offer little that is striking to the traveler or visitor. Time was when they were members of an almost independent republic whose hopes were high, and whose history serves at least to show that the New England town system cannot thrive in an unfriendly soil.

CHAPTER VIII.

THE SAYBROOK ATTEMPT AND ITS FAILURE.

THE Saybrook colony was the offspring, in one sense, of the English king's committal to the policy of "thorough." There was in the kingdom, in addition to the comparatively helpless lower-class victims of Laud, an unknown number of gentlemen of good family who were thoroughly indoctrinated with Puritanism, or with kindred forms of dissent. These had as yet escaped serious persecution, partly through family and social influences, partly through the English reserve which, by checking any too violent expressions of dissent, had enabled family and social influences to have their full effect. About 1634–35 there were strong indications that the period of peace for this class was approaching its limit. Wentworth, in Ireland, was constructing the covered way by which the liberties of England were to be assailed. The heart of all Protestant Europe was yet faint and sick at the hideous atrocities of Tilly's musketeers at the sack of Magdeburg: was any more mercy to be expected by English cities at the hands of Wentworth's Irish musketeers? And who was to suppose that the supple body known as a parliament under Elizabeth and James would take the law into its own hands against Charles? Or that Puritanism would develop a soldiery before which the king's men would faint and fly? Patient and reserved men forgot that other Englishmen were as reserved, as patient and as dangerous as they, and concluded that hope was gone from England, and that there was no refuge but across the Atlantic.

It may be that the supposititious, or at least unverifiable grant to Warwick by the Council of Plymouth in 1630 was a pious fraud, designed to provide some such refuge, if the fear of confiscation of charter rights should deter Massachusetts from receiving refugees. The difficulty is to understand why the declaration of a baseless claim by the Say and Sele patentees, in the country and during the life of the original owner, should not have been met by a prompt contradiction. This is the strongest secondary evidence of the validity of the grant to Warwick in 1630, and its transfer to the Say and Sele Company in 1631, — that in 1634–35 the latter patentees made active and public preparations to enforce their claims to Connecticut and to remove there themselves, without exciting any complaint or opposition on the part of the Plymouth Council or their later grantees. That broad excuse, "the confusion of the times," may serve as a partial but hardly as an entirely satisfactory explanation.

John Winthrop, Sen., the governor of Massachusetts, had led the great Puritan migration to that colony in 1630. His son, John Winthrop, Jr., did not reach Boston until October, 1635. He was then a young man of twenty-nine, of good natural parts, well improved at Cambridge and Dublin and by travel on the continent, and he had already shown that philosophical, equable and judicial temperament which made him a trusted leader of men throughout his life. One of the bitterest critics of the early Massachusetts system hesitates before the beauties of the younger Winthrop's character, and calls him "perhaps the brightest ornament of New England Puritanism." His father's connection with the Say and Sele associates must have been close, and they must have seen in the son the qualities they needed. It thus happened that the son, on his way to Boston, was diverted into an interest in Connecticut, which finally made him more vitally important to that colony than the father had ever been to Massachusetts.

Articles of agreement were entered into July 7, 1635, between John Winthrop, Jr., of the one part, and Viscount Say and Sele, Sir Arthur Hasselring, Sir Richard Saltonstall, Henry Lawrence, Henry Darley and George Fenwick of the other. Robert, Lord Brooke, did not sign, but was a party in interest. Winthrop was to be fully compensated for his time and trouble, was to act as " governor of the river Connecticut in New England, and of the harbor and places adjoining," for one year, and was to build a fort at the mouth of the river, with a garrison of fifty men, reserving 1,000 or 1,500 acres of good ground, near the fort, for its maintenance. His commission as governor was signed, sealed and delivered to him July 18.

Winthrop arrived at Boston just a week before the first considerable migration to the Connecticut Valley. It is said that the intruding settlers made an agreement with him that, if the real owners, " their lordships," should require them to remove from their new settlements, they were to do so on receiving satisfaction for their improvements, or corresponding locations elsewhere. The agreement is referred to in the preamble to the Massachusetts commission to the provisional magistrates of Connecticut; but it is curious that it does not seem to be referred to in the elaborate series of instructions to Winthrop, and letters to the king and various English noblemen in regard to the charter, although it would have materially strengthened their case under the Fenwick purchase, as showing constructive permission from " their lordships " to settle, in default of notice to quit. Winthrop, to whom the instructions were addressed, was the very person who in 1635, as agent for the proprietors, had given them conditional permission to settle in the Connecticut Valley; and yet, in 1661, they allow themselves to appear to his majesty as originally sheer interlopers. In spite of the authority of the father's journal, the statement seems to lack some particulars essential to a clear understanding of it.

The mouth of the river had already been seized by an English force, in order to keep it from the Dutch; but the works constructed must have been of the most primitive character. A party of twenty men, sent by Winthrop, arrived at the fort and took possession November 24, 1635; and a little later came Winthrop himself and Lyon Gardiner, who soon became commander of the fort. For some years the garrison endured even more than the usual monotony of a frontier fort. Its men were ambushed and attacked during the Pequot struggle, but were restricted to a defensive warfare. Even settlement was really hindered by the fort. It drew danger, from Dutch or Indians, as the candle draws the moth; and its direct protection was only efficient enough to keep its people within the fort, and in a few scattered buildings very near it.

George Fenwick had visited the place the year of Winthrop's assumption of control. About midsummer of the year 1639 he returned with much more parade. He had two vessels, which brought also his wife, Lady Alice Boteler, and his family. The name Saybrook was given to the settlement in honor of the two leading proprietors, Lord Say and Lord Brooke; but the contemporary genius for misspelling, reacted upon by the neighborhood of the river and the Sound, made it read Seabrook for many years upon the Connecticut records.

The first minister was Rev. Thomas Peters, followed in 1646 by Rev. James Fitch, who removed in 1660 to settle at Norwich with most of his church, there to become very much entangled with the affairs of the Indians and the management of their lands. Besides these, Captain John Mason, a renowned man of war and major general of the Connecticut colony's militia, and Thomas Leffingwell, were the leading men; but there were many other Saybrook names which the Norwich migration transferred to that part of the commonwealth and subsequently far beyond its borders.

The tract of land usually considered as under the jurisdiction of Saybrook was about ten miles in length, divided midway by the Connecticut River, and extending six or eight miles back from Long Island Sound. Small as this territory was, it was of great importance as controlling the only water exit from the Hartford region, and as the seat of the representative of the only paper title within the future commonwealth. The authorities of Connecticut showed their usual acuteness by forming close relations with Fenwick. He was admitted to the first conference which formed the New England union in 1643; and, as that confederation recognized only the four colonies of Massachusetts, Plymouth, Connecticut and New Haven, Connecticut shrewdly appointed him as one of her commissioners in 1643 and 1644, with Edward Hopkins as the other. Fenwick was thus identified with Connecticut as closely as he could have been without an actual transfer of the rights which he represented. His second term of service as commissioner, in 1644, enabled him to render most important service to Connecticut in her boundary disputes with Massachusetts, which colony laid claim before the commissioners to the Pequot country. Fenwick interposed a protest against any decision which should in any way impeach his principals' title to the territory in dispute, and the commissioners decided to postpone the decision until the patentees could be heard from. The delay served to enable Connecticut to secure a firmer hold on the conquered territory before a final decision became imperative.

This diplomatic stroke had hardly been dealt when the Connecticut general court appointed a committee to treat with Fenwick for the sale of Saybrook. The logic of events had been too much for the Saybrook colony. The state of things at home was no longer what it had been in 1634. Whether Jenny Geddes ever threw her stool or not, a train of events had been started, bringing calamities to royalty and relief to the persecuted; the once supple parliament had taught

Wentworth the real meaning of "thorough;" and, above all, Cromwell and his Ironsides had charged at Marston Moor. Puritan gentlemen in England had other things to think of than emigrating to Saybrook; and Fenwick was hopelessly isolated. Connecticut had the purpose and power of growth, but there was no longer hope for Saybrook.

The agreement of sale was made December 5, 1644. Fenwick made over the fort, its appurtenances, and the land in the neighborhood to the colony of Connecticut. Lands not yet disposed of were to be distributed by a committee of five, of whom Fenwick was to be one. The rest of the Warwick patent, from Saybrook to Narragansett Bay, was to be brought by Fenwick "under the jurisdiction of Connecticut, if it came into his power." In return, Fenwick was to have the use of the buildings within the fort for ten years, with an impost on exports of corn, biscuit, beaver and cattle which should pass the fort during that time. As security to Fenwick, the general court ordered in the following February, in its ratification of the agreement, that every master of a vessel should land at the fort while passing it, and deliver to the commandant of the fort a note of the dutiable part of his cargo. In 1646 the amount was limited to £180 per annum, the total duty collected during the ten years being about £1,600.

The imposition of the duty nearly disrupted

the New England union. In 1647 Massachusetts filed a protest against it before the commissioners of the union. She claimed that Connecticut had no right to levy on the Massachusetts towns of the upper Connecticut Valley a tax which was to inure to Connecticut's sole benefit in the acquisition of Saybrook. In 1649 the commissioners of the other three colonies decided against the protest of Massachusetts. Thereupon the Massachusetts commissioners exhibited an order of their general court, levying a tax on all goods of the other colonies imported into or exported from Boston, ostensibly for the repair of the castle in the harbor. The suspiciously opportune circumstance of the castle's need of repairs just at this time excited considerable anger in the other colonies; and this was intensified in 1653 by the refusal of Massachusetts to join the other colonies in a war against the Dutch and Indians. Perhaps the feeling in the latter case was the greater on account of the attitude assumed by Massachusetts, that of an advocate of peace and righteousness, averse to an offensive war; whereas the fact, as it seemed to contemporary observers, was that the governing desire of the Bay colony was to convince the other colonies of their impotence, and of their folly in supporting the refusal of Connecticut to yield to Massachusetts even in the petty affair of the impost. With the expiration of Fenwick's ten years' term the retaliatory measures were quietly allowed to disappear: probably the castle had been put into good repair by that time.

With the conclusion of the agreement of 1644, Saybrook subsided into the position of a Connecticut township. Fenwick continued to reside at the fort, but took no prominent part in Connecticut affairs. The Connecticut general court requested him to return to England at his earliest convenience, and act as its agent in procuring that grant of the entire jurisdiction under the patent which he had promised to get "if it ever came within his power to do so." Lady Fenwick died at Saybrook about 1648, and her husband soon after returned to England, giving up the last vestige of the commercial city which was to have graced the mouth of the Connecticut. He died in 1657, before the colony applied for a charter.

The Connecticut authorities were diligent in disseminating the idea, and were perhaps honest in their own belief, that Colonel Fenwick's sale had been a transfer of the patent and of the jurisdiction thereunder, for this gave the colony a quasi-legal standing which it had not before. When Massachusetts, during the impost and boundary disputes, impugned the standing of Connecticut as a colony unauthorized and unwarranted by law, the latter colony always replied that it had a charter or patent in England, but that "the confusion of the times" prevented it from showing anything more than a copy. It was when the confusion began to disappear, and the validity of the excuse with it, that the colony took steps to secure a charter from the king. In the instructions to Governor Winthrop, the colonial authorities lay great stress on the Fenwick sale as involving the equitable transfer of the patent itself, although the terms of the agreement contradict them. They go so far as to say, "Had we not been too credulous and confident of the goodness and faithfulness of that gentleman [Fenwick], we might possibly have been at a better pass;" and they direct the governor to take steps to recover from Fenwick's heirs the amount paid to him. They even sequestered the colonial estate of Mrs. Cullick, Fenwick's sister and his New England heir, until £500 were repaid and further claims were remitted. It would be far more than even-handed justice to the fathers of the Connecticut colony to admit that they were the simple victims of the wiles of George Fenwick: if he could so easily delude them, he was more successful than their other contemporaries. They seem to have understood perfectly in 1644 the wares for which they were then bargaining, and were quite aware that this part of the consideration was purely contingent. So impossible was it in 1661 for the contingency to be fulfilled that the letter of the colony to the king takes conspicuous care not to mention the Fenwick agreement at all. Perhaps its attitude toward the Fenwick family may best be explained as that of men who had bought a contingency, found it less valuable than they expected, and were unwilling to confess their error even to one another.

On the other hand, the romantic life and death of Lady Fenwick ought not to give to her husband's character that generous glamour which Connecticut historians have been too prone to allow him. It should not be forgotten that he deliberately sold and appropriated the proceeds of property of which he was not the sole owner, only the agent. The colonial authorities yielded to his demand for £1,600 for property which was not his, rather than see it sold to the Dutch; and they paid the sum agreed upon. But the substantial iniquity of the transaction undoubtedly stirred them to a greater eagerness to make use of the invalidity of one feature of the agreement in order to secure substantial justice in others. On the whole, the merits of the case seem to be with the colony.

CHAPTER IX.

CONNECTICUT UNTIL THE UNION.

It is much to be regretted that the fathers of the Connecticut colony seem to have been too much immersed in the struggle for existence to give us any record of the appearance of men and things in these early years. In this respect, Connecticut is unfortunate beyond any of her sister commonwealths. Hartford, the subsequent capital of the colony and state, may be taken as an example. There does not seem to be any surviving map, plan, picture, sketch or verbal description of the town, or of any public or private building, until about the time of the Revolution. Even the zeal of the antiquary finds "no thoroughfare" inscribed almost immediately on every clue which would have been a promising one in Massachusetts. The contemporary letters, journals, etc., seem to take existing things for granted. The minds of the writers were occupied almost exclusively with the actions of men; and the pregnant incidental hints as to social features, manners and customs, topography, etc., which are so frequently furnished in other colonies by writers who had no notion that they were furnishing them, are not found in Connecticut. This was due to the peculiar nature of the early struggles in the colony. Difficulties of soil, commerce and general industry were no new matters with them: their wits were working mainly to know what other men might do or could do; how Massachusetts men would act about the boundary line; how the Dutch would act about Long Island and the territory west of the Connecticut River; how Englishmen would settle their home government; and what would be the influence on the fortunes of the little congeries of towns which, formed without a legal title, had never acquired one except from a man who never had it and did not profess to sell it. Determined as they were to maintain the integrity of their colonial existence, the impediments were enormous, and almost all of them lay in possible human action. It is no wonder, then, that the early official and unofficial records of Connecticut deal so largely with this one side of human history, and give us so little of any other.

Antiquarian zeal has overcome some of these difficulties. The process of tracing back land titles through the records of land transfers has given us an excellent map of Hartford in 1640, which, though partly conjectural, gives what is probably a very close representation of the town. It lies on the west bank of the Connecticut River, where the river runs nearly due south. Running eastward, through the southern central part of the town, is the "little river," or "riveret," a swift-flowing brook, whose depth varied with the seasons. The bulk of the town was thus to the north of the little river, and to the west of the Connecticut. Like the city of Washington, it was at first a city of magnificent distances. Its first settlers laid it out on a scale so generous that it was not necessary to enlarge the city limits until 1853, or to add more than one highway to the original roads during the century and a half between the settlement of Hartford and its incorporation as a city in 1784. Only one tenth of the township was included in the city limits of 1784; the city now covers the whole township, and its streets have increased from thirty to three hundred in number within the present century.

At the mouth of the little river is the Dutch post Good Hope, still in the possession of its original owners in 1640, as Berwick-upon-Tweed long marked the remnant of the English claims in Scotland. Alongside the main river was a strip of meadow land, and along the rising ground which bounded it on the west ran the highway from Boston, which passed through the three river towns, and afterwards became the highway to the whole territory to the south. On the north bank of the little river, fronting a road along its edge, there were placed in succession the houses of Governor

Haynes, of Rev. Mr. Hooker, of Rev. Mr. Stone, and of Elder Goodwin, " Meeting House Alley " separating Hooker and Stone. Meeting House Alley ran from the little river to a square (now State House Square), some distance in the rear of Stone and Goodwin, and nearly in the topographical center of the town, which contained the market place, the jail, and the meeting house. The mass of the lots on this side of the town, except those fronting on the little river, lay east and west, perpendicular to the Boston highway and the parallel roads. The lots to the south of the little river lay mostly north and south, perpendicular to the highway along the little river and the parallel streets. Almost all the meadow land on this side of the little river, down to the Dutch settlement, was owned by Edward Hopkins, the colony's leading merchant; and to the southwest of his tract was the estate of the Wyllys family, on which was that which was to be the Charter Oak. Further up the little river were the tanyard, located on an island; and the mill, on the northern shore. Outside of the town were the cow pasture, the ox pasture, the landing, etc., and the roads were named according to the places to which they led.

Few particulars are known of the size or appearance of the meeting house, or of any other building. All the buildings were very certainly small, though the erection of a sawmill in 1667 is an indication of an early improvement in house-building. The windows were hardly more than openings for light and air; and their size was reduced by the scarcity of glass, and the necessity of using oiled linen or other translucent material as a substitute. The meeting house was too small to admit of galleries, or of anything more than the merest suggestion of a pulpit. There was no plaster. Instead of pews there were plain and hard benches, and artificial heat was unknown, even in the bitterest weather. Indeed, the Hartford church had no stoves until about 1815; and what Lodge calls " the ferocious practice " of baptizing newly born infants in church must have had an additional horror in the depth of winter. Finally an armed guard, suggestive of Indian neighbors, was an inseparable accompaniment to religious services, and was provided with seats near the door. In the other Connecticut towns, religious and other meetings were called by beat of drum, one of the inhabitants making an annual contract for the service. Hartford alone had a bell, brought from Cambridge, which was probably at that time the only church or public bell on the continent, with the exception of the one at Jamestown, Va. Its contents now make part of the bell, recast in 1850, belonging to the First Congregational Church of Hartford. New Haven had no church bell until 1681.

One of the most difficult and delicate functions

of a church committee in Connecticut and New Haven towns was the seating of the congregation. A transfer of a family from one seat to another betokened a social rise or fall. In the smaller towns, such transfers were usually made by a majority vote at a town meeting; and the town records have numberless entries of permissions granted to fortunate and rising men to sit "in the justice's pew," or "in the cross pew by the second pillar," or "in the second pew on the right," the proper places for their wives, on their side of the house, being as carefully specified.

Finally the meeting house was used for a long time for every variety of secular purposes, not only as a place for town and other meetings, but as a place of deposit for arms, military provisions, and lost or stolen property. The Hartford church building was not merely the scene of ecclesiastical councils: the meetings of the New England commissioners, of deputies from other commonwealths, and even the exciting conferences with Andros in regard to the charter, took place here. It was not until toward the middle of the next century that the towns began to see the incongruity of secular business in a dedicated house of worship, and began to erect townhouses and other distinctively public buildings.

Bad as were the roads of the United States almost everywhere until the era of turnpikes set in, and railroads in their turn forced the turnpikes up to a higher standard, the roads of Hartford and its neighborhood had a certain evil preëminence. The excellence of the soil was reflected in the bad character of the roads. Its tenacious clay only needed moisture enough to become a weariness to the flesh of horses and of men. Within the last thirty years, says one authority, wagons have been seen sunk to the hub in the native clay of Pearl Street, close to the center of the city. In 1774 the town prisoners for debt represented to the general assembly that the roads were for a considerable part of the year so miry and impassable that no one came to the jail to bestow alms on the prisoners; and they petitioned that the jail limits should be enlarged. What the roads must have been in still earlier days passes speculation. It may perhaps be that the early years of John Fitch, of Windsor, spent in annual experiences of the horrors of Hartford roads, were the influence which turned his attention to improving the waterways of the country by endeavoring to perfect the steamboat.

Mr. J. C. Parsons "cannot discover that any land in the town is now in possession of the descendants of the original owners, having been continuously in the possession of the family; some, through female heirs, may possibly be so held." This state of things is common to most Connecticut towns, but it does not imply that the original stock is dying out. It is only a symptom of the universal readiness to transfer property and assume new property relations. There is hardly a Connecticut town in which the names of the first settlers are not as absolutely numerous as at the settlement; if there is any relative decrease, it is due to the superimposition of a foreign population. The old names, even the Christian names, show a remarkable persistence, and an equally remarkable persistence in the characteristic of property-holding, even though their possessors have exchanged family for other property. The original fecundity is shown in the fact, that, in spite of this persistence, it is the old family names which have shown a disposition to drift out of the commonwealth by emigration. For this there have been four main channels: in early years, to Vermont, and so over the border into New York; later, to Pennsylvania (Wyoming) and to central New York; later still, to the Western Reserve of Ohio, and so throughout that State and the West; and of recent years, to New York city, and thence in every direction. In addition to these main channels, isolated routes of migration have been innumerable, so that Connecticut names are now to be found in every part of the Union. Such a steady stream of migration could not but have hastened this process of alienation of family property. Those who migrated soon disposed of their share of the patrimony, and it regularly passed away from the name, though not necessarily from

Connecticut names and stock. The absence of ancestral holdings in the State is merely a redistribution of the original holdings.

The Massachusetts man and woman of 1637-38 are the exact social representatives of the early Connecticut settlers, except so far as the poverty and meagerness of the Massachusetts life of the time were still further intensified by the difficulties of an absolutely new settlement. There are said to have been but thirty plows at the time in all Massachusetts: what estimate shall we make for the new and struggling Connecticut colony? We have, unfortunately, no such Pepys as Judge Sewall for early life in Connecticut, but Sewall's hints as to the hardships of early Massachusetts life may well be reinforced and transferred to our commonwealth. The utter lack of a multitude of things which have come to seem absolute necessaries in the eyes of their descendants; the difficulties of travel and communication; the complete isolation from the outer world through the grim months of a New England winter, during which the sacramental bread in the churches was sometimes frozen on the plates; the bitterness of the winter cold even in private houses, where the ink sometimes froze in the inkstands within a few feet of the great fire; the utter inadequacy of medical and surgical attendance; the ignorance of and antagonism to the art of amusement in every form; the incongruous mixture of the civilized and the savage, in a society in which a minister, trained in an English university, might be called away from writing a treatise on the dealings of the English commonwealth with its former king, or with the American churches, to drive a drunken Indian out of his kitchen, or chaffer with a hunter for food or clothing, — these were social conditions from which the early settler did not escape by removing from Massachusetts to Connecticut, and they are more fairly within the province of the Massachusetts historian.

There are, however, certain visible distinctions between the drift of public events in Connecticut and in Massachusetts which make it difficult to believe that there was not some hidden differentiation between the people of the three migrating towns and of the five which were left, which has colored their whole subsequent history.

The difficulties between king and parliament were at their height when the Connecticut colony was founded; and for more than half a century the relations of the house of Stuart to its various opponents formed the critical public question for the New England colonies. Throughout this period there was probably no great difference between the underlying purposes of the two colonies under consideration. Both meant to preserve the public privileges which they had gained, to extend their territory and jurisdiction, and to evade or resist the interference of the home government with their autonomy. But the methods of Massachusetts were peculiarly her own. There were strong reasons, in the history, traditions, and consistent public teachings of the colony, why she should pose as the pronounced champion of colonial liberties. On every occasion she seems to have felt it to be incumbent upon her to assume a more or less decided public attitude, and equally incumbent upon her strongest neighbor, Connecticut, to support her by a similar course. In very many cases Connecticut did so; in fact, the most common criticism of her policy by her own people was that she was too apt to " trot after the Bay horse." But every case in which Connecticut chose to follow a policy of her own seemed to the Bay colony only an instance of unmanly defection rather than of independent action.

The consistent policy of Connecticut, on the other hand, was to avoid notoriety and public attitudes; to secure her privileges without attracting needless notice; to act as intensely and vigorously as possible when action seemed necessary and promising; but to say as little as possible, yield as little as possible, and evade as much as possible when open resistance was evident folly. Much of the difference must have been due to the different circumstances of the two colonies. Massachusetts, secure in the possession of a charter, must have felt always that, even if beaten down from any claim, she could fall back, in the last resort, upon her legal privileges. Connecticut, while without a charter, must have felt the same hesitation in following some of the leads of her neighbor which an unarmored vessel would feel in following some of the motions of an ironclad ; but the steady continuance of her policy after she had obtained a charter seems to argue some structural difference in the people. Her line of public conduct was precisely the same after as before 1662. And its success was remarkable : it is safe to say that the diplomatic skill, forethought, and self-control shown by the men who guided the course of Connecticut during this period have seldom been equaled on the larger fields of the world's history. As products of democracy, they were its best vindication.

The period closed in 1691 with the loss of the original charter of Massachusetts, the imposition of a new and restricted charter upon her, and the palpable and even conscious inability of her public men to make good by action the positions assumed in the past. The mortification of this defeat was aggravated by the pronounced success of the Connecticut policy. The best of New England's historians has not hesitated to avow and to reiterate his conviction, not only that Connecticut left Massachusetts in the lurch, but that she allowed her application for a charter to be used by the royal agents as an essential instrument in the disintegration of the New England union and the final humiliation of Massachusetts.

Such a conclusion assumes far too much. It would have been just, in the first place, if Connecticut had ever imitated the Massachusetts positions, and had given Massachusetts to understand that she had entered the union for the purpose of upholding the Massachusetts policy. On the contrary, the Connecticut policy was a matter of notoriety among New England public men from the beginning. The accusation of Massachusetts was wholly an afterthought to cover her own want of forethought in sacrificing democracy to class influence, and in thus drifting into a position where she was hopelessly stalemated. It must always have been baseless, except on the supposition that Connecticut was in some manner bound to follow her neighbor's lead, and to surrender her own right of judgment in every great emergency, a course which Connecticut was not bound or likely to take. In the second place, an admission of the legality, with an impeachment of the justice, of Connecticut's policy, assumes that a decided adherence by Connecticut to the Massachusetts policy would have resulted in obtaining a more complete autonomy for all the New England colonies, and would have saved the union. But this is mere conjecture, and improbable as well. It is no more probable, at least, than that Massachusetts would have scored a success equal to that of Connecticut by following a similar line of policy. It is no answer to this to say that Massachusetts preferred failure, after an heroic resistance, to success attained by shifty and temporizing measures: the less said about the heroism shown by the dominant class of Massachusetts, in the events which culminated in 1691, the better. Its nullification of the articles of union in 1652-54 had taken the life out of them: they never again showed any vitality, and the Connecticut charter simply gave decent burial to the corpse.

The facts are, that these commonwealths were then hardly fitted for complete autonomy; that the Connecticut policy obtained about as much as was practicable or best at the time, while the Massachusetts policy obtained considerably less. The spirit which still moves the Connecticut workman to invent anything rather than expend a foot-pound of energy uselessly, seems to have actuated the people from the beginning. They would receive Andros, for example, most deferentially, make no sign of resistance until resistance could take its most vigorous and effective form: then the work was done thoroughly, and almost absolute silence followed until the next opportunity for decisive action. No one can study the history of the commonwealth without being struck with the individuality of the people, as shown in their public career; or, without believing that that individuality was not due simply to circumstances, to their thirty years' struggle for a charter, but that it belonged to them even in Massachusetts, perhaps even in old England.

From their first settlement, Hartford and "ancient" Windsor seem to have gone quietly and steadily on in their natural course of development. Wethersfield had migrated without a minister, and, for this or some other reason, its course of development ran ill from the first. Within its first half dozen years of life, its neighbor towns and New Haven were compelled to offer "loving counsel" as to Wethersfield difficulties; and Davenport, of New Haven, put his into the wise suggestion that the minority should migrate again. The minority who acted on this advice settled at Stamford and formed a New Haven town. In 1644 another portion of the Wethersfield minority, as has been said, removed to the New Haven jurisdiction and formed part of the town of Branford.

There seems to have been no defined method of turning a settlement into a political "town," beyond the mere act of the general court in receiving its deputies, until after the charter was obtained. It is difficult, therefore, to assign any exact date to the political birth of the early Connecticut towns. The growth of the family may be traced in the steady increase in the number of deputies in the general court itself. There were seventeen deputies in 1649; twenty in 1650; twenty-two in 1651; twenty-five in 1654; and twenty-six in 1656–57, this number remaining the maximum until after the union was consummated under the charter. The increase came from the successive recognition of the new towns of Saybrook, Stratford, Farmington, Fairfield, Norwalk, Middletown, New London, Norwich, and the Long Island towns — Huntington, Southampton and East Hampton; but there can be no pretense at accuracy in saying when each of these towns was first represented in the general court. Town recognition seems really to have taken a somewhat different line, hinging on those ancient and important functionaries, the constables. Professor H. B. Adams has said: " We do not suppose that this has always been a conscious standard for legislative action in the recognition of towns, or for the actual determination of town or parish units; but we claim that without a constable, or some power representing the corporate responsibility of the community for the preservation of the local peace, a town would be an impossibility." His evident hesitation in making an assertion which would seem almost a truism to the Connecticut historian is another illustration of the unwisdom of confining the study of the New England town system to its phases in Massachusetts, as if it had been a thing peculiar to that commonwealth. In fact, it can be studied better, for many purposes, in Connecticut than in Massachusetts; for the town in Connecticut was almost as free as independency itself until near the period of the charter, while in Massachusetts it was circumscribed from the beginning by commonwealth power. Professor

Adams will find his supposition, doubtful as it may be under the comparatively artificial Massachusetts system, emphatically confirmed under the more natural Connecticut system. We know, for example, that the Indian purchase on which the town of Norwalk rests was made in 1640, and that settlement began about 1650; and we infer from various circumstances that the purchase and settlement of Middletown took place about 1646–47. But the record of their " incorporation " is no more than a vote of the general court, September 11, 1651, that " Mattabeseck [Middletown] and Norwalke " should be towns and should choose constables. As the collection of taxes and the announcement of elections were among the functions of the constable, it seems probable that the express or tacit recognition of the town's constable was in effect until the charter, a recognition of the town itself and of its right to choose deputies. The records really show no other. The difficulty of the general court in dealing with new towns was about parallel with the difficulty of the congress of the confederation in dealing with the quasi State of Vermont.

A parallel indication of the growth of the colony is to be found in the tax-lists. The first distinct increase of taxable property comes December 1, 1645, when the general court granted a "rate" of £400, "to be paid by the country." Of this amount £340 was to be paid by the three original towns; £45 by Stratford and Fairfield; £15 by Saybrook; and £10 each by Tunxis (Farmington) and Southampton, L. I. In 1652 the "rates" were still confined to the towns just named, Southampton being omitted. It is an indication of the prosperity resulting from sixteen years' work that the assessed value of the property in these seven towns was now £70,000, as follows: Hartford, £20,000; Windsor, £14,100; Wethersfield, £11,500; Farmington, £5,200; Saybrook, £3,600; Stratford, £7,000; and Fairfield, £8,900. In the following year, three new towns, Pequot (New London), Mattabesek (Middletown), and Norwalk, are recognized in a draft of men for an armed force, as well as in the rates; and the assessed value rises to £79,700. In 1661, just before the receipt of the charter, the assessed value rises to £84,137. The usual tax assessed upon this amount was a penny or a halfpenny, constituting a "rate" or a "half rate."

Long Island had never been more than nominally under the jurisdiction of the Dutch. They had planted a few farms at its western end, but the rest of the island was a wilderness. Among the multitude of conflicting and unintelligible grants made by the council of Plymouth before its dissolution, was one to the Earl of Stirling, covering Long Island. The grantee seems to have claimed ownership only, not jurisdiction. In practice, therefore, when his agent sold a piece of territory, the new owners became an independent political community, with some claims against them, but no direct control. The island was thus in much the same position as the Connecticut territory before the first irruption of settlers, and offered much the same attractions as a place of refuge for persons or communities who had found the connection between church and state grievous. A company from Lynn, Mass., bought the township of Southampton from Stirling's agent, April 17, 1640. There were at first but sixteen persons in the company, Abraham Pierson being their minister. This was the church which, first removing to Branford in 1644, when Southampton became a Connecticut town, finally settled at Newark, N. J. Easthampton was settled about 1648, by another Lynn party, and was received as a Connecticut town, November 7, 1649. The town of Huntington, though part of it was bought from the Indians by Governor Eaton, of New Haven, in 1646, really dates from about 1653. May 17, 1660, it was received as a Connecticut town. There were thus three Connecticut towns on Long Island, in addition to Southold, the New Haven township. Between these and the really Dutch settlements at the western end of the island, there were English settlements in the neighborhood of Hempstead; but these acknowledged a much closer dependence on the Dutch authorities.

Hardly any of the expansion of Connecticut, prior to the grant of the charter which gave a legal basis to its claims, was due to accident. In almost all of it we can see very clearly a provident determination on the part of the people to give their commonwealth respectable limits, and to turn to account every favoring circumstance in that direction. Hardly was the Pequot war under way when the general court resolved to send thirty men to occupy "the Pequoitt Countrey & River in place convenient to maynteine our right that God by Conquest hath given us." And from this moment Connecticut maintained her right by conquest to the whole of the present eastern part of the State with a vigor which was in itself strong promise of success. One secret of the commonwealth's success, in this as in the Saybrook and other cases, was the policy which it followed with adverse claimants, a policy which the politico-religious constitution of New Haven prevented it from imitating. Instead of engaging in a struggle with a rival, the Connecticut democracy always endeavored to adopt him, to make its interests his, and so to secure even a better title out of conflict. In the case of the Pequot country, it was John Winthrop, Jr., the former agent of the Saybrook proprietors, who developed an inchoate rivalry with the colony for possession of the coveted territory; and Connecticut's policy, carefully applied, not only strengthened her title to the Pequot country, but gave her one of the best of her long line of excellent governors, and was in the end one of the chief means of obtaining her long desired charter. Winthrop's attention had been turned to the Pequot country. Fisher's Island, "against the mouth of the Pequot River," was granted to him by the Massachusetts general court, October 7, 1640, with a reservation of the possibly superior title of Connecticut or New Haven; and Connecticut, instead of taking any exceptions to the grant, promptly confirmed it. In 1644 Massachusetts gave Winthrop authority to "make a plantation in the Pequot country." He went to the place in the following spring, and in the autumn of 1646 had gathered a few families there, and was beginning to put up houses. The claims of Massachusetts were grounded on the fact that her troops had taken part in the conquest of the Pequots; and the case was decided against her by the New England commissioners in July, 1647. Connecticut at once gave Winthrop a commission, September 9, 1647, to execute justice in his town "according to our laws and the rule of righteousness." May 17, 1649, the court established the boundaries of the new town and named its magistrates. One of these two dates, and most probably the former, is to be taken as the town's entrance to the list of Connecticut towns. On the latter date, the court suggested the name "Fair Haven," but the people preferred that of New London.

The last of the Connecticut towns before the charter was Norwich, an offshoot of Saybrook. Its settlement was approved, under the name of "Mohegan," by the general court in 1659; and it was summoned, October 3, 1661, under the name of "Norridge," to send representatives.

The divergence between the Connecticut colony and its sister and rival of New Haven had become marked long before Monk began his march for London. The attempt has been made in this chapter to state some of the elements of strength of Connecticut. It had become a strong, well-balanced political unit, with a clear notion of a territorial goal to be striven for, and of the line of policy to be pursued in striving for it. Its democracy gave every man a personal interest in the maintenance of the colony's claims; and the results were another proof that "everybody knows more than anybody." Its towns were as free as towns could well be; the right of suffrage was as nearly as possible universal; it can hardly be said that there were any dissatisfied elements to be placated, or else to fester in the vitals of the commonwealth; and the steady bias of the commonwealth toward civil and religious freedom had enabled it to find elements of increased strength in what might have been elements of intestine weakness. For twenty years or more, the "loving brethren" of Connecticut and New Haven lived on in entire satisfaction with one another's corporate existence. The time had then come when the growing commonwealth found that the separate existence of New Haven was a complete obstacle to the natural course of development of Connecticut. The comparative weakness of New Haven will come out in the narrative of the events which led to the union; but it is fair to say in advance that one of the most effective of these weakening elements in New Haven was the apparent agreement of a part of her people with Connecticut rather than with their own colony. Freedom was more attractive in the long run than restriction.

CHAPTER X.

THE TWO COLONIES UNTIL THE UNION.

THE organization in which the idea of the American Union first cropped out, to exist a while and then to die away almost unnoticed, was the New England union of 1643. As Massachusetts was the most distinguished and influential member of this confederation, the full account of its origin and history should in fairness be reserved to Massachusetts historians. It will not be improper to say here that such a union had been proposed by Connecticut in 1637, just after the settlement; but Massachusetts received the proposal with a demand that her right to Agawam (Springfield) and to free navigation of the Connecticut should be recognized. Connecticut's answer was so "harsh" that the further consideration of the matter lapsed for some years. It soon turned out that Massachusetts had right on her side, so far, at least, as the jurisdiction over Springfield was concerned; and the extreme confusion of English affairs, through the struggle between king and parliament, was an inducement to the New England colonies to suspend all minor differences, and combine for common defense against the Indians and the Dutch. In 1643 the union was formed, consisting of Massachusetts, Plymouth, Connecticut, and New Haven. Connecticut had not yet advanced far enough on the road to a clear comprehension of her future to make any objections to New Haven's separate existence; but New Haven's hurry to organize a systematic government and take part in the confederation seems to show at least a dawning suspicion of a possible conflict between her own interests and those of her neighbor. There was not yet any considerable superiority of one colony over the other: their respective populations are estimated at 3,000 for Connecticut and 2,500 for New Haven.

The leading reason for the formation of the union was probably the inability of the home government, during the confusion of the civil war, to afford protection to the New-Englanders against the claims of the Dutch colony of New Netherland. With the most amicable feelings on both sides, the Dutch colony, thrust in between English colonies to the south and to the north of it, must have been pressed more hardly as the English colonies grew, until at last the question of the annexation or independent existence of New Netherland must have called imperatively for settlement. But the feelings on neither side were really amicable. The New England settler was an Englishman; and the Englishman of that time had a chronic disposition to regard the Dutchman as a commercial rival, and an habitual intruder into places where he had no good excuse for being. As the New England Englishmen found themselves forced into nearer relations with the New Netherland Dutch, the two parties met with many of the old animosities still unhealed. The grant to the New Netherland company by the States General of Holland, October 11, 1614, had covered all the territory "between New France and Virginia, the sea-coasts of which lie between the fortieth and forty-fifth degrees of latitude," that is, from about the present location of Philadelphia to the Bay of Fundy. This nominal jurisdiction was really confirmed by the States General to the Dutch West India Company in 1621 for twenty-four years; but in course of time the growth of English settlement compelled the Dutch to modify this nominal claim, and to rely on the discoveries of Hudson to support their claims to the district between the thirty-eighth and forty-second degrees of latitude, or from about the mouth of the Potomac to the mouth of the Connecticut. As the greatest concession to the English, based on the English charters then in existence, they claimed the coast from Cape May to the mouth of the Connecticut, from latitude 39° to latitude 41°. In answer to all these official and unofficial claims, the English finally relied on the voyages of the Cabots as entitling them to the whole coast, including the parts explored by Hudson, which they declined to take as real discoveries. But at first, with the possible expedition of one Captain Argal, of Virginia, about 1614, who is said to have compelled "the pretended Dutch governor" at the mouth of the Hudson to submit to the king of England and promise tribute, the English for many years quietly acquiesced in the Dutch settlement. Their objection was to the extent, not to the fact, of the Dutch colony.

The Delaware company, including nearly all the leading men of New Haven, had been formed for colonization purposes. Following the New Haven policy of purchase, the New Haven settlers had sent an agent in 1640, who bought from the natives a tract of land on both sides of the Delaware River. In the following year the New Haven civil authority asserted its *jurisdiction* over the purchased territory; and a company was sent out which settled on the west shore of the Delaware, near what is now known as Salem Creek. This was under the governorship of Kieft; and William the Testy sent two ships in 1642 with a detachment of troops, who attacked the settlement, burned its houses and made the settlers prisoners. Remonstrance for this step was almost the first business of the commissioners of the New England union; but they got no satisfaction from Kieft. In 1649 Governor Eaton made another appeal to the commissioners for help; but the commissioners were not disposed to enter upon a quarrel at the time. They would refuse to assist any persons from any other colony who should attempt to settle the Delaware purchase without the consent of New Haven; but they would not maintain the claims of New Haven against the Dutch by force. The failure of the scheme was a blow from which independent New Haven never recovered. Her richest men had ventured their all and lost it, and the colony was in sore straits for some years.

The Dutch West India Company perceived clearly the growing strength of the English colonies. In reply to the appeal of the new Dutch governor, Stuyvesant, for authority to repel force by force, and for material aid, the home corporation declined to think of war, which, they said, "cannot in any event be to our advantage: the New England people are too powerful for us." Thus left in the lurch by his superiors, Stuyvesant could do no more than take the best terms obtainable; and it is creditable to him that he kept his colony in existence more than ten years longer. His first step was to go to Hartford, to meet the New England commissioners in negotiation, arriving there September 11, 1650. He took high ground from the beginning. He insisted on having the negotiations conducted in writing; and, in his first letter, he not only protested against the presence of the English in Connecticut as an infringement on the undoubted rights of the Dutch, but dated the letter at "New Netherland," thus calmly assuming every point in dispute. The commissioners were not to be caught. They refused to receive the letter and thus acknowledge that Hartford was within the Dutch territory. He finally yielded the point, and a long correspondence resulted in an agreement to submit all the questions between Dutch and English to four arbitrators, two to be named by the governor, and two by the commissioners. Stuyvesant named Englishmen as his agents, and the four agreed upon a settlement of the boundary matter, ignoring all other points in dispute as having occurred under the administration of Kieft. It was agreed that the Dutch were to retain their lands in Hartford; that the boundary line between the two peoples on the mainland was not to come within ten miles of the Hudson River, but was to be left undecided for the present, except the first twenty miles from the Sound, which was to begin on the west side of Greenwich Bay, between Stamford and Manhattan, running thence twenty miles north; and that Long Island should be divided by a corresponding line across it, "from the westernmost part of Oyster Bay" to the sea. The English thus got the greater part of Long Island, a recognition of the rightfulness of their presence in the Connecticut territory, and at least the initial twenty miles of a boundary line which must, in the nature of things, be prolonged in much the same direction, and which in fact has pretty closely governed subsequent boundary lines on that side of Connecticut. If these seem hard terms for the Dutch, and indicative of treachery on the part of their two English agents, it must be borne in mind that, by the terms of his instructions from his principals, Stuyvesant had to take the best terms he could get. The treaty of Hartford was dated September 19, 1650.

Peter Stuyvesant was probably not satisfied with the treaty, even though he was compelled to accept it. At all events, he soon furnished fresh occasion for negotiation. In the spring of 1651, the New Haven people fitted out another vessel for their Delaware Bay settlement. It touched at New Amsterdam, and its appearance put the last of the Dutch governors into a terrible rage. He arrested officers and passengers, and only released them with sounding threats of the fate of any future New Haven expedition to the Delaware, on their promise to return at once to New Haven. Again the New Haven adventurers appealed to the New England commissioners, and those officials this time espoused their cause. They wrote to Stuyvesant, charging him with a breach of the treaty, though it is not easy to see on what grounds; and a resolution was passed, promising protection to any Delaware settlement against all comers, provided it should number a hundred and fifty men. Still there was no collision.

In the following year, vague rumors of an impending Dutch and Indian war nearly brought about the long expected struggle. As the New England colonies came nearer to the Dutch, the resulting complications with the Indians increased. The two Connecticut colonies, as has been said, had no difficulties with their own Indians after the downfall of the Pequots. Their main difficulties arose in the southwestern corner of the present State, in the district where now is the town of Greenwich. The district had been bought by its first owner, Robert Feake, as a part of the New Haven jurisdiction; but the Dutch had seduced the first inhabitants, under Captain Patrick, who had a Dutch wife, to come under their jurisdiction and accept a place as a Dutch town. It had been agreed at Hartford that Greenwich should be restored to New Haven; but the usual vices of a border settlement seem to have prevailed here. Later, in 1656, the deputies of Stamford at New Haven complained bitterly of the conduct of the people of Greenwich, of "their disorderly walkeing among themselues, admitting of drunkenness both amonge the English and Indians, whereby they are apt to doe mischeife both to themselues and others: they receive disorderly children or seruants who fly from their parrents or masters lawfull correction; they marry persons in a disorderly way, beside other miscariages." It was in this Alsatia that the troubles seem to have begun which broke out first in the war of 1643 between the Dutch and Indians, when the Dutch called in Captain Underhill, of Stamford, as their commander-in-chief, and in the course of which Mrs. Hutchinson, who had found refuge here from her Massachusetts enemies, was done to death by the Indians. Other Indian outrages took place at intervals in the neighborhood. A Stamford Indian, found guilty of one of the most atrocious of these, was taken to New Haven and executed by decapitation. "He sat erect and motionless," says the New Haven record, "until his head was severed from his body." There was enough trouble with the Indians in this quarter to make it a source of universal alarm when, in the spring of 1652, it was rumored that Stuyvesant had induced all the Indians to unite against the English, and had supplied them with ammunition. The evidence of the existence of the plot was in the affidavits of a number of the Indians themselves, a class of evidence which ought of itself to have been Stuyvesant's complete vindication. A majority of the commissioners, however, believed it, and based upon it an ultimatum to Stuyvesant. The accusation naturally made Stuyvesant very indignant, and he demanded a committee of investigation. The commissioners sent three distinguished New-Englanders to New Amsterdam to act as such committee. The tone of their letters was not conciliatory, or calculated to inspire the governor with confidence in his judges; and he refused to answer any questions except such as should be approved by persons whom he should select. His reason doubtless was his diffidence of his familiarity with the language in which the examination was to be conducted. But, as the persons whom he selected had "been complained of for misdemeanors at Hartford, and one of them had been laid under bonds for his crimes," the committee took the whole proceeding as a fresh affront, and judges and accused parted in still higher exasperation with one another. On the report of the committee, whose members had obtained new evidence of Stuyvesant's duplicity and treachery on their way home, all the commissioners except those of Massachusetts declared for war. Massachusetts referred the question to her ministers, who declared that, while they believed the evidence against the Dutch governor, it was not sufficient to justify a war before the judgment of the rest of the world; and that the colonies should stand on the defensive, without declaring war. One of their number, who claimed to write on behalf of "many pensive hearts," took more warlike ground, and threatened the commissioners with the curse of the angel of the Lord against Meroz unless they declared war upon Stuyvesant. But the resolution of the majority was more satisfactory to the Massachusetts general court, and it steadfastly refused to take part in an offensive war. The whole controversy is particularly interesting for the reason that it was the first in our history which shows the tendency which has finally controlled American constitutional law. All the parties acknowledged the binding character of the articles of union; and the controversy went mainly to the construction of them, to the interpretation of the powers of the commissioners under them. The occasion was not, as it would have been in England, a dispute as to what the governing body had better do, but a dispute as to what the governing body had a right to do, thus showing that in the latter case there was behind the nominally governing body a recognized popular sovereignty superior to it. This debate of 1652 might very well be taken as the beginning of constitutional law, in the peculiar phase of the term which obtains in the United States and other countries having a written constitution.

The unusual bitterness of the controversy had come largely, not from academic differences as to the construction of the articles, but from the general suspicion that the Bay colony was moved by the question of the tolls at the mouth of the Connecticut River, already referred to, and by a desire to convince the associate colonies that Massachusetts was their real head. Some of the western towns of Connecticut even made ready for war on their own account; and it was when all prospect of war, either by colonial or home power, had vanished, that Ludlow in disgust left the colony which he had helped to plant, and went to Virginia. Indeed, the New England confederation was in a state of extreme confusion, and almost *in articulo mortis*. The commissioners had declared war; Massachusetts had really introduced the first instance of nullification; and the other colonies found it equally difficult to make war, in obedience to the commissioners, without Massachusetts, or to keep the peace and satisfy their own people. Connecticut and New Haven kept a small cruiser in commission. New Haven decided guardedly that it would not do to begin war under present circumstances; and it was not until April, 1654, that the Hartford general court formally "sequestered" the Dutch fort of Good Hope, and banished the Dutch ensign from Connecticut soil. But both had great difficulty in restraining their people, and a small insurrection had to be quelled in Stamford.

The relations between England and Holland had not been improved by the establishment of the English commonwealth. At the execution of Charles I., the Dutch States General had waited in a body on his son, recognized him as Charles II., and refused even a reception to the English envoys. Cromwell's successful battle of Dunbar, in September, 1650, and his still more successful battle of Worcester just a year later, brought the Dutch to their senses, and they asked an alliance with the Commonwealth. The English parliamentary leaders, however, wished to make a successful navy the counterbalance to their too successful army. They passed the Navigation Act of 1651, which cut their rivals out of the carrying trade. There was an "accidental" collision between the two fleets in May, 1652, when Blake called upon Van Tromp to lower his flag, and Van Tromp answered with a broadside. Again, in the autumn, Blake and De Ruyter met in the Channel in an indecisive conflict; and in November Van Tromp drove Blake into the Thames, and sailed the Channel with a broom at his masthead. A few months later, Blake, issuing forth again into the Channel with a horsewhip at his masthead, drove Van Tromp in his turn into harbor.

While the two great marine monsters were thus rolling heavily into collision, it was but natural that the little fish across the Atlantic should take a keen personal interest in the matter. Every accidental victory of Blake was to them an additional hope of a parliamentary fleet, which should deal out justice to the wicked Dutch governor and his Manhattan associates. New Haven was especially elate, for the relations of her leading men with Cromwell had always been particularly close. It was the battle of Naseby which had brought about that almost solitary touch of romance in Connecticut history, the "phantom ship" of New Haven. The New Haven people, feeling more reason for relying on the rising fortunes of the Cromwell interest, equipped a ship of one hundred and fifty tons, freighted her, and sent her to England with an agent to endeavor to procure a charter from the new power there. It was in January, 1647, that she sailed, and the ice in the harbor had to be cut in order to open the way for her. Nothing more was ever known of her: the seventy souls on board had gone to their account, and the material loss was so severe a strain on the colony that its leaders began to cast about for a new location, in Ireland, Jamaica, or elsewhere, — the Jamaica proposition being Cromwell's own. In June, 1649, so the story goes, the long-lost ship was seen beating up the harbor towards New Haven. As the townspeople gathered to watch her, at first incredulous, then joyful, then hesitating and awe-stricken, it was seen that there was but one man on her deck; that he was leaning on his sword, and looked sadly on the gathered multitude. As she drew nearer, he pointed once to the sea, and then New Haven's phantom ship vanished from sight.

In June, 1653, the joyful news was received that Cromwell had taken sides with the majority of the commissioners, and had enjoined Massachusetts to desist from her opposition; and that a fleet of commonwealth ships was at Boston, ready to help the New England union to remove the Dutch flag from Manhattan. The Massachusetts general court was angry, but not angry enough to resist openly. It still refused to raise troops for the war, but consented to allow the parliamentary commissioners to raise men in Massachusetts, if they could. Arrangements for an expedition of eight hundred men, to attack New Netherland, were in progress, when they were stopped by the news of peace between England and Holland, which had been concluded April 5, 1654. Stuyvesant thus obtained another lease of life.

There was at first a strong disposition in Connecticut and New Haven to allow the union to lapse because of what they regarded as the perfidious conduct of Massachusetts. New Haven had even formally voted not to choose commissioners. But Massachusetts urged a continuance of the union so feelingly that commissioners were chosen as usual, and their meeting proved to be an exceedingly amicable one. From that time the union went on through the rest of its brief existence with little apparent friction. But it is as evident as anything can be that the heart had been taken out of it by the course of Massachusetts in 1652. Nullification is nullification, whether the moving cause be worthy or unworthy; and after Massachusetts had once successfully nullified the plain provisions of the articles, her confederates could never again feel that perfect confidence in her future action which is essential to the usefulness and even the existence of a league government. A stronger tendency is evident every year to reduce the functions of the commissioners to matters of administrative routine, while the several colonies diverge more and more strongly in the protection of their own interests and in their peculiar development.

For six years after the peace between England and Holland, the two Connecticut colonies went on in their course of development with few events of exceptional interest. Successive deaths were thinning out the ranks of the original settlers. Hooker died in 1647. John Haynes, the first governor of Connecticut, died in 1654, and his family seems to have become extinct soon after. Henry Wolcott, one of the most influential leaders of the same colony, died in 1655. He was more fortunate in his descendants: there was hardly a time for the next two centuries when a Wolcott was not in some post of trust and honor in the service of the Commonwealth. In 1657 and 1658 died Edward Hopkins of Connecticut, and Theophilus Eaton of New Haven. Hopkins had been governor of his colony in alternate years from 1640 until 1654, Haynes being chosen in the other years. He had married the sister of David Yale, a Boston merchant; and his bequest to the towns of Hartford and New Haven founded the Hopkins grammar schools in those cities, as Elihu Yale's beneficence long afterward gave the impetus to the college which bears his name. Eaton had been chosen governor of New Haven every year from the settlement in 1638 until his death. His loss was almost irreparable to his colony, coming as it did just before the crisis in her history. It is impossible here to do justice to his public services and his private worth. But there are some indications that in these respects he had surmounted obstacles which the official records have not fully detailed. His biographers claim that his numerous family "was under the most perfect government." If the facts found by the church trial of 1644, in which Mrs. Eaton (the governor's second wife) was censured, are to be taken as proved, Eaton's home life must have been a constant thorn in the flesh. Mrs. Eaton seems to have been in the habit of venting a very ugly temper in the most outrageous language to the whole family, from her husband down to "Anthony the neager." She slapped the face of "old Mrs. Eaton," while the family were at dinner, until the governor was compelled to hold her hands; she pinched Mary, the governor's daughter by his first marriage, until she was black and blue, and "knocked her head against the dresser, which made her nose bleed much;" she slandered Mary, falsely impeaching her character; and in all points she seems to have been the type of the vulgar notion of a stepmother. She, the wife of one of the "seven pillars," put the church to shame by becoming a pronounced Anabaptist, walking out from the communion service, arguing with Mr. Davenport from her seat in the audience, and expressing loud and exasperating approbation when he used the familiar formula, "On this point I will be brief." There seems to have been a good deal of human nature under the surface, even in New Haven.

Davenport was still in New Haven: it was not until 1668, after the union of the two colonies had been accomplished, that he removed to Boston. In both Connecticut and New Haven, the healthy condition of the body politic was shown by the fact that new men were coming up prepared to take the places of those whom death was so rapidly removing. First among these was John Winthrop. Chosen governor in 1657, deputy governor in 1658, and governor again in 1659, he became at once so necessary to the people of Connecticut that they changed the provision in their constitution forbidding the immediate reëlection of a governor, and he was reëlected annually until his death in 1676. His son, Fitz John, following in his father's course, was governor from 1698 until his death in 1707. The Wyllyses, Talcotts, Wolcotts, Treats, Shermans, and other families were sending a stream of young men into public life, and all of them were well fitted for it. One of the ablest of the new men was John Allyn of Hartford. Nominated to the board of assistants in 1661, he was chosen secretary of state in 1664, and held that office for twenty-eight years between that date and his death in 1696. The personalities of the men of the time get little attention, unless their work is theological, as in the case of Hooker or Davenport, or their non-essential characteristics are such as to strike the public attention and so win some advantage for the colony, as in the case of Winthrop. The mass of the leaders pass slowly across the stage, doing their work like men, but leaving us hardly any notion of their personal appearance or traits. The influence of the feeling is shown in the refusal of the Wyllys family to erect any monuments in their family burying ground. Said one of them: " If Connecticut cannot remember the Wyllyses without a monument, let their memory rot." In few cases is this general tendency more disappointing than in that of John Allyn. Hardly any trace of him is left beyond the cramped but legible writing in which he kept the records, and the work which those records detail. And yet it is quite evident that, whenever work was to be done requiring stubborn tenacity of purpose and cautious shrewdness of method, John Allyn's name always appears in the center of it. Like so many of his contemporaries, he seems to have been entirely satisfied with the reward offered by the consciousness of effective work; and we can only wonder now how much the commonwealth of Connecticut owes to John Allyn.

Eaton's place at New Haven had been taken by

William Leete, who served as governor of that colony from 1661 until the union of the colonies. He was one of the original settlers, and one of the seven pillars of the church at Guilford. After the union, he became deputy governor, 1669-75, and then served as governor from Winthrop's death until 1680, dying in 1683.

CHAPTER XI.

THE CHARTER AND THE UNION.

MONK'S march to London came in the opening days of the year 1660. On the 25th of April, Charles landed at Dover; and in July the momentous tidings reached Boston. On the vessel which brought them came Whalley and Goffe, two of the regicides: England was no longer a place for them. They stayed in Boston and Cambridge until the following February, treated at first with distinguished consideration by the authorities as well as by private persons. The first intelligence that they were under the ban of the new government made such a change in their treatment that they fled to New Haven, arriving there March 27. A royal warrant for their arrest followed them from Massachusetts through Hartford, but the messengers found their errand blocked at New Haven by the most exasperating obstacles. They had to yield to the magistrates' cautious regard for the Sabbath; their documents were read aloud in public meeting, instead of being treated as secret-service business; and, when the Sabbath came, they were regaled with a sermon from the significant text: "Hide the outcasts; bewray not him that wandereth; let mine outcasts dwell with thee, Moab; be thou a covert to them from the face of the spoiler." Davenport and his people were evidently in full accord with the regicides. Leete and the magistrates seem to have seen the consequences of their action; but they continued to make use of every legal obstacle to thwart the arrest, and the messengers finally returned to Boston empty-handed, though the two judges had been concealed at New Haven, or within three miles of it, throughout their visit. The "Judges' Cave," on the summit of West Rock, sheltered them for a month, and then they set out on their wanderings. Sometimes in New Haven, Guilford, or Milford, sometimes in their old refuge or like spots, they continued to escape their pursuers for some three years. In 1664, finding that special royal commissioners had arrived, charged with their arrest, they went to Hadley, in western Massachusetts. Their choice of a final refuge shows again the secret tie which seems to have bound together the New Haven people, the minority of the dissatisfied Connecticut churches, and the Cromwellian element in England; for Hadley's settlement had been due to the secession of a minority of the Hartford and Wethersfield churches. This was the scene of their asserted appearance to head the settlers in repelling an Indian attack; and here Whalley died about 1674, and Goffe probably five years later. Their burial-place is really uncertain, though some have believed it to be in New Haven.

The authorities of Connecticut were as anxious as those of New Haven that no harm should come to the regicides, and the fugitives found as frequent and as secure refuge in Hartford as anywhere else. But the difference of method showed itself in this as in other cases. When the regicides were really not within their jurisdiction, the Connecticut authorities always seized the opportunity to make their zeal in the king's service evident. They overwhelmed the royal commissioners with warrants, letters of authority, and proclamations; the colony was in a ferment because of their haste to lay hands on the criminals; they were his majesty's most faithful servants. Under the like circumstances, the New Haven authorities always showed a decorous satisfaction in saying No to the commissioners, which went far to discount the sincerity of their denials when the fugitives were suspected to be concealed within their jurisdiction with their privity. They could not but have been reported to the home authorities as a dangerous colony, the remaining quintessence of Cromwellianism; and such reports could not but have had a strong influence on the fortunes of the two colonies in the charter struggle which followed immediately.

The records of Connecticut show nothing done

in regard to the Restoration until March 14, 1660 (61), though the vote then passed refers to a previous decision at an informal meeting of the magistrates and deputies. On the date just given, the general court voted that Charles II. should be proclaimed king; that an address should be prepared and sent to him, asking for "the continuance and confirmation of such privilidges and liberties as are necessary for the comfortable and peaceable settlement of this colony;" and that the £500 which the Cullick estate was to pay the colony should be reserved to pay the expense of the application. The court of election, May 16, approved a draft of an address offered by Governor Winthrop, appointed a committee to revise and complete it, and named the governor as the colony's agent in England in regard to the patent. This last is the first open mention of what must have been the burning desire of every Connecticut leader, — the obtaining of a charter to give legal title to what had been done by popular authority. At the session of June 7, the court finally approved the address which had been completed, renewed the governor's appointment as agent "to procure us a patent," and authorized him to draw on the treasurer for £500. From that time there is not a word about the charter in the records until they are blazoned with the triumphant entry of its reception in October, 1662, more than a year afterward. In the interim, the colony, having done all that it could do, waited in sober patience. Just as Winthrop was embarking for England, New Haven at last proclaimed Charles II. king, more than a year after the news of his accession had been received; and the step was not taken until remonstrances had been received from friends at home, warning the colony of the evil impression which its continued silence was making there. The form has been called grudging and half-hearted. In reality, it almost demands the space for insertion in full, for the sake of the refreshing contrast which its simple and manly terms offer to the servility of the style which the habit of the times at court seems to have extorted from Connecticut. It is as follows:

"Although we have not received any form of proclamation, by order from His Majesty or Council of State, for proclaiming His Majesty in this Colony; yet the Court, taking encouragement from what has been done in the rest of the United Colonies, hath thought fit to declare publicly and proclaim that we do acknowledge His Royal Highness, Charles the Second, King of England, Scotland, France, and Ireland, to be our sovereign lord and king; and that we do acknowledge ourselves, the inhabitants of this colony, to be his Majesty's loyal and faithful subjects."

Winthrop set sail for England in August, 1661.

He took with him the address and petition to his majesty, which had cost the whole intellect of the colony such prolonged labor; a letter of instructions from his principals; and letters to Lord Say and Sele, and the Earl of Manchester, two old Puritans, now of the king's privy council. The instructions directed him to consult with Say and Sele, Brooke, and such of the original patentees as he could find; to endeavor to obtain a copy of the Say and Sele patent, and have it confirmed to the colony, with such amendments as could be obtained; and, in case the Say and Sele patent could not be come at, to apply for a new patent for the colony, with bounds extending " eastward to the Plymouth line, northward to the limits of the Massachusetts colony, and westward to the Bay of Delaware, if it may be." The southern limit is not mentioned, unless a recommendation to include the adjacent islands be considered as carrying the limits beyond New Haven and over Long Island. A contemporary protest from Connecticut against the appointment of a boundary committee, cited by Atwater, would go to show that such was the case. " We conceive you cannot be ignorant of our real and true right to those parts of the country where you are seated, both by conquest, purchase, and possession, though hitherto we have been silent, and altogether forborne to make any absolute challenge to our own." The address to the king is of the most inflated style of

the Stuart period of English. It begins with a
regret that its authors are separated by so vast an
ocean from those who are under the immediate influence
and splendor of so great a monarch, in the
princely palace of his renowned imperial city, the
glory of the whole earth; and that a too early
winter had hindered them from long since prostrating
themselves by an humble address at their
sovereign prince's feet. It described the settlement
of the colony just at the beginning of the
sad and unhappy times of the wars in England,
which its people had since been bewailing with
sighs and mournful tears. It told how the people
of Connecticut, all through the civil war, had
been hiding themselves behind the mountains in
that desolate desert, as a people forsaken, choosing
rather to sit solitary, and wait upon the Divine
Providence for protection, than to apply to any
of the illegitimate governments which had arisen
in England, their hearts still remaining entire to
his majesty's interests. It implored his majesty,
now that the beams of his sovereignty had not
only filled the world's hemisphere, but had appeared
over the great deeps in the New England
horizon, to accept " this colony, your own colony,
a little branch of your mighty empire." And it
pleaded their poverty as an excuse for their presentation
of nothing more than their hearts and
loyal affections to his majesty. It is hard to see
how Winthrop could have read the document with
a straight face.

The gratitude of the colony was a lively sense of favors to come : the petition which accompanied the address was as straightforward as the address was circumgyratory. It asked that the king would grant to the colony a patent in the terms of that formerly granted to the Say and Sele associates, or of that granted to Massachusetts; and that it might include immunity from customs, in order that the colony might recoup by commerce its losses in the Pequot war. The letters to Manchester and Say and Sele besought their coöperation, which was heartily given.

Winthrop's winter in London was spent to good advantage. New England historians have wearied themselves in detailing his advantages for such a negotiation in such a court, — his natural powers of mind, developed by sound university education ; his gentle manners, polished by continental travel ; the manly beauty of his face and person ; and the kindly, mature, and solid judgment which governed the whole man. The story is also told of a ring given to Winthrop's grandfather by Charles I., and now returned by the ambassador to the new king ; and the charter of Connecticut is attributed almost equally to the tactful courtesy of Winthrop and the filial affection of Charles. One can hardly help a suspicion, however, that the £500, which the Connecticut leaders had placed at Winthrop's disposal, had a more considerable influence on the result than the histories have yet admitted. The new court had required some time to get warm in its seat before showing plainly the depths of venality to which it was prepared to descend. The time for the disposition of places, and of all kinds of court favors, by bargain and sale, had now fully come; and it was about this time that Samuel Pepys seems to have had his eyes opened to the fact that this was the way in which many of those about the court did get their incomes. At any rate, there seems to have been no final accounting for the balance of the £500 between Winthrop and the colony. Winthrop had gone primarily on his own business: so says the resolve of May 16, 1661. The colony had ordered the munificent sum of £80 to be paid to the governor as his salary for the year; and it would not have been likely to have passed over a further claim of £500 for mere expenses, unless those expenses had been somewhat in the nature of a secret-service fund.

There is a sentence in the petition to the king which may possibly have some significance. "May it please your majesty graciously to bestow upon your humble supplicants such royal munificence, according to the tenor of a draft or instrument, which is ready here to be tendered, at your gracious order." That Charles II. should have drawn up and offered to a Puritan commonwealth a charter under which, as Chalmers, sound royal authority, says, "over their acts of assembly there was no power of revisal reserved, either to the king or to his courts of justice, nor was there any obligation imposed to give an account of their transactions to any authority on earth," is hardly a conceivable theory. That a charter drawn up by Winthrop, and passing through some of the many secret channels existing at the court, should have passed the scrutiny of the king, more through favor for the channel through which it had come than through filial affection or liking for a chance acquaintance, is at least more easy to believe. For no more democratic charter was ever given by a king than that which Charles signed for Connecticut, April 23, 1662, giving it a government which lasted for a century and a half, until the adoption of the new constitution in 1818.

The charter constituted a body politic and corporate, under the name of "Governor and Company of the English Colony of Connecticut in New England in America," to consist of Winthrop, John Mason, seventeen associates named, and such other persons as should be made free of the company thereafter (*i. e.*, admitted voters), with all the powers of an English corporation and with a common seal. The freemen were to choose from time to time a governor, a deputy governor, and twelve assistants ; each " town, place, or city " was to send two deputies ; and the governor, assistants, and deputies together were to constitute the general assembly, with power to change times of election, to admit freemen (that is, to establish the requisites for the right of suffrage), to constitute judicatories, to make laws not contrary to those of England, to define the duties of officers and the manner of their election, to impose fines and penalties or revoke them and pardon offenses, to repel warlike attacks by force, and to hold the territory within the limits granted in trust for the freemen of the colony. Until the second Thursday of the following October, Winthrop was named governor, Mason deputy governor, and twelve of the charter members assistants. All the freemen and their descendants were to have the rights of natural-born English subjects. Finally, the territory of the colony was to cover "all that part of our dominions in New England in America bounded on the east by Norrogancett River, commonly called Norrogancett Bay, where the said river falleth into the sea, and on the north by the line of the Massachusetts Plantation, and on the south by the sea, and in longitude as the line of the Massachusetts colony, running from east to west; that is to say, from the said Narrogancett Bay on the east to the South Sea on the west part; with the islands thereunto adjoining." Connecticut was thus to have a domain stretching from Narragansett Bay to the Pacific Ocean; and the charterless and defenseless colony of New Haven was included within these limits.

The charter was first produced and shown in this country at a meeting of the New England commissioners at Boston, September 4, 1662. The New Haven commissioners must have sent the startling intelligence home at once, so that both the interested colonies must have known of it about the same time. The Connecticut general court records for October 9 note that the "patent or charter" was this day publicly read in the presence of the freemen, and that a committee of three had been appointed to take the charter into their custody in trust for the colony. Hartford was then declared the capital; the civil and military officers of the colony were confirmed in their places; and a formal letter was drawn up to the constables of the towns, directing them to collect the taxes, and to distrain the property of delinquents. Such laws as were not in conflict with the terms of the charter were validated and confirmed. The right of suffrage was regulated by an order that all candidates for the privilege should bring a certificate from a majority vote of their town that they were persons " of a civil, peaceable and honest conversation," twenty-one years old or upward, and taxed in the lists for at least £20 estate. This was a widening of the elective franchise, for the qualification had been fixed at £30 since 1657. In addition to these enactments, a long series of resolutions was passed, all intended to strike at the weak spot of New Haven, and break up the political organization of that colony. Their details will be reserved until the statement of the events which gave them success has been made.

On its part, the New Haven general court, at its meeting of October 15, merely appointed a day of fasting and prayer for guidance " in this weighty business about joining with Connecticut colony." Immediately after the fast, a New Haven town meeting disapproved any such union. At the freemen's meeting, November 4, and the general court meeting on the following day, a letter from Connecticut was read, enclosing a copy of the charter, and demanding the consummation of the union. Two answers were sent. The first intimated mildly that New Haven was not " expressly included" within the charter jurisdiction, and asked that the New Haven colony might remain " distinct, entire, and uninterrupted, as heretofore," until they could hear from Winthrop. The second, from the freemen, argued that the charter only empowered Connecticut to acquire and hold lands within the limits assigned, but did not authorize it to interfere with the lands already acquired by New Haven ; and it besought the Connecticut authorities to wait until they could make application for a charter, and learn his majesty's real intentions, to which they meant to submit. Here the public records become silent until the following spring.

But the inherent weakness of the New Haven confederacy, arising from its peculiar ecclesiastical system and its restrictions on the right of suffrage, had already become visible, and were having their influence on the proceedings of both parties to the controversy. For some ten years before, an underlying spirit of dissatisfaction seems to have cropped out from time to time; but the final outburst seems to have been due, at least indirectly, to the Quakers. The New England commissioners had recommended the several colonies, in September, 1656, to take measures against the Quakers. Connecticut complied so far as to direct that any town which harbored Quakers should be fined; but the execution of the penalties against the sect was finally left " to the discretion " of the magistrates. They seem to have exercised so much discretion that the heretics, despairing of any chance of martyrdom in this quarter, gave Connecticut a comparatively wide berth. New Haven, on the contrary, went into the matter with more spirit. The court of magistrates itself undertook the trial of offenders, and every trial increased the number of criminals. The public and indignant criticisms of the Quakers and their harborers upon the methods and manners of the New Haven jurisdiction must have been as fire to tow, when there were so many others dissatisfied by reason of more temporal circumstances. About 1660, the general court begins to have especial trouble in regard to letters attacking their civil organization and practice. It looked upon all such offenses as not merely civil offenses, but as offenses "against the King of Peace, that had so long continued peace amongst them;" and it punished them most rigorously. The number of its assailants rapidly became greater, as did the exasperation of the court, which was hardly ever out of hot water from 1660 until the union was accomplished. In 1661 the dissatisfaction had risen so high that several of those chosen as magistrates refused to take the oath; and the general court decided to make public declaration of its position. It acknowledged that the non-freemen had complained that "just privileges and liberties" were denied them; but it declared that this denial was a part of the fundamental system of the colony, established by law, from which it would not be diverted by any agitation; and it added the hint that it was only necessary for the dissentients to join the church in order to qualify themselves for the enjoyment of the rights to vote and hold office. This declaration must have added fuel to the flame; and the court's meeting in May, 1662, gives evidence of this. The record admits that there was "great discouragement upon the spirits of those that were now in place of magistracy;" and it was no wonder. Cases were multiplying of men who, when arrested, denied the authority of the colony to make laws now that the king was proclaimed, and demanded of the marshal "whether his authority came from Charles the Second?" These were awkward questions for New Haven to answer. As they multiplied, the embarrassment of the court, and the hesitation of the doubtful mass of citizens, increased with them. The want of a legal basis to the colony's authority was already painfully evident, even while its only antagonists were its own ill-disposed citizens : what was to be the difficulty of the case when Connecticut should set up her claims, and become an eager refuge and support to every one who should resist the authority of New Haven?

It was at this session that Bray Rossiter of Guilford, and his son John, the Mother Carey's chickens of the coming storm, first appeared on the scene. The father, as an allowed physician, had claimed exemption from taxation; when that was refused, he excepted to the colony's right to tax; and now he, with others of Guilford, was haled before the general court to answer to the charge of having sent some offensive papers to the court, and of having spread others abroad, "to the disturbance of the peace of this jurisdiction." Most of the accused apologized, the lamest apologies being gladly accepted by the court; but their statements all pointed to the Rossiters as the ringleaders, and the court hardly knew what to do with them. There were present, says the record with half concealed bitterness, " Mr. Allen and Mr. Willis, of Connecticut, waiting to see an issue of the business, pretending to be friends to us and friends to peace, laboring with Mr. Rossiter and his son to bring him to some acknowledgment of evil." Finally a written statement was accepted from him in which he " owned that in several passages and expressions he had been very rash and inconsiderate," and agreed to submit to the government " while he continued under it." The Connecticut charter was soon to relieve him from conscientious scruples as to the last-named clause. It is noteworthy that, in examining one of the parties, the court said that it " had met with this business both from Stamford and Southold ; " and Southold sent no deputies to this session. A summons was sent to the Southold deputies to see that the taxes were paid, and to report for prosecution all persons refusing payment. It is evident that the New Haven jurisdiction was already among the breakers.

This was the state of affairs when the two general courts met in October, and the Connecticut body heard their invaluable charter read to the freemen. Then followed the first series of orders by which Connecticut spread out her jurisdiction over her neighbor. The people of Southold wrote that they had had notice from " Mr. Willis, of Connecticut," that they were within Connecticut's limits ; and that they had appointed Mr. Young to be their deputy. Young was admitted as a freeman and deputy, and was appointed magistrate for Southold ; and the people of that place were directed to choose a constable, to whom Young was to administer the oath of fidelity to Connecticut. Similar applications were received from "several inhabitants" of Stamford and Greenwich, of Huntington and Oyster Bay, on Long Island; and these towns, with Mystic and Pawcatuck in the district claimed by Massachusetts, were directed to choose Connecticut constables, for the constable seems still to have been the pivot of town authority. The court went further, and ordered that word be sent to the inhabitants of Westchester that they too were within the colony's chartered limits, and that they should follow the same procedure. In the new pride of the charter, the colony was ready to throw down the gantlet not only to New Haven and Massachusetts, but to the Dutch also. So fully had the colony taken its position, that, at the meeting of the following March, it was necessary to do no more, except to vote £20 to Mr. Rossiter.

The letter to New Haven, and the answers of the New Haven committee and freemen, already mentioned, occupied the winter; but the forces which were disintegrating New Haven met no check. The Connecticut committee, in March, 1663, proposed nearly the same terms of union, which were finally adopted; but New Haven rejected them, on the ground that she had appealed to the king and could not prejudice her appeal. In May, New Haven sent another remonstrance to

Connecticut; but it is noteworthy that her officers, then elected, took the oath "for the year ensuing, or until our foundation settlements be made null." In August, her committee showed further signs of weakness by proposing a series of a dozen questions as to the terms on which a treaty of union could be effected; and the answer of the Connecticut committee certainly gave them full assurance of perfect equality and security for all their rights, except the exclusive privileges of church-members, under the New Haven system. In September, the New Haven delegates complained to the New England commissioners of the action of Connecticut, particularly of the appointment of constables, " who are very troublesome to us." Connecticut answered, and Massachusetts and Plymouth decided that, as New Haven had been recognized as an independent member of the confederation, any infringement on her jurisdiction would be a violation of the articles of union; and that any such act in the past ought to be recalled. All this time, however, the Connecticut authorities were quietly allowing their new agents in the New Haven towns to carry on their work; and the results were that before the end of the next year the unfortunate colony of New Haven was deeply in debt, unable to collect taxes, and unable even to pay the salaries of her officers.

At the meeting in December, 1663, the New

Haven court had received some poor encouragement in two letters, one from Winthrop, the other from the English privy council. Winthrop's letter was to John Mason, deputy governor, and the Connecticut general court; but he had sent a copy to New Haven. He remonstrated against the appointment of constables in New Haven towns, and wished that all such proceedings should be suspended until his return home, when he hoped to arrange an amicable union of the two colonies. His language as to his own previous pledges is curiously ambiguous: "And further I must let you know that testimony here doth affirm that I gave assurance before authority here, that it was not intended to meddle with any town or plantation that was settled under any other government; had it been otherwise intended or declared, it had been injurious in taking out the patent not to have inserted a proportionable number of their names in it." Who can make out from this whether Winthrop means to endorse this asserted promise of his or not? The course of the two governors, indeed, is almost inexplicable. Winthrop obtains a charter, covering New Haven; the New Haven authorities assert, without contradiction, that he had twice promised in writing, before setting out for England, that he would not have New Haven included under his colony's jurisdiction; and Winthrop finally makes this curiously roundabout admission, with which all parties seem afraid to meddle further. On the other hand, while Leete, the New Haven governor, fulfills all his duties through the crisis with punctuality, his action always carries a suspicion that it is perfunctory; his heart does not seem to be in the work. No one who has followed the records carefully will be at all surprised by the assertion of Hubbard and Mather, that the action of Winthrop in so framing the charter as to include New Haven was by the special desire of Governor Leete himself; nor by the assertion of the Connecticut governor and council in 1675, when Leete was deputy governor and present, with several of the former New Haven leaders, that "their [New Haven] conjunction with this colony was desired by the chief amongst them." Leete's action was repudiated by Davenport, in a letter to Winthrop, as "his private doing, without the consent or knowledge of any of us in this colony;" "not done by him according to his public trust as governor, but contrary to it." And yet, so far from repudiating Leete, the people reëlected him governor. The facts probably are that Leete and other New Haven leaders were quietly tired of the whole New Haven system, and despaired of their ability to maintain it longer; that Winthrop ascertained this fact just before leaving for England; and that much of the fury of words which was expended on the negotiations was meant to allow events to take their course, while the honest and conscientious upholders of the old system were being satisfied and convinced of the futility of further resistance. The times were out of joint for New Haven; and while the leaders were not disposed to help overturn their fathers' work, they were no more disposed to stand in the way of events. No doubt Winthrop was relieved to find on his return that Connecticut had gone on obstinately in her course; and no doubt also Leete was no less relieved to impart the news.

The privy council's letter was no more than a circular to the governors of the New England colonies; but as it was directed to New Haven among the rest, that colony took this as an evidence that the king had had no intention of absorbing them in the rival colony. A sounding proclamation was issued at once. It rehearsed the special orders of the council in regard to New Haven, being careful to note the addition of his majesty's sign manual "in red wax;" it stated the embarrassment which the colony was under in fulfilling the king's directions by reason of the refusal of some ill-disposed persons to pay their legal taxes; and it cautioned all such persons to cease their opposition at once. It is almost pitiful to see the eagerness with which the colony, which had settled here in primitive independence, now seized on this straw of royal recognition; and, however one may admit the necessity and benefit of the union, he can hardly help wishing that the manly little colony had not been forced into it.

Connecticut had succeeded in stirring up a hornet's nest in almost every quarter. Her general assembly had appointed agents for the colony, with the powers of magistrates, in the New Haven towns on the mainland and Long Island, in the Dutch towns of Hempstead, Jamaica, Flushing, and Westchester, and in the Narragansett or Rhode Island country as far east as Wickford. Stuyvesant had appeared before the commissioners at Boston, in September, 1663, to protest on behalf of the Dutch; and the commissioners, while recommending a reference of the matter to them at their next meeting, took ground against any violation of the boundaries agreed upon in the treaty of 1650. The people of the Narragansett country were memorializing the Massachusetts general court. New Haven's protests found a sympathetic audience in the majority of the New England union. Connecticut hardly seemed to have a friend. The state of affairs, however, had one favorable aspect: each of the other parties had too many interests of its own to attend to for any unswerving support of New Haven. Connecticut agreed not to make any present claim of exclusive jurisdiction over the Dutch towns; and a more temporizing policy as to the Massachusetts contest left New Haven finally isolated. Nevertheless, that sturdy colony again resolved in December to make no treaty with Connecticut until affairs had been restored again to their original condition. It also ordered that distraint be made for unpaid taxes. This last step brought about a significant hint of a readiness to resist by force. On the last day of the year, the Rossiters, who had gone to Hartford and secured a Connecticut constable and magistrates, created a terrible hubbub in Guilford before daylight. Guns were fired; the inhabitants were roused and thrown into great confusion; and assistance had to be summoned from New Haven and Branford to keep order. Though this was accomplished, the object of the Rossiters was accomplished with it, for it was agreed that tax collection and distraint should be suspended for the present.

New Haven's position was now desperate. There was no money in the treasury; the towns were divided within themselves; there was no physical force to constrain the disloyal; and the authorities were either discouraged or fainthearted. Leete called a special session of the general court in January, 1663 (4), and laid the state of the case before it. It still stubbornly voted not to treat; and it named Messrs. Davenport and Street a committee to draw up its grievances in writing. The committee's work is commonly known as " New Haven's Case Stated." It is the most dignified and pathetic document in the whole controversy. It stated the origin of the colony; its title by purchase; its recognition by the Dutch, by parliament, by the king, by the united colonies of New England, and by Connecticut herself; the promises of Winthrop; and the turbulent and seditious practices of Connecticut toward her sister colony, contrary to righteousness and peace; and it demanded that reparation be offered for the past, and security for the future. The document was in the form of a letter to the Connecticut general assembly; and it is to be regretted that Connecticut's answer was by no means so dignified. Its tone is that of triumph and exultation; and its writers were evidently out of patience with long waiting. There are indications, however, in a most amicable contemporaneous correspondence between the two committees, that both parties had about accepted the fact of union as inevitable, and had pretty well agreed on its terms. At any rate, the New Haven general court ceased from this time to do any important business.

The inevitable conclusion was hastened by an unexpected event. It was now March, 1664, the month in which King Charles made his grant of the territory then in New Netherland to his brother, the Duke of York. The grant covered the whole of Long Island, and the mainland from Delaware Bay to the Connecticut River, thus including both Hartford and New Haven within its limits. Little as they liked Connecticut, the New Haven people liked the duke less; and the only apparent security against his government, for both colonies, was in the charter of Connecticut. The news of the grant was brought to Boston by the fleet and army of Nichols in July; and the downfall of the Dutch government at Manhadoes followed in August. In the same month, Leete called a meeting of his general court, and informed them that their committee recommended submission. With great confusion and dissatisfaction, a vote to that effect was passed, then reconsidered, and then passed again in about the same words; but the people were still so stubborn that the vote amounted to little.

In September, the New Haven delegates were admitted for the last time, and against the protest of Connecticut, to seats in the meeting of the New England commissioners. In October, the Connecticut general assembly appointed a committee to demand the submission of New Haven, and to admit New Haven freemen as Connecticut freemen; and it also appointed Leete and other New Haven leaders agents of Connecticut, with the powers of magistrates, to administer justice, and ordered all other officers to retain their places and perform their duties until the next election. In November, the representatives of Connecticut attended a meeting of royal commissioners at New York, to settle the limits between New York and Connecticut. This erudite body assigned Long Island to " the Ducke off Yorke," and all plantations lying eastward of a certain creek or river called

"Momoronack, which is reputed to be about twelve miles to the east of Westchester," to Connecticut. This was accepted as the king's decision by the much-enduring New Haven colony. The general court, with "as many of the inhabitants as was pleased to come," voted to submit, but "with a *salvo jure* of our former right and claim, as a people who have not yet been heard in point of plea." Connecticut had renewed her first offers of ample security for equality under the charter, and in her answer to the notice of submission asked that all unpleasant reflections might be "buried in perpetual silence." When the general assembly met at Hartford in March, 1665, deputies from the former New Haven towns were present; the proceedings were harmonious; and Leete and three other New Haven leaders were chosen magistrates or assistants. The colony of New Haven had ceased to exist, and ecclesiastical supremacy had given way to democracy.

In October, 1665, in probable pursuance of terms before agreed upon, the general assembly ordered that two county courts be held at New Haven in June and November. These introduced trial by jury into the former New Haven territory, while they preserved to the people all that could be granted of their former autonomy. In May, 1666, the general assembly proceeded to divide the commonwealth into four counties, the boundaries of New Haven county extending "from the east bounds of Guilford unto the west bounds of Milford." This made a change in the commonwealth's judicial system. Until 1665, the highest judicial body was the particular court, composed of the governor or deputy and the magistrates. From 1665 until 1711, the particular court was succeeded by the court of assistants, seven of the twelve assistants chosen by the general assembly. The superior court was introduced in 1711, and the supreme court of errors and appeals, composed of the governor and assistants, in 1784. From 1807 until 1855, the latter was composed of superior court judges sitting in bank, and, since 1855, of district judges. The commonwealth's court of assistants, however, did not sit at New Haven until 1701.

Connecticut has played no small part in the development of the American Union, and in the peaceful conquest of the great western continent; and her part would have been sadly marred if the integrity of her natural boundaries had been broken by the continued existence of the separate colony on the south. Her leaders of 1662-65 were bound by every regard to the future of the commonwealth to insist on the absorption of New Haven; their insistence showed their foresight. And yet, even though the commonwealth emerges from the struggle with its natural outline unbroken, one may be pardoned a feeling of regret as New Haven sinks beneath the surface after her persistent fight for life. The county of New Haven does not quite fill the void left by the republic of New Haven.

CHAPTER XII.

THE COMMONWEALTH. 1662–1763.

BEFORE the grant of the charter, the general court of Connecticut had begun to show the characteristics of a real commonwealth government. No exact point of time can be stated at which the transformation took place; but there is a plain difference between the generally recommendatory tone in which the court was in the habit of addressing the towns in 1640, and the decidedly mandatory tone into which it had grown in 1660. As soon as the charter had given it the consciousness of a legal title to existence and authority apart from its town units, its drift in the assumption of powers heretofore left to the towns became somewhat stronger, until the essential commonwealth interests had been brought under its jurisdiction. And yet it never lost the influence of the forces which had founded the colony. The Connecticut towns, while they were generally content to confine their work to the matters of purely local interest which had been left to them by the general assembly, had never any hesitation in resisting, by all peaceable means, any action of the supreme

THE COMMONWEALTH. 193

legislative body which seemed to them unjust; and the general assembly, in its turn, was always disposed to treat such town resistance mildly, and to seek for an accommodation rather than resort to force.

During the century which followed the grant of the charter, Connecticut had but nine governors, excluding Andros. All of these, with the exception of Wolcott, who was dropped by reason of accusations of extortion, served until death or advancing age compelled the choice of another; and as the elections were annual, the long terms of service speak well for the satisfaction of the people with the rulers of their choice, and for the conservatism and "steady habits" of the Connecticut people.

For some years after 1665 the colony went on in comparative quiet, developing new towns in every direction, and disturbed only by boundary disputes with its neighbors, by King Philip's war, and by the temporary recapture of New York by a Dutch fleet and army in 1673-74. The latter alarm was short-lived. The forces of New England were set in array; the English towns on Long Island returned gladly to the jurisdiction of Connecticut for protection; but peace between England and Holland restored the province of New York to the duke in 1674. The king issued a new patent for the province, in which he not only included Long Island, but the territory up to the

Connecticut River, which had been assigned to Connecticut by the royal commissioners. The assignment of Long Island was regretted, but not resisted; and the island which is the natural sea-wall of Connecticut passed, by royal decree, to a province whose only natural claim to it was that it barely touched it at one corner. The revival of the duke's claim to a part of the mainland was a different matter, and every preparation was made for resistance. In July, 1675, just as King Philip's war had broken out in Plymouth, hasty word was sent from the authorities at Hartford to Captain Thomas Bull at Saybrook that Governor Andros of New York was on his way through the Sound for the purpose, as he avowed, of aiding the people against the Indians. Of the two evils, Connecticut rather preferred the Indians. Bull was instructed to inform Andros, if he should call at Saybrook, that the colony had taken all precautions against the Indians, and to direct him to the actual scene of conflict, but not to permit the landing of any armed soldiers. "And you are to keep the king's colors standing there, under his majesty's lieutenant, the governor of Connecticut; and if any other colors be set up there, you are not to suffer them to stand. . . . But you are in his majesty's name required to avoid striking the first blow; but if they begin, then you are to defend yourselves, and do your best to secure his majesty's interest and the peace of the whole colony of Connecticut in our possession." Andros came and landed at Saybrook, but confined his proceedings to reading the duke's patent, against the protest of Bull and the Connecticut representatives. It may have been thought that this success would meet the approval of the Hartford authorities, but they were made of sterner stuff. While commending the officers and men engaged, they added significantly: " We wish he had been interrupted in doing the least thing under pretense of his having anything to do to use his majesty's name in commanding there so usurpingly, *which might have been done by shouts, or sound of drum, etc., without violence.*" This lesson of unhesitating resistance was not lost on succeeding officers of the colony. In October, 1693, Benjamin Fletcher, the hot-tempered governor of New York, appeared at Hartford with his majesty's commission to act as commander-in-chief of the New England militia. In spite of the assembly's protest, he ordered out the militia, and went to the parade ground to review them. The commanding officer was Captain Wadsworth, who had saved the charter from Andros. Fletcher began to read his commission. Wadsworth ordered the drums to beat; and, says Trumbull, "there was such a roaring of them that nothing else could be heard." Fletcher angrily demanded silence, and the drummers hesitatingly complied. The instant the reading of the commission was renewed, Wadsworth shouted, " Drum,

drum, I say!" Again the rattle began, and again the governor struggled for silence. When he had obtained it, Wadsworth turned to him and said, "If I am interrupted again, I will make the sun shine through you." He then gave final orders to his drummers, and the governor retired without having his commission read.

Connecticut suffered comparatively little from the horrors of King Philip's war; the lesson to her Indians had been too sternly taught for that. It is a little curious to notice how close the storm of war came to her northern and eastern boundaries without overpassing them. There were burnings and massacres through the western borders of Massachusetts, and battles in Rhode Island; but the Connecticut men regularly fought outside of their own colony. The colony, however, must have been kept in a constant state of alarm by the near approach of hostilities, and her troops were freely furnished, and took an active part. She kept in the field about one third of the New England forces. It was Major Treat, with a Connecticut force, who relieved the Essex men at Deerfield, and drove off the Indian besiegers of Springfield and Hadley; and in the great swamp fight, Connecticut's contingent of three hundred men lost eighty killed and wounded, or about half the total loss. In sober, manly, and striking language, the general assembly gave them a fitting epitaph: "There died many brave officers and sentinels, whose memory is blessed, and whose death redeemed our lives. The bitter cold, the tarled swamp, the tedious march, the strong fort, the numerous and stubborn enemy they contended with, for their God, king and country, be their trophies over death. Our mourners, over all the colony, witness for our men that they were not unfaithful in that day."

Andros had come out as governor of New York on its recovery from the Dutch in 1674. All the letters of the Connecticut council, as the upper house of the assembly was called under the charter, show a standing distrust of Andros, which was a fitting prelude to their intercourse ten years later. Such distrust, in the case of an able man as Andros seems to have been, was certainly inevitable. The state of affairs was worthy of notice. The Empire State of New York has little reason to envy the prosperity of the State of Connecticut in 1886 ; the case was far otherwise in 1674. At that time, an able, enterprising cavalier officer, sent out as governor of the duke's province of New York, found his energies crippled with the management of a territory consisting of two fairly important towns, a few straggling settlements on the Hudson, and some disaffected New England townships on Long Island. This western half of Connecticut was just the strip of territory needed to make New York a province in reality, and to enable him to do essential service against his majesty's enemies in Canada; the duke had at least a claim to it; and the royal governor could not be expected to appreciate at their full value the objections of a set of Hartford Puritans to this most necessary absorption. A boozing, incompetent governor of New York was an immense relief to the Connecticut authorities: a man of Andros's abilities had to be, and always was, dealt with at arm's length. His offers of help against the Indians were accepted cordially, but were always restricted to the exact service required. The letters which passed between the two parties show a constant sense of the real situation, in their mixture of distinguished courtesy with occasional railing, and in the constant readiness of Connecticut to bristle up in defense of some point which the governor was always ready to assure them was not of the least importance. The intercourse, however, gave Connecticut a very fair knowledge of Andros's character and methods, which must have been of service in the coming struggle.

In the later years of Charles II., royal commissioners, headed by Edward Randolph, gave New England much distress, urging upon the home government the general neglect of the navigation acts, and the offensive independence of this quarter of America. Massachusetts suffered most; and her charter, like the franchises of London, was vacated on a writ of *quo warranto*. Charles died in 1685, and his brother, James II., succeeded him. In July, 1686, Governor Treat received two writs of *quo warranto* against the colony of Connecticut, issued the previous year, calling upon it to show title for its exercise of political powers or abandon them. In December came another. In both cases, according to the colony's subsequent letter to King William, the time set for appearance had elapsed before the serving of the writ, so that the colony could make no defense, as perhaps was intended; but an attorney was appointed, and every preparation made for what resistance was possible. Andros had been succeeded by Dongan as governor of New York in 1682; and the king was represented in New England by Joseph Dudley, a recreant Massachusetts man, as president of the royal commissioners. Dudley undoubtedly did part of his work by endeavoring to persuade Connecticut to surrender her charter peaceably to the crown, promising to exert all his influence to procure her one equally favorable. The colony was not to be cajoled: aware of her impotence for open resistance, she followed her traditional policy, arguing and expostulating, never yielding a jot, but not resorting to action until the time for action was fully come.

In December, 1686, the Hartford authorities were called upon to measure their strength again with their old antagonist. Andros had landed at Boston, commissioned as governor of all New

England, and bent on abrogating the charters. Following Dudley's lead, he wrote to Treat, suggesting that by this time the trial of the writs had certainly gone against the colony; and that the authorities would do much to commend the colony to his majesty's good pleasure by entering a formal surrender of the charter. The colony authorities were possibly as well versed in the law of the case as Andros, and they took good care to do nothing of the sort; and, as the event showed, they thus saved the charter.

The assembly met as usual in October, 1687; but their records show that they were in profound doubt and distress. Andros was with them, accompanied by some sixty regular soldiers, to enforce his demand for the charter. It is certain that he did not get it, though the records, as usual, are cautious enough to give no reason why. Tradition is responsible for the story of the charter oak. The assembly had met the royal governor in the meeting-house; the demand for the charter had been made; and the assembly had exhausted the resources of language to show to Andros how dear it was to them, and how impossible it was to give it up. Andros was immovable; he had watched that charter with longing eyes from the banks of the Hudson, and he had no intention of giving up his object now that the king had put him in power on the banks of the Connecticut. Toward evening the case had become desperate. The little democracy was at last driven into a corner, where its old policy seemed no longer available; it must resist openly, or make a formal surrender of its charter. Just as the lights were lighted, the legal authorities yielded so far as to order the precious document to be brought in and laid on the table before the eyes of Andros. Then came a little more debate. Suddenly the lights were blown out; Captain Wadsworth, of Hartford, carried off the charter, and hid it in a hollow oak-tree on the estate of the Wyllyses, just across the "riveret;" and when the lights were relighted, the colony was no longer able to comply with Andros's demand for a surrender. Although the account of the affair is traditional, it is difficult to see any good grounds for impeaching it on that account. It supplies, in the simplest and most natural manner, a blank in the Hartford proceedings of Andros which would otherwise be quite unaccountable. His plain purpose was to force Connecticut into a position where she must either surrender the charter or resist openly. He failed: the charter never was in his possession; and the official records assign no reason for his failure. The colony was too prudent, and Andros too proud, to put the true reason on record. Tradition supplies the gap with an exactness which proves itself.

Having done all that men could do, Treat and his associates bowed for the time to superior force. Andros was allowed to read his commission, and

Treat, Fitz-John and Wait Winthrop, and John Allyn received appointments as members of his council for New England. John Allyn made what the governor doubtless considered to be the closing record for all time. But it is noteworthy that the record was so written as to flatter Andros's vanity, while it really put in terms a declaration of overpowering force, on which the commonwealth finally succeeded in saving her charter from invalidation. It is as follows:

"At a General Court at Hartford, October 31st, 1687, his excellency, Sir Edmund Andross, knight and Captain General and Governor of His Majesty's territories and dominions in New England, by order of His Majesty James the Second, King of England, Scotland, France, and Ireland, the 31st of October, 1687, took into his hands the government of the colony of Connecticut, it being by His Majesty annexed to Massachusetts and other colonies under his excellency's government. "FINIS."

The government was destined to last far longer than either the governor or his government. But, while it lasted, Andros's government was bitterly hated, and with good reason. The reasons are more peculiarly appropriate to the history of Massachusetts, where they were felt more keenly than in Connecticut; but even in Connecticut, poor as was the field for plunder, and distant as it was from the "ring" which surrounded Andros, the exactions of the new system were wellnigh intolerable to a people whose annual expense of government had been carefully kept down to the lowest limits, so that, says Bancroft, they "did not exceed four thousand dollars; and the wages of the chief justice were ten shillings a day while on service." The feeling in Connecticut is well represented in the story of the answer made to Andros himself, when he asked somewhat suspiciously for the reason of the proclamation of a fast-day: "Sir, *this kind* goeth not out but by prayer and fasting." There were not lacking incitements to premature insurrection; there were letters from hot-headed friends in England, telling them that they were "but a company of hens" if they did not revive their charter by force; and the Andros party had private intelligence implicating various leaders in some vague plot for a revolt. But the people were, as ever, self-restrained. The letters of Treat and Allyn to Andros are models of courtesy, as of faithful stewards who thought only of his interests. The colony waited patiently for the precise moment when it could strike most effectively, and then it struck once and for all, with all the strength that was in it.

April, 1689, came at last. The people of Boston, at the first news of the English Revolution, clapped Andros into custody. May 9, the old

Connecticut authorities quietly resumed their functions, and called the assembly together for the following month. William and Mary were proclaimed with great fervor. Not a word was said about the disappearance or reappearance of the charter; but the charter government was put into full effect again, as if Andros had never interrupted it. An address was sent to the king, asking that the charter be no further interfered with; but operations under it went on as before. No decided action was taken by the home government for some years, except that its appointment of the New York governor, Fletcher, to the command of the Connecticut militia, implied a decision that the Connecticut charter had been superseded. Late in 1693, Fitz John Winthrop was sent to England as agent to obtain a confirmation of the charter. He secured an emphatic legal opinion from Attorney General Somers, backed by those of Treby and Ward, that the charter was entirely valid, Treby's concurrent opinion taking this shape: "I am of the same opinion, and, as this matter is stated, there is no ground of doubt." The basis of the opinion was that the charter had been granted under the great seal; that it had not been surrendered under the common seal of the colony, nor had any judgment of record been entered against it; that its operation had merely been interfered with by overpowering force; that the charter therefore remained valid; and that the peaceable submission of the colony to Andros was merely an illegal suspension of lawful authority. In other words, the passive attitude of the colonial government had disarmed Andros so far as to stop the legal proceedings necessary to forfeit the charter; and then prompt action, at the critical moment, secured all that could be secured under the circumstances. William was willing enough to retain all possible fruits of James's tyranny, as he showed by enforcing the forfeiture of the Massachusetts charter; but the law in this case was too plain, and he ratified the lawyers' opinion in April, 1694. The charter had escaped its enemies at last, and its escape is a monument of one of the advantages of a real democracy. For fifty years, every man in the commonwealth had felt the maintenance of the commonwealth to be his own personal concern, and had been willing not only to die for it, but to live for it, work for it, and exercise the highest sort of self-control for it. Out of this mass there had been evolved a class of representative men, who were in the highest degree capable of seeing and doing just what was needed. Democracy had done more for Connecticut than class influence had done for Massachusetts.

The settlement of the boundaries of the colony was a longer and more fruitful source of dissension than the legal government. On the west, the agreement of 1664 was superseded in 1683 by a new one between Connecticut and Governor Dongan of New York, Andros's successor, in which the quadrilateral, at the southwest corner of Connecticut, first makes its appearance. It was agreed that the starting point of the line should be Lyon's Point, at the mouth of " Byram Brook," between the towns of Rye and Greenwich ; thence up that brook to the " wading place," where the common road crossed it ; thence eight English miles north-northwest into the country ; thence easterly to a line parallel to the first, beginning twelve miles east of Lyon's Point as the Sound runs, and to a place in that line eight miles from the Sound; thence along this north-northwest line to a point twenty miles from the Hudson ; thence northerly to the Massachusetts border, by a line " parallel to Hudson's River in every point." If the quadrilateral first described came at any point nearer than twenty miles to the Hudson, the other northerly lines were to be run so much further to the eastward as to give New York an equivalent tract of land. This threw Rye into New York, and recognized New York's old claim that Connecticut was to come no nearer to the Hudson than twenty miles' distance. It also gave up the line agreed upon in 1664, running north-northwest from Mamaroneck, crossing the Hudson near West Point, and leaving the district east of it, including Newburgh, Poughkeepsie, and Kingston, under Connecticut. It has since been rectified in various points, and the proposed line parallel to the Hudson has been straightened, but otherwise it is the basis of the present line. Rye revolted to Connecticut in 1697; but the king's confirmation of the line of 1683 in 1700 forced the town to return to New York. The whole line was established by survey in 1725 and 1731, re-surveyed by New York in 1860, agreed upon by both States in 1878 and 1879, and ratified by congress in 1880-81. It should be added that the unnatural junction of Long Island with New York in 1664 carried with it the island called Fisher's Island, off the southeast corner of Connecticut, which had been granted to Winthrop by Connecticut in 1641; and it thus gave the southern boundary of Connecticut its odd appearance, running from the mouth of Pawcatuck River, at the eastern end of the Sound, to the center of the East River, at the western end.

The northern boundary of the colony was not fully settled for more than a century. When Connecticut was settled, the Massachusetts southern line was in the air; and in 1642 that colony sent two men, Woodward and Saffery, to run the line according to the charter. The surveyors are said to have been ignorant men; and Connecticut authorities call them *lucus a non lucendo*, "the mathematicians." They began operations by finding what seemed to them a point "three English miles on the south part of the Charles River, or of any or every part thereof:" thence the southern Massachusetts line was to run west to the Pacific Ocean. The two mathematicians, however, either hesitating to undertake a foot journey to the Pacific, or doubting the sympathy of casual Indians with the advancement of science, and being sufficiently learned to know that two points are enough to determine the direction of a line, did not run the line directly west. Instead, they took ship, sailed around Cape Cod and up the Connecticut River, and found what they asserted to be a point in the same latitude as the first. In fact, they had got some eight miles too far to the south, thus giving their employers far too much territory; but they had fulfilled their principal duty, which was to show that Springfield was in Massachusetts. An *ex parte* survey, and of such a nature, could not of course be recognized by Connecticut. The oblong indentation in Connecticut's northern boundary is a remnant of the ignorance of Woodward and Saffery; for Massachusetts claimed a line running just north of Windsor, and Connecticut finally reclaimed all but this oblong. She made *ex parte* surveys of her own in 1695 and 1702, and then both colonies appealed to the crown. This was evidently a dangerous tribunal for both; and in 1714 they agreed on a compromise line much as it is at present. Connecticut received, in return for her concessions, 107,000 acres of wild land in Massachusetts, which was sold for about $2,500 and the proceeds given to Yale College. As surveys became still more accurate, it was found that the present towns of Enfield, Suffield, and Woodstock, which had fallen to Massachusetts by the agreement of 1714, were really south of the line, so that Massachusetts was governing territory outside of her charter limits. In 1749 Connecticut accepted the petition of these towns to be restored to her jurisdiction, and they have since been Connecticut towns. Massachusetts continued to claim the towns, but did not attempt to enforce the claim until 1804, when she finally abandoned it. In 1822 and 1826, the line was run as it now is, leaving the indentation to Massachusetts, perhaps as a memorial to Woodward and Saffery.

"How the boundary on the east was ever fixed," says Bowen, "seems a puzzle;" and he cites, very appropriately, Rufus Choate's description of it in one of its stages: "The commissioners might as well have decided that the line between the States was bounded on the north by a bramble bush, on the south by a bluejay, on the west by a hive of bees in swarming time, and on the east by five hundred foxes with firebrands tied to their tails." Connecticut claimed all the Narragansett country, up to Narragansett Bay, by conquest from the Pequots; and Massachusetts, on the ground of her essential assistance to Connecticut, claimed a division of the spoils. Rhode Island was considered an unchartered nonentity by both. In 1658 the New England commissioners really gave judgment against Connecticut, assigning the Mystic River as the boundary between Massachusetts and Connecticut, thus handing over the whole of Rhode Island and the eastern part of the present State of Connecticut to the Bay colony. The present township of Stonington thus became a Massachusetts town, and was called Southerton; and the Atherton Company, a Massachusetts association, whose leader, Captain Atherton, had bought large tracts of land in Rhode Island from the Indians, and which had acknowledged the jurisdiction of Connecticut, now passed under that of Massachusetts. The Connecticut charter in 1662, by carrying that colony up to Narragansett Bay, instead of clearing matters up, complicated them still further. Rhode Island then had an agent in London, soliciting a charter, which was granted in 1663; and it assigned as the western boundary of that colony the Pawcatuck River from its mouth to its source, and thence a due north line to the Massachusetts boundary. To prevent a conflict, Winthrop had made an agreement with the Rhode Island agent, which was made a part of the Rhode Island charter, that the Pawcatuck River should receive the additional title of "*alias* Norrogansett or Narrogansett River;" and that, wherever the Connecticut charter spoke of the Narragansett River, the Pawcatuck River should be taken and deemed to be the one intended! Connecticut at once repudiated this action of Winthrop as *ultra vires*, erected a town government at Wickford, and set the all-penetrating power of the Connecticut constable to work there. Then followed a period of great confusion, Rhode Island arresting Connecticut town officers, and *vice versa*, in the disputed territory, and Connecticut preparing to make her claims good by force, for the New England commissioners in 1664 had decided the dispute in her favor.

In the mean time, Randolph's royal commissioners, whose history in New England was that of a common and public nuisance, took the Narragansett dispute under consideration in 1665, without giving the parties any hearing or notice of it, and decided it in their usual impartial fashion. They decided that neither Connecticut nor Rhode Island had the slightest claim to the territory in dispute ; and they took it away from both, and erected it into a separate territory, to be known as the King's Province, belonging solely to his majesty. The title of the Atherton Company to their land purchases was decided in the same summary way: it was adjudged null and void, and the settlers were ordered to leave the King's Province. It adds to the oddity of the decisions that no one seems to have asked the commissioners to interfere.

The country in dispute was in reality almost a wilderness, with very few settlers. Connecticut therefore allowed the Randolph decision to go with a protest, until it became obsolete as the royal commissioners faded like an unhappy dream out of New England's memory. From time to time she appointed commissioners to meet those of

Rhode Island, though the meetings came to nothing. Proclamations and arrests enlivened the lot of the lonely dwellers in the Narragansett country; but settlement was retarded by the knowledge that the settler had to buy into a lawsuit of the most vexatious character. Rhode Island southwest of Providence was thus practically unsettled except by Indians, when the events of King Philip's war embittered the controversy by reinforcing the feeling of Connecticut men that the Narragansett country rightfully belonged to them by conquest as well as by charter. Their soldiers had fought in the swamp fight at Kingston, where the power of Philip was broken; their patrolling parties had afterwards scoured the country, and swept it of Narragansetts; and all the time Rhode Island had looked idly on, and had never struck a blow for the coveted territory, for her neighbors or for herself. After renewed confusion, a new set of royal commissioners, in 1683, decided every point in the Narragansett controversy in favor of Connecticut. The prospect for Rhode Island was therefore dark. All of its present territory west of Narragansett Bay and southwest of Providence had been adjudged to Connecticut. All east of the bay, if the grounds of this decision were to hold good as a precedent, belonged to Plymouth. And Massachusetts, to the north, was in waiting with a variety of claims, and a general willingness to act as residuary legatee of the late colony of

Rhode Island. It must have seemed certain that the existence of the stout little colony was to be limited to its first fifty years, and that its time had come. But its salvation came from the inability of its enemies to agree. The decision of the commissioners was not confirmed or considered by the home government, owing to the troublous times of James II.; and Rhode Island was enabled to deny its weight altogether. Then came Andros, who took Rhode Island's view of the case, and put her into possession of the disputed territory. She held to it, in spite of intermittent attempts of Connecticut to exercise jurisdiction over it, and in spite of a decision of the English attorney general in 1696 in favor of Connecticut. Indeed, her persistency, and the ugly possibility of an appeal to England for a general decision, began to incline Connecticut to a modification of her claims. Under the charter of Rhode Island, her western boundary was to be the Pawcatuck River to its head, and thence due north to the Massachusetts line. If the Pawcatuck River be followed up to its source, as still given on Rhode Island maps, that point will be found in a pond just east of where the swamp fight took place, near Kingston, within a half dozen miles of Narragansett Bay. A line due north from this point would pass just west of Providence, and would leave Rhode Island only a narrow strip of territory on the west shore of the bay. Connecticut, giving up her first claim to abut on the bay, now held to a literal interpretation of the Rhode Island charter; and it is not easy to see how her legal claim to the bulk of the disputed soil could be gainsaid. Rhode Island, however, was really fighting for her life; and her struggle was so persistent that Connecticut at last abandoned her old claim. In 1703 commissioners from both colonies agreed to follow the Pawcatuck River up to a branch called the Ashaway, thence a straight line to a point twenty miles due west of the extremity of Warwick Neck in Narragansett Bay, the northwest corner of the Atherton tract, and thence due north to the Massachusetts line. A subsequent attempt of Rhode Island to revive her ancient claim to the Mystic River as her western boundary led Connecticut to renew her resistance to the settlement of 1703; but the English board of trade in 1723 reported in favor of the moral claim of Rhode Island, and showed a disposition to make the dispute an excuse for uniting the two colonies in a royal government. Connecticut therefore joined in 1727-28 in running the line of 1703, which, slightly straightened in 1840, has since remained the boundary. The legal grounds of Connecticut's claim seem to have been good; but common justice to the different relations to the territory in dispute, which was vital to Rhode Island and only important to Connecticut, and common justice also to the obstinate fight made by the smaller colony, may fairly give reason for satisfaction in the final settlement. But it should not be forgotten that this was a case in which the smaller colony, if sufficiently determined, as Rhode Island evidently was, had a great advantage. She was ready to risk everything on an appeal to England; for, if she lost this territory in default of an appeal, she had little else to live for. In every crisis of the controversy, therefore, Rhode Island had a weapon in reserve to which Connecticut had no shield, for the last thing she wished was to come again under the general jurisdiction of an English tribunal: she had too many larger interests, outside of the Narragansett country, which such a tribunal would undoubtedly bring into question, while Rhode Island had hardly anything else to risk. This weapon, brought promptly and resolutely into play by Rhode Island whenever it was necessary, gave her a victory, to which she was fairly entitled by circumstances, at any rate.

Two disputes as to the soil of the colony remain to be stated. In 1635, just before the council of Plymouth disbanded it undertook to divide up the whole of New England into eight parcels, which it distributed among its members. The only one which gave any annoyance to Connecticut was that of the Marquis of Hamilton, running from the mouth of the Connecticut River to Narragansett Bay, and extending sixty miles back into the country. Hamilton sent over an agent to examine his grant; but, being a royalist, he was unable to make any serious effort to colonize during the commonwealth period. At the Restoration, his wife, now Duchess of Hamilton, opposed the charter of Connecticut; and her claims were referred to the royal commissioners for New England, who reported against them in 1665, but in 1683 referred a new claim to the king. The ground taken by Connecticut was mainly that of limitation, — that the Hamilton family, having utterly neglected to prosecute their claim to the territory for far longer than twenty years, and until others had settled and improved it, were debarred from entering it now. On this ground, endorsed in 1696 by the law officers of the crown, the council of trade finally decided in favor of Connecticut in 1697.

The other case, which kept the colony in trouble for years and was finally extinguished by the Revolution without any real decision, was the claim of the Mohegan Indians. John Mason, one of the founders of Windsor, afterwards settled at Saybrook, was the military man of the colony. The records generally refer to him as "the Major." After the Pequot war, he and his family seem to have had an hereditary friendship for the Mohegans, which was a burden to the white parties to it. The Mohegans seem to have made treaties of land cession with prodigal generosity when drunk, and to have lied about them circumstantially when sober. In 1640 they ceded their lands to Connecticut by an instrument which gave that colony power to establish plantations where it would, reserving certain lands to the Indians, and agreed to prevent other whites from settling in their territory without the consent of the Connecticut magistrates. The territory covered New London county and part of Windham; and it would be difficult to frame a more complete transfer than that made by the Indians. Mason settled at Norwich, in the Mohegan country, in 1659.

Two different stories were told by the Indians about the deed of 1640. One was that it was given to Mason by Uncas when the latter was at war with the Narragansetts; and that it was only to be used by Mason if Uncas were conquered, as he was not. This story was varied from time to time by another, quite inconsistent with the first, but less severe upon their friend Mason. It was that the deed of 1640 was understood by them as a mere trusteeship in Mason, as a man who understood the English people and English law, and could maintain the rights of the Indians. Mason's name is not even mentioned in the deed. Nevertheless Mason seems to have accepted this version.

In 1671, the year before his death, acting as if the deed of 1640 had been made to him as trustee instead of to the colony of Connecticut specifically, Mason deeded back a large tract to them, entailing it upon them and making it inalienable. In 1680, again, Uncas obtained from Connecticut a confirmation of his remaining lands, expressly resigning all jurisdiction over all of them. Within a year or two he died; his tribe was split into fragments; it was impossible to trace any legitimacy of blood; and the Indian claims fell into confusion worse confounded. The grandson of Mason, and the son of Mr. Fitch, the minister of Norwich, who were fast friends of the Indians, made their cause their own, and in 1705 they brought it to trial before a royal commission, headed by Governor Dudley of Massachusetts, and composed of his party. The trial was a curious one. If there was any cause of action for the plaintiffs, it was impossible to find it; the judges were determined to make the case a point of attack on the charter of Connecticut; and the defendant protested and refused to appear, on the ground that the commission had no powers to adjudicate the colony's title to existence. The commission decided against Connecticut, and the colony appealed to the crown. From that time the case dragged along until the Revolution, decided again and again in favor of the colony, and appealed by the Mason family, whose personal interests had become interwoven with the Mohegan claims. After the Revolution, the Indians, content with the State's reservation, made no further movement to reopen the case.

The commonwealth, its legal existence having been maintained and secured and its boundaries established, had a quiet and generally uneventful history so long as peaceful relations with the mother country were kept up. Buttressed on all sides by other colonies, as in King Philip's war, it suffered little from the colonial wars except in men. But its immunity from immediate danger had no effect in checking its readiness to make common cause with the other colonies. Soldiers were provided freely by the colony, and did their part manfully. But the brief story of Connecticut's colonial wars will fall better under the financial history with which they are closely connected.

CHAPTER XIII.

ECCLESIASTICAL AFFAIRS. 1636–1791.

It was probably inevitable, under the circumstances of time and place, that the first effort to establish a democratic commonwealth should be complicated with an ecclesiastical system entirely foreign to its real nature. Religious homogeneity almost compelled it. To the first settlers in Connecticut, though not for the same reason as in New Haven, civil and ecclesiastical affairs were convertible terms. The township and the church were coterminous: the town, by which term, as distinguished from the territorial *township*, was meant the body of voters within the township, settled civil and ecclesiastical affairs indifferently in the same town meeting; and as about all the voters were at first church-members and agreed closely in creed and methods, the dual system produced little friction for a time. It was inevitable that lapse of time should disturb the original homogeneity and bring trouble. The effort in New Haven to put off the evil day by the practical absorption of the state in the church led to the downfall of the commonwealth. The long contin-

ued efforts in Connecticut to reconcile church and
state under a free town system gave rise to difficulties whose history might fill volumes, and task
the learning of an expert in church history. Mather, no mean expert, said of one of the opening
struggles that its origin was as obscure as that of
the Connecticut River. The attempt of a mere
layman to penetrate such a labyrinth must necessarily be hazardous; and we are to venture in
no further than relation is found to the peculiar
development of the commonwealth.

It will easily be seen that a reconciliation between churches which acknowledged no earthly
master, and a commonwealth legislature whose
final authority was to be supreme, was a work of
no little difficulty. The long and comparatively
successful maintenance of the concordat in Connecticut seems to have been due to the character
of Hooker and the impress which he left on the
ecclesiastical traditions of the colony. He and
Davenport were fair types of the methods of the
two colonies. Both were masterful men, even for
that time. Davenport applied his force directly,
and failed. Hooker relied on influence, and succeeded. Most of Hooker's successors, in spite of
an occasional slip into direct aggression, followed
his methods with like success. With no official
voice in legislation, and no direct appeal even to
their arbitration, there was hardly an important
piece of legislation which was not tested by their

approval or disapproval; and it is to their honor that they were content with the substance of power, based on the confidence of their people. Only this mutual confidence made the concordat possible. Many an act of the general assembly, which seems an interference with the liberty of the churches, was based in reality on the tacit approval of the ecclesiastical element of the colony. They were the voice of the ecclesiastical, speaking through the civil power.

At the beginning, the Connecticut and New Haven churches alike were Congregational and Calvinistic. Each church claimed complete control of its own affairs. In cases of doubt or dispute, it would submit to the decision of a council of neighbor or allied churches; but the selection of the churches which were to form the council was always a matter for mutual agreement, or fresh disputes, between the two parties. The church knew no superior. It was begun by a common agreement in articles of faith by those who proposed to become members. The ceremony of the selection of the "seven pillars," already described, was peculiar to the churches of New Haven, Milford, and Guilford, and seems to have been in their cases an expedient of the leaders for the establishment of their politico-ecclesiastical system. A well-organized Connecticut church was at first supposed to have two ministers. One was the pastor, whose duties were mainly the exhortation, encouragement, and pastoral care of the members; the other was the teacher, whose work was the doctrinal defense of the church and the instruction of its people. The ruling elder was the executive officer of the church; but its success depended largely on the coöperation of the ruling elder with the pastor. The functions of the deacons were those which have always been familiar in those officers. Back of all of them was the vote of the church, a Calvinistic democracy, undefined in its powers, and ready, on occasion, to claim the full powers of an ecumenical council. When the union had been completed, there were fifteen of these churches in the colony: the Long Island churches, organized in the same way, had passed under the dominion of New York.

The first churches were mostly small. Those of Hartford and New Haven were of course the largest. The church of Wethersfield, when it split and the defeated party removed to Stamford, numbered but seven communicants, the orthodox majority numbering four and the heterodox minority three. Pierson's church at Southampton, on Long Island, numbered but sixteen. This paucity of numbers, however, was due to the promptness of the first settlers in organizing their churches. The church really began with the settlement. The first item in the Norwalk town records provides for the restraint of wandering swine; the second, for the erection of a minister's house; the third, for a pound.

The first great church dispute, which rent the Hartford church from 1654 until 1659, has been so complicated with the names of the actors and with doctrinal points, that one who is not a profound theologian can hardly make anything of it. There are indications, however, that an explanation may be found in the effort to accommodate the original church and state system to the changing conditions of the people, and that the actors, however prominent, were merely floating on the surface of opposing currents whose nature even they did not understand quite clearly. Three points are of interest: the church establishment; the connection of church and state, or rather town; and the change in the people, with its effects.

The first code of Connecticut, in 1650, required that all persons should be taxed for church as well as for state; and the taxes for support of the minister, and for other ecclesiastical purposes, were to be levied and collected like other taxes. So long as a trace of the establishment lasted, even down to the adoption of the constitution of 1818, the connection with the civil power continued. The church society used the civil tax lists in levying its rates; the conditions of suffrage in society meetings were the same as in civil town meetings; and the penalties for voting by unqualified persons were the same. The civil power collected the taxes for the church by distraint. If the church refused or neglected to support its minister, the general assembly settled the proper rate of maintenance and enforced it on the church; and if a church remained without a minister for more than a year, the general assembly could name a proper amount for ministerial purposes, and compel the church to raise and expend it. The principle of such connection was the ecclesiastical system of the commonwealth from 1639 down to 1818; and the successive " enfranchisements " of other sects were simply permissions to them to use the secular arm according to what had been at first the special privilege of the establishment.

Considering the churches recognized in 1650 as established, the commonwealth forbade any persons to form a new church within the colony without consent of the general court and of the neighboring churches. The man, therefore, who, not being a member of one of the established churches, found himself within the territory of a church, was unable to vote in purely church matters; but he was compelled to vote taxes and pay taxes for the support of a minister in whose call he had had no voice. From their establishment, the churches had been strict in regard to baptism, and their inquisitions into the personal experience of candidates for membership were searching. As the numbers increased of those who could not respond to such inquisitions and were thus barred from the church, dissatisfaction must have increased with them. It often took the shape of complaints that the children of such persons were refused baptism; but it may be suspected fairly that the natural wish to share in the control of the church whose expenses they helped to pay had a great deal to do with it. Either the right of suffrage must be restricted to church-members, or all the voters must be let into the church. In New Haven, church-membership had swallowed democracy; in Connecticut, was democracy to swallow church-membership?

The Cambridge platform, adopted by a council of the New England churches held at Cambridge, Mass., in 1648, was intended to be the model for the church system of New England, and it governed the Connecticut churches for sixty years. Its importance was more in its recognition of church independence than in any formulation of a creed. But, in spite of its recognition of church independence, there was in it the seed of state interference, so far at least as Connecticut churches were concerned, for it insisted "that the magistrate is to see that the ministry be duly provided for." In Connecticut the magistrate was really the town; and the town's democracy would hardly be willing to support the church without at least trying to control it. The attempt was soon made by the general court, as the mouthpiece of all the towns, in the course of its efforts to settle the Hartford difficulty.

In February, 1657, the general court called for a council of the New England churches at Boston, to consider certain propositions of the general court. The object of these propositions was well understood to be the widening of church-membership. The New Haven churches rejected the suggestion of such a council, and the purely independent element in Connecticut sympathized with them, for the decision of such a council looked straight to state interference as a means of enforcing it. Nevertheless the council met, and sustained the new rather than the old view. It declared that baptized infants were bound, on arriving at years of discretion, to " own the covenant " and become formal church-members; and that the church was bound to accept them, if they were not of scandalous life and understood the grounds of religion, and was bound to baptize their children, thus continuing the chain of claims to church-membership to all generations. This made church-membership rather an affair of the head and of morals; and it was deeply execrated by the New Haven churches, and by at least a strong minority of the Connecticut churches, for it really gave every baptized person a voice in church government. It was commonly known as the Half-way Covenant.

In 1664 the general court formally approved the council's decision, and " commended " it to the churches under its jurisdiction, which now covered New Haven. So far as it ventured to do so, the general court thus made the Half-way Covenant, with its loose system of admission to the church, the ecclesiastical law of the commonwealth. But it was from the first a political rather than an ecclesiastical idea; it never was welcome to the Connecticut churches, and some of them never accepted it.

To return now to the Hartford difficulty, which had been woven into every step of the progress toward the Half-way Covenant. Its nominal beginning was after the death of Hooker in 1647. Goodwin, the ruling elder, wanted Michael Wigglesworth as Hooker's successor; and Stone, the surviving minister, refused to allow the proposition to be put to vote. The Goodwin party, twenty-one in number, including Deputy Governor Webster, withdrew from the church; the Stone party undertook to discipline them; a council of Connecticut and New Haven churches failed to reconcile the parties; the general court kindly assumed the office of mediator, and succeeded in making both parties furious; and finally a council at Boston in 1659 induced the Goodwin minority, now some sixty in number, to remove to Hadley, Mass.

A larger struggle followed Stone's death in 1663. There were now two young men, Whiting and Haynes, in the places of Hooker and Stone; and the new incumbents, in addition to their opposition to one another, seem to have been about equally tactless. Haynes headed the Half-way

Covenant party. He was supported by the church, and the ratification of this form of church discipline by the general court in 1664 strengthened his position. Whiting, with those who still held to the primitive doctrine of the necessity of individual experience and strict investigation of it before admission to the church, was compelled to remain in a church which must have seemed to him and his party almost a heterodox body. Five years of this sort of life was necessary to convince both parties of the necessity of a compromise.

In May, 1669, the general court advised that all persons approved in law and sound in the fundamentals of the Christian religion should "have allowance of their persuasion and profession in church ways;" that is, that they should have liberty to constitute another church within the town limits. This innovation had evidently become inevitable. In October, Mr. Whiting appeared before the court, applied for permission to form a new church, and received it. The Second Church of Hartford was thus formed the next year by Mr. Whiting and thirty-one families; and the first breach in the original identity of town and church was accomplished. Further, as the members of the new church necessarily received the privilege of diverting their share of the taxes to the support of their own church, the principle of this more democratic precedent guided the slow emancipation of all the other sects down to 1818. But it is not a little odd to find that the new church, founded as a protest against the Half-way Covenant, adopted that practice from its very first meeting.

However unwillingly the churches might accept the Half-way Covenant, it could not but affect their church-membership very seriously. The number of "strict Congregationalists" steadily decreased, while the number of "large Congregationalists," leaning to Presbyterianism, was as steadily increasing. "A church without a bishop, and a state without a king," was still the theory; but the state had now a regulator in the shape of a supreme legislature, and this was enough to bring about a desire for a similar regulator for the church. The general court evidently leaned toward a council of the churches, much after the fashion of a Presbyterian synod, as a fly-wheel to keep the churches in harmony on points of fundamental importance, while allowing disagreement on minor points. The ministers had been in the habit of holding neighborhood meetings, and, after the union, county meetings; but these were voluntary, and their proceedings were limited to the special objects for which they had been called. This, however, was a germ for an establishment; and the absolute power of individual churches to decide upon the qualifications of candidates for the ministry, and certain scandals resulting therefrom, furnished the occasion.

In 1708 the general court directed that the churches of each county should send their ministers and "messengers," or·lay representatives, to meet at their county town; that the county assemblies should settle upon what they considered the best system of church order; and that delegates from the county assemblies should meet at Saybrook, at the coming Commencement, to draw up for the general court's adoption a commonwealth church system.

The synod met in September, adopted the Savoy Confession as modified by the Boston synod of 1680, and formed the Saybrook platform as an ecclesiastical system for the commonwealth. It directed that "consociations" of neighboring churches should be formed in each county; that a church, or an excommunicate person with the consent of the church, should have the right to bring disputes before the consociation; that a pastor or church refusing to be bound by the decision of the consociation should be put out of communion; and that there should be an annual meeting of delegates from all the consociations. The scheme was at once ratified by the general court, and the churches united by it were "owned and acknowledged established by law;" but permission was reserved to any church to "soberly differ or dissent from the united churches hereby established." This was about the measure of rights given to dissenters in England by the act of 1689, under William and Mary. The dissenting churches were to be taxed for the support of the established churches. The establishment was a modified Presbyterianism. There was no formal coercive power; but the public provision for the minister's support, and the withdrawal of it from recalcitrant members, formed a coercive power of no mean efficacy. With its adoption, the Congregational churches of Connecticut passed into their semi-Presbyterian stage of existence; indeed, toward the end of the century, President Dwight uses the terms " Congregational " and " Presbyterian " as about convertible.

The Saybrook platform brought order at once into the Connecticut system; but worse than disorder came with it. The tendency of such an orderly system to a barren intellectualism, difficult enough to resist at the best, became far stronger when the church was dependent on the state for material support. Within thirty years, the worst symptoms of a purely state religion began to show themselves, and it required all the vitality of the churches, and a tremendous internal convulsion, to banish them. The great revival of 1741, beginning in the church of Jonathan Edwards at Northampton, Mass., and intensified by the preaching of Whitefield, Gilbert Tennant, and others, struck the first blow at the hitherto secure position of the Saybrook platform. Wandering revivalists disturbed many of the ministers, and their complaints found a sympathetic audience in the general court. That body passed an act in 1742 which protected the churches rather more than the Saybrook platform had given any reason for anticipating. It forbade under penalties the entrance of an ordained minister into the parish of another minister to preach there without the invitation of the settled minister and his church; it increased the penalty in the case of an unlicensed person; and it ordered any foreigner or stranger, licensed or unlicensed, who should preach in violation of the act, to be sent as a vagrant from "constable to constable" out of the colony.

The Connecticut churches had changed very much since the time of Hooker, but not enough to make it likely that such legislation as this would pass unchallenged. Churches all over the colony became divided within themselves; the "new lights," as the maintainers of freedom for the new methods were called, were hurried by zeal into the most fantastic doctrines and practices; and the colonial ecclesiastical system was again all at sea. One church chose a minister, ordained him, quarreled with him, silenced him, cast him out of the church, and delivered him up to Satan, and all within the space of a year. The extravagance of the new lights afforded the "old lights" a fair opportunity of proceeding to extremes with a good grace. General court and assembly joined in arresting, excommunicating, and prosecuting ministers who violated the act and church-members who went to hear them. When Whitefield made a second tour through the colony in 1745, the general court even denounced him by resolution as a promoter of errors and disorders, and cautioned the ministers not to admit him to their pulpits, and church-members not to listen to him. Before 1748, the different consociations had expelled about all the "new lights" among their ministers, one of the consociations remarking complacently in one case that it had now blown out one new light, and that it meant to keep on until it had blown out all the rest.

Meanwhile separations among the churches had gone on apace. When a minister was disbarred by any of the consociations, that portion of his flock which agreed or sympathized with him left their church with him, and organized a church of their own. When a schism arose in a church from any cause, it was not long before it ran into some phase of the old and new light controversy, and a separation took place. There were thus a number of separate churches in the colony, and their position was peculiar. From its foundation, the law of the colony had been that any man who should refuse to contribute according to his ability to the support of the settled ministers should be compelled to do so by levy and distraint, as in the case of other taxes. At the same time, provision was made, and in 1669 and 1708, as has been said, was enacted into statute, that members of unestablished churches might "have allowance of their persuasion and profession in church ways or assemblies without disturbance." This, however, was intended to secure quiet to licensed dissenting churches, and to enable members of new Congregational churches, when licensed by the general court, to transfer their share of the taxes to their own ministers. Unlicensed Congregational churches were worse off than either, for they were taxed for the support of the Established churches, and were open to prosecution besides.

This arrangement had worked very fairly for some sixty years. When a separation took place, as in Hartford, it was ratified by the general court, and the members of the new church paid their rates only for the support of their own minister. No one was legally a minister unless recognized by the general court, and then he was entitled to a measure of state support. About 1706 the ecclesiastical calm had been interrupted by the Church of England. One of its missionaries began to preach in Stratford, and in 1722 another was permanently settled there. It was but natural that the members of this church should object to supporting their own minister and paying rates for the Congregational minister as well; and they had a strong disposition to appeal from the laws of Connecticut to those of Great Britain, which was the last thing the colony wanted. It is a tradition that the establishment of the Episcopal Church in New Haven was secured by an offer to pay the fines for dissidence, coupled with a demand for a copy of the proceedings for transmission to the home government. In 1727 the general court passed an act which cut the tie that had so long bound town and church together. Hitherto there had been but one church in a town, unless the general court permitted a separation. Now any society of the Church of England might be formed in a town; its members were thereupon excused from paying rates to the settled or Congregational minister; their obligation to pay taxes was transferred to their own minister; and the old church was to be known as the "prime ancient society." The latter, however, still retained the taxing power over all persons not members of any church. In 1729 the act of 1727 was extended to cover the case of Quakers and Baptists.

The new churches formed by the new-light schism claimed to be Congregational: the tyrannical legislation of 1742 had taken them out of the scope of the act of 1669, and their members were still held bound for taxes to support the very ministers from whom they had seceded. Some congregations became nominal Baptists in order to get the benefit of the act of 1729. Others simply refused to pay, and the settled ministers put every engine of the law in motion against them. Their property was levied upon and sold for a small fraction of its real value; in default of satisfaction by property, they were arrested and taken to jail, with the scandalous accompaniment of the scenes naturally arising from a violent resistance; and a faint flavor of the Inquisition began to pervade the ecclesiastical system of the colony. When the cause of the new lights took this form, the end was not far distant. One church after another, on the occasion of almost any dispute with its minister, took the opportunity to repudiate the Saybrook platform, and to reassert the primitive freedom of the churches; the number of malcontents was steadily increasing; and about 1780 the general court gave up the struggle and the Saybrook platform together. In 1791 it practically granted the right of free incorporation to all religious bodies; but persons unconnected with any church were still required to pay rates to the established Congregational organization until the constitution of 1818 made all such contributions voluntary.

In spite of the act of 1727, other sects than the Congregational were really exotics. It was not until 1789 that the first Methodist society was founded at Stratford, where the Episcopalians had begun their organization. The Baptists and other sects had existed in small numbers; but all the sects were weak, and membership in them was to some extent a removal from the sympathies of the mass of the people. To the Episcopalians, whose church had lorded it at home as the Congregational church now lorded it in Connecticut, this state of affairs must have been particularly exasperating. Their feeling of isolation was increased by the difficulty which they experienced in obtaining a bishop. It was not until 1784 that Bishop Seabury was consecrated by the Scottish bishops, having failed of ordination at the hands of the English bishops, on account of the necessity that the candidate should take the oath of allegiance to the crown.

For one reason or other, every dissenting sect in Connecticut had its own grievances, and felt itself to be more or less an alien to the commonwealth. This worst political feature of any ecclesiastical restriction showed itself again and again in local politics before the Revolution, still more during the Revolution in the development of the Tory party in the State; and it was the basis of almost all party opposition after the Revolution, until, coalescing with the rising tide of democracy, it overthrew the charter itself in 1818.

The establishment of Yale College, as it was an essential part of the colony's ecclesiastical system, may best find a place here. The Connecticut general court, in establishing a free-school system in 1644, had done so on the express ground that it was "one chief project of that old deluder, Satan, to keep men from the knowledge of the

Scriptures;" and the selectmen of the towns were cautioned, as a fundamental part of education, to see to it that parents and masters gave children weekly instruction in "some short orthodox catechism." A college was evidently needed as the capstone to the system; and New Haven, under the impulse of Davenport, began thinking of such an institution in 1641. It was allowed to slumber because of the protest of the leading men of the Bay: they urged that all the resources of all New England were barely enough to support Harvard, and that an attempt to establish a new institution would merely ruin both. In 1652 the project was formally given up for the time, but the New Haven authorities had been directed, five years before, to reserve one of the home lots for the college.

When the time seemed to have come, in 1698, for reviving the project, the general synod of the colony took the work in hand, intending to call the new college "The School of the Church." During the following year, the notion of church control was given up; but ten ministers were named as trustees. Their first meeting probably took place in the year 1700; and it was later in the same year that the famous meeting took place at Branford, when each minister laid upon the trustees' table his contribution of books, saying, "I give these books for the founding of a college in this colony." The whole number was about forty volumes: so small was the germ from which has sprung one of the great institutions of learning of the United States.

In October, 1701, the general court chartered the college, in order to enable it to hold lands and receive gifts and bequests; and an annual grant amounting to about £60 sterling was voted to aid in its support. The trustees fixed upon Saybrook as the place for the college, and Abraham Pierson as its first rector. But Mr. Pierson was settled as minister at Killingworth, and his people would not consent to his removal. Until his death, the library and students remained at Killingworth; but the Commencements took place at Saybrook. The first of them was on the 13th of September, 1702, when Nathanael Chauncey, the first graduate, took his degree. Degrees, apparently honorary, were given at the same time to four others who had already been graduated at Harvard. It is a pleasing circumstance to record that a large part of the instruction of the early classes had been given by the trustees, in default of other instructors.

Mr. Pierson died in 1707, and Mr. Andrew was chosen in his place. Part of the students went to his residence at Milford, and the rest to Saybrook; and the college was thus divided until 1716. When the trustees met at the Commencement of 1716, they found the college almost broken up. Divided instruction and government, aided by the eager struggles of other towns to obtain the final location of the college, and crowned by an outbreak of smallpox, had scattered the students in every direction, and there were the germs of half a dozen possible colleges. In October the trustees voted to fix the college at New Haven, and persisted in spite of an opposition which divided the whole colony and was carried into colonial politics. In 1717 the general court endorsed the removal, and voted a grant to aid in the erection of buildings. All through these years, good friends in England had been sending over books, the foundation of the noble library which is now so great an ornament to the college. One of these benefactors was Elihu Yale, a man of New Haven ancestry, who had gone into the East India trade and become a "nabob." He had shown a strong interest in the college; and it would probably be doing the excellent trustees no injustice if one presumes them to have thought that his interest would be increased if the institution were removed to New Haven and named after him. At any rate, the first Commencement held at New Haven, in 1718, was marked by the adoption of the title YALE COLLEGE, with a dedicatory memorial to Mr. Yale. Yale started in the race long after her rival at Cambridge; and it is interesting to speculate on the results of the equality which she would have attained at the beginning, if Mr. Yale had been able to carry out the generous intentions which he certainly felt for the college which bore his name. Unfortunately, he died intestate before he could do what he meant to do; and the college received no more aid from him. Never was human distinction so cheaply purchased as that which has perpetuated the otherwise almost unknown names of John Harvard and Elihu Yale.

If a college were a living thing, one might fancy Yale drawing a long breath of satisfaction as it struck its roots deep into its new soil. It had found its proper place: New Haven would not be New Haven without the college, nor would Yale be quite Yale without New Haven. But its troubles were by no means over. The dissatisfaction at the removal would not down: there was an irregular Commencement in progress at Wethersfield while the college was receiving its new name; and an attempt by the sheriff to remove the library from Saybrook led to a riot, in which many of the books were lost. These difficulties were healed by the prudence of the general court, and Timothy Cutler, of Stratford, was chosen rector in Mr. Andrew's place. He proved to be a most efficient and popular head; but in 1722 the good people of the colony were astounded to learn that the new rector, one of the tutors, and two neighboring ministers, had embraced Episcopacy, and were going to England to be ordained. They carried out their intention, and became the fathers of the Episcopal Church in Connecticut. But they left the college in distress; and it was not until 1725 that a successor to Mr. Cutler was found, in the person of Rev. Elisha Williams. Under his rectorship Yale at last began to prosper. Berkeley, subsequently Bishop of Cloyne, made his visit to America, and recognized Yale's claims to a leading educational place by gifts which were, for the time, very munificent; and Mr. Williams at his resignation in 1739 left the college firmly established.

His successor, Rev. Thomas Clap, of Windham, was the first in the long line of distinctively Yale presidents. His predecessors had been Connecticut ministers, set for a time over a special work. He sank everything else in his presidency. He introduced the modern systems of cataloguing the library; he formulated the laws and customs of the college; and in 1745 he obtained a new charter for "The President and Fellows of Yale College." The day of the "collegiate school" had gone by, and the real Yale College had fairly begun its career. In 1750-52 the general court aided in erecting Connecticut Hall, and allowed President Clap to hold a lottery to complete the work. In 1755, when disputes connected in one way or other with the new-light controversy were distracting the Connecticut churches, President Clap showed his executive ability and promptness by establishing Yale as a separate church, thus removing it from the scene of active strife; and further, in order to avoid any conflict over the matter, he very shrewdly refused to ask the general court for permission, claiming the right, as an incorporated college, to do so. The opposition to the college seized this opportunity to attack it before the general court, on the ground that it was "too independent;" but President Clap appeared as its attorney, and defended it successfully. He seems to have been one of those college presidents who, endowed by nature with abilities sufficient for eminence in any department, have devoted them all to the development of the college.

The college preacher who had been called in 1755, Rev. Naphtali Daggett, retained his position until his death in 1780, having acted as president for a time on the death of Mr. Clap in 1767. During his professorship in 1779, the British made their attack on New Haven. Among the hasty levies which went out to oppose them was the stout old college preacher, armed with his shotgun. When the others took to their heels, he stood his ground, loading and firing in the most unministerial fashion. A British detachment charged him and captured him; and the officer in command inquired, not very gently, "What are you doing here, you old fool, firing on his majesty's troops?" "Exercising the rights of war," said the doctor, grimly. He was to be exercised in the rights of war in a different way. In his own words, "They damned me, those who took me, because they spared my life. Thus, 'midst a thousand insults, my infernal driver hastened me along farther than my strength would admit in the extreme heat of the day, weakened as I was by my wounds and the loss of blood, which, at a moderate computation, could not be less than a quart. And when I failed in some degree through faintness, he would strike me on the back with a heavy walking-staff, and kick me behind with his foot. At length, by the supporting power of God, I arrived at the green in New Haven. . . . I obtained leave of an officer to be carried into the Widow Lyman's and laid on a bed, where I lay the rest of the day and the succeeding night, in such acute and excruciating pain as I never felt before."

President Ezra Stiles, called in 1777, was a worthy successor to President Clap. He was succeeded by Timothy Dwight in 1795, by Jeremiah Day in 1817, by Theodore D. Woolsey in 1846, by Noah Porter in 1871, and by Timothy Dwight in 1886. Modern Yale began under President Dwight, in 1795. Able as preceding presidents had been, he was the first who reached a really national reputation. At the same time the rising opposition to Yale control in the State reacted by intensifying its support, so that it was for the time the ruling power. John Wood, in 1802, thus describes the political structure of Connecticut, from a democratic standpoint: "This State has not formed any constitution since the Revolution; but ancient superstition and the prejudice of custom have established an hierarchy, which is directed by a sovereign pontiff, twelve cardinals, a civil council of nine, and about four hundred parochial bishops. The present priest, who may be honored with the appellation of pope, is Timothy Dwight, President of Yale College. . . . The annual Commencement at Yale College takes place in September, a short time previous to the election of the legislature. At this time, the president is attended by his twelve cardinal members of the corporation, the governor, the lieutenant governor, and seven other senior members of the first legislative house (which compose the lay part), and the greatest part of the clergy. On this occasion, the governor and other civilians are subordinate to the president, and they feel deeply impressed with a sense of their subordination, knowing that he can kill or make alive at the next annual election, — that he emphatically holds the keys which command their political damnation or salvation. The pope, being thus surrounded by his cardinals, his civil councils, and his parochial bishops, determines the order and detail of the ensuing election. Each one returns home with a perfect understanding of the part he is to act." He then goes on to draw a highly colored picture of the manner in which the clergy, the "parochial bishops," control the elections under direction of Pope Dwight.

All this was but a deeply prejudiced view of the feeling which Connecticut, and particularly the clergy, were coming to have toward the college. The little State's little college was fast becoming a national institution. Its former meagre system, under which instruction was given by the president and a few tutors, was giving place to the organized staff of professors which now numbers a hundred. From the beginning of this century, Yale's development has not only been strong, natural, and healthy: it has also tended steadily into university development. The original college has been the nucleus around which have been clustered successive coördinated departments of study. The Medical School was added in 1813; the Theological School in 1822; the Law School in 1824; the Sheffield Scientific School in 1847; the Art School in 1864; and the Peabody Museum of Natural History in 1866. In 1886 the title Yale College was changed to that of Yale University. In its sphere, the State's development has been limited by circumstances, while that of the college has been free from necessary limitations; naturally, therefore, the devotion of the State to the college has not been able to keep up the closely paternal relations which John Wood found so exasperating in 1802. But the State and city cannot but be proud of the institution which Davenport conceived, Clap preserved, and Dwight sent on its way to its present rank as a great university.

CHAPTER XIV.

FINANCIAL AFFAIRS. 1640-1763.

A DEMOCRACY usually finds its vulnerable side in financial errors, and any decadence in the quality of its individual units is most quickly reflected here. Connecticut's success in repairing her own blunders is an evidence that there was at least no decadence in her colonial history. The commonwealth shared with the other New England colonies the early difficulties arising from want of metallic currency, or from clumsy attempts to supply the want by various attractive but fallacious expedients. At first, the little ready money which the settlers brought with them served for their trade with one another, while the Indian trade was carried on by means of Indian money. It soon became necessary to use the Indian money, wampum, wampum-peage, or simply peage, in traffic among the whites; and it passed current at the rate of six pieces, later four pieces, to the penny, or a fathom for five shillings. The use of this was not uncommon even during the early years of the next century. In addition, there were all sorts of substitutes for money: beaver-skins, codfish, farm products, live stock, bullets, and nails served either for small change or for large payments. Much of the legislation, in Connecticut and in other New England colonies, which has been stigmatized as a sort of sumptuary legislation, fixing prices for goods, was really intended to put a legal value on them so that they might serve as currency, either in liquidating private debts or in paying taxes. In case of doubt, the goods were "prysed," or appraised, by arbitrators selected by the two parties.

"Bay shillings," of the Massachusetts coinage of 1652, became current in Connecticut soon after their issue, in spite of the efforts of the Bay colony to keep them at home. But clipping soon put them into doubt, and the colonists were driven back to primitive substitutes. The journal of Mrs. Knight, who passed through Connecticut in 1704, tells us that there were then in use in that colony four distinct sorts of currency. "Pay" was barter, property at the prices which the general court had affixed to it in acceptance for taxes for that year. "Money" was metallic currency, or wampum for the token money. "Pay as money" was property, at rates fixed by the parties, not by the general court. "Trust" was a price, with time given. The court records often speak of the first as "country pay," not because the articles came from the country, as one might suppose, but because its rates of value were fixed by the " country," a term often used for the colony or state, and that in strict accordance with good English precedents. Payment " in specie " meant payment in articles specified by the agreement, or, in default of that, in articles at rates specified by the general court's acts. It was not limited to money until gold and silver were made the *only* legal tender. The "money" used in larger payments was mainly Spanish pieces-of-eight, that is, of eight reals, afterwards supplanted by the Spanish milled dollar, each about equivalent to six New England shillings; and the persistence of this equivalent value of six shillings to the federal dollar long afterward is a curious survival of ancient values. As all these substitutes varied in value or in price, and as the real money was generally of somewhat doubtful quality, all the difficulties of arithmetic were added to the natural difficulties of trade; and, as always happens under such circumstances, the sharpest and least scrupulous reaped all the profit, while the mass of the people, too busy with other things to study the intricacies of finance, paid the piper. Not content with this state of affairs, the colony was imprudent enough to seek relief in the thorny paths of paper money emissions. This part of the commonwealth's history is intimately connected with her wars.

The first set conflict of Connecticut with the Canadian French came after the recovery of the charter. The accession of William and Mary to the English throne had been followed at once by war between England and France, in which the colonies were involved without any great desire for it. Connecticut's position was peculiar. She was shut off from any imminent danger by New York and Massachusetts; and yet she was in a position from which she could give quicker and more effective aid to the exposed settlements of those colonies than their centres of power could render. Help from Hartford could reach Albany or the towns of western Massachusetts sooner than it could be sent from New York or Boston. Connecticut was therefore usually at war in defense of her neighbors rather than of herself; but her aid was never given grudgingly or scantily.

At the first rumor of war, Connecticut had sent Captain Bull to Albany with a detachment for the defense of that place, and another detachment to New York city for a similar purpose. Leisler then held New York city, while the Albany district was in a state of incipient rebellion against him. Suddenly the French and Indians burst into Schenectady, where no sufficient watch was kept, massacred the people, and burned the place. Bull had warned the people to keep a better watch, but to no purpose. Leisler and his opponents both charged the calamity upon the false security produced by the intrigues and promises of the opposite party; and all the thanks received by Connecticut came in the form of accusations by both parties that she had encouraged the rascals of the opposition. There is a good commentary on her disinterestedness in the fact that De Callières' plan of campaign contemplated only an attack on Albany and New York, with no design on Connecticut.

In conjunction with the other New England colonies and New York, Connecticut agreed to take part in the land expedition up the Hudson, which was to coöperate with Governor Phipps's sea expedition against Quebec. Fitz John Winthrop was placed in command of the joint forces, with Milborn, Leisler's son-in-law, as commissary. Milborn does not seem to have known enough to provide food or transportation for the army; and, in default of these very necessary factors of success, Winthrop was compelled to retreat. Leisler took the side of his son-in-law, heaped volumes of abuse upon Winthrop, and finally ordered him under arrest. It is said that the Indians attached to the army released him, "to the universal joy of the army." The Connecticut general court expressed itself emphatically in his favor, and the tone of Leisler's letters is enough to confirm their judgment. For the remainder of the war, Connecticut's part was confined to furnishing troops whenever any of her neighbors called for them.

The case was much the same in Queen Anne's war, which broke out in 1702, but was aggravated by the programme pursued by Governor Cornbury of New York, a cousin of the queen, and Governor Dudley of Massachusetts. Dudley's object was to unite all the New England colonies under his government; but he was shrewd enough to persuade Cornbury that he meant merely to attach Connecticut to New York. So Connecticut was kept busy in satisfying the requisitions of her neighbor governors for troops and material aid of all kinds, while the two governors were all the time planning to vacate the charter of Connecticut. A bill for that purpose was brought before parliament, and was only defeated by the most untiring efforts of Ashurst, the colony's agent. Dudley's attempt to enforce the Mohegan claims, already mentioned, was a part of the scheme.

Dudley's whole scheme proved abortive in 1705; and the colony no doubt took great satisfaction, when he next sent a request for troops in 1707, in returning a flat refusal. Two years after, in 1709, on a requisition from the queen for three hundred and fifty men to attack Quebec, and for four hundred more for a land expedition against Montreal, Connecticut promptly filled her quota; and about one hundred of her men were among the dead who were the principal result of the campaign. The next year, three hundred men were raised and took part in the capture of Port Royal. In the following year, four hundred men were raised to give stupid Hovenden Walker the pleasure of wrecking them in Canadian waters.

Until 1709 the colony had fought through all its work on a money basis, raising or lowering the tax-rates from time to time as necessity required or permitted. Its limit had now been reached. The taxes had risen to seven or eight pence in the pound, a ruinous rate for a poor and struggling agricultural commonwealth, whose own governmental expenses were kept down to the lowest point. In June, 1709, "the great scarcity of money, the payment of the public debts and charges of this government, especially in the intended expedition to Canada," led the general court to order the issue of £8,000 in paper currency. It was to be received at a premium of five per cent. in payment of taxes; no legal-tender clause was inserted, as in other colonies; and a special tax of ten pence in the pound was ordered for payment in two annual parts. Further levies made it necessary to order the issue of £11,000 more in the same year, with the provision of a tax for payment in six annual parts. From this time the issues went on with bewildering rapidity. In all cases it speaks well for the underlying good sense of the authorities that provision was made for special taxation for the redemption of each issue; but the evil consequences of such issues could not be altogether avoided. The original avoidance of the legal-tender feature lasted until 1718, and then it was introduced under a bashful cover. Debtors who tendered bills of credit were relieved from execution and imprisonment. Further, counterfeiting had become alarmingly common; and the general court had come to rely more and more, in every emergency, on fresh emissions of bills of credit. And in 1733 the once cautious colony had become so demoralized as to establish what was really a land-bank, issuing £30,000 in bills, and dividing the amount in loans equally among the five counties. In spite of continuous efforts to provide in advance by taxation for the redemption of each issue, the balance against the colony was growing larger; the purchasing power of the paper was depreciating; and, though this effect was disguised from most people by the legal-tender feature, yet there was not a man in the colony who could not appreciate it, as it came in the rise of prices of commodities: silver rose in price from 8s. per ounce in 1708 to 18s. in 1732, and to 32s. in 1744. As usual, the price of labor lagged behind in the rise, while the price of all that the laborer ate or wore was rising faster, so that the laborer paid the cost of most of the factitious increase of business. The authorities themselves became careless, so that, for the first time in its history, the accounts of the colony became so puzzling during this period that it is practically impossible to make anything out of them. The best that can be made of them is that, down to 1740, £156,000 of paper had been issued, but that all but about £6,000 of this had been redeemed by taxation;

and that there were still outstanding about £33,000 issued and loaned to the various counties, making about £39,000 in all for which the colony was now responsible.

From the time of Walker's luckless expedition there was peace in the colony for nearly thirty years, such peace as the colonists might have had nearly always but for the fact of the existence of a "home government." In 1739 this "home government" saw fit to declare a war against Spain, which swept France into its circle in 1744, and was only ended by the peace of Aix-la-Chapelle in 1748. It was only when the French took part in it that the more northern colonies became fully involved: until then, Oglethorpe and the new colony of Georgia bore the brunt of the conflict. But the northern colonies did not altogether escape: the home government had prepared an entertainment for them, in Admiral Vernon's Carthagena expedition, more elaborate than Walker's and almost as unlucky. Connecticut contributed her proportion of the men, one thousand in number, whom New England sent to Carthagena, of whom hardly a hundred returned; and the expenses of the armament called for a further issue of £45,000 in paper, £8,000 to be applied to the redemption of former issues, or "old tenor," and £23,000 to be loaned out, and the interest applied to redemption purposes. This issue was called "new tenor." In obedience to a demand of the

FINANCIAL AFFAIRS.

board of trade, the legal-tender provision was struck out. The extension of the war to France in 1744, and the brilliant and successful expedition against Louisburg, brought fresh expense, which Connecticut met by fresh issues of "new tenor," bringing her whole emissions for the war up to the enormous sum of £131,000, on a tax valuation of a little more than £900,000 in 1743. These bills soon began to depreciate in their turn, but never fell quite so low as those of the old tenor; at the worst, one of the former was equal to three and a half of the latter. Steadily enforced taxation, and the receipt of some £29,000 in coin, which was the colony's share of the parliamentary grant in reimbursement of the expenses, were sufficient to wipe out the outstanding paper, which had amounted in 1751 to about £340,000, reckoning both old and new tenor in old tenor, as was customary. By 1756 the colony had pretty nearly got rid of her paper. This consummation had been helped by an act of parliament in 1751, forbidding the issue of legal-tender paper and of paper currency of any kind, unless limited to the taxes of the current year, or secured by taxes payable within five years. It was also helped by the more uncomfortable fact that the colony took advantage of the depreciation of her own paper to redeem it at about eleven per cent. of its face value.

Connecticut's experience with the treacherous expedient of paper currency had not been sufficient to guard her against all future resorts to it, but it was sufficient to save her from its worst phases for all time to come. In June, 1704, Queen Anne had issued her proclamation, stating a table of values for the various foreign coins then current in Great Britain and the colonies. Such money, at the English equivalents there named, now got the popular name of "proclamation money," or "lawful money," the state of affairs being what would now be called a resumption of specie payments. During the paper flood, the proclamation had been little regarded, but it now came into operation. When the French and Indian war broke out, Connecticut at once met its initial expenses by the issue of paper payable within three years in "lawful money," with interest at five per cent., and without any legal-tender clause; and this policy was followed steadily through the war. In all cases, a tax was laid to redeem each emission; the paper, being of varying value according to the amount of accrued interest, circulated very little as currency; and there was little depreciation or confusion. The whole amount issued was £359,000, and it all seems to have been paid at maturity or before.

Connecticut took her full part in the warlike operations for which all these issues were intended. She had sent eleven hundred of her sons, and a sloop of war of her own, on the expedition to Louisburg in 1745, when the colonies, abandoning all reliance on the shiftless home government, surprised it and themselves by taking a fortress which, by all military rules, should have been impregnable. Her part in the French and Indian war has been somewhat obscured by her strenuous opposition to the plan of union devised at Albany in 1754, at Franklin's suggestion, as if she had been an obstacle to the efficient prosecution of the war. The plan proposed a general government of the colonies by a president-general and a grand council; and one secret of Connecticut's opposition to it seems to have been its provision that all nominations of commissioned officers, by land and sea, should be by this central government. From the time of Andros down, every attack on the charter of Connecticut, either by the crown or by neighbor colonies, had come in the form of an attempt to get control of the colony's militia; and the colony had come in her turn to have an almost fanatical determination to commission her own officers. It was this, rather than any unreasonable democracy, which led her into opposition to the plan which always seemed to Franklin the fairest that could have been devised for both parties.

At the beginning of the war, Connecticut was called upon for one thousand men as her share of the army which was to win the battle of Lake George. The contingent of the much larger colony of Massachusetts was but a trifle larger; but Connecticut not only met the call at once, but authorized the governor to raise five hundred more, if they should be needed. Her senior officer, Phineas Lyman, was second in command of the army, of which William Johnson, of New York, was commander in chief. The fortune of the two halves of the battle was similar in one respect. Major Williams, of Massachusetts, who commanded the routed advance party, was killed almost at the first fire; and it was Nathan Whiting, a New Haven officer, who rallied the men and managed the retreat to the main body. Johnson, having been wounded enough to justify him in retiring, left the field at the beginning of the main action; and it was Lyman, of Connecticut, who for five long hours carried on the fiercest conflict then on record in colonial history, in which almost the entire French regular force was put out of existence. The real victor did not have even the satisfaction of seeing his name misspelled in the "Gazette." Johnson, according to President Dwight, had the ineffable meanness to ignore him altogether in his report, and to accept the honor of knighthood for the victory which Lyman had won. The histories have treated Lyman very much as his superior officer did.

In the unfortunate campaigns of 1756 and 1757, Connecticut regularly raised more than twice the number of men assigned to her as her quota. Her men underwent every vicissitude of the war; and her public men must have had a training in democracy such as their fathers had never quite enjoyed. In this war, the characteristics of democracy and aristocracy were for the first time brought directly into contrast on American soil. The Connecticut democracy had produced a class of men of its own; all were tested as to their ability, advanced as they were competent to serve the public, and then kept in office until they were ready to retire to a well-won old age. Rotation in office and favoritism were equally incomprehensible to the Connecticut mind. Now it was brought to meet the varying product of the English aristocratic system: sometimes a gallant soldier, like Howe or Wolfe; sometimes a statesman of genius, like Pitt; more often an imbecile, like Webb or Loudoun or "Mrs. Nabbycrombie," who owed to family or court influence a position for which Connecticut would never have paid them more than one year's salary.

Lyman, commissioned as major general, was senior officer of the Connecticut troops, and Whiting his second. Under them were most of the men who afterwards became distinguished as the commonwealth's contribution to the defense of American independence, the most prominent of whom was Israel Putnam. A native of Salem, Mass., of which his forefather had been one of the first settlers, he had removed to Pomfret, Conn., in 1739, and it was near that place that his adventure with the wolf gave him a reputation throughout the colony for absolute fearlessness. Entering the war as a lieutenant, he came out with the grade of lieutenant colonel, having gained his advance, with the thanks of the colony's legislature, through a succession of wood-ranging adventures which would need a volume for the telling. Lyman, however, would have led Putnam in revolutionary rank and success, but for his unfortunate trust to court honor and gratitude. Going to England in 1763, to secure a grant of land for the disbanded soldiers, he lingered there for eleven years, in all that hope deferred which maketh the heart sick; returned in 1774, broken in mind as well as in spirit; and died in West Florida the following year.

The Connecticut troops were in all the campaigns of 1758; they took their share in the awful butchery of Ticonderoga, and in the second capture of Louisburg. The colony's efforts were so exhausting that, when it was called on for 5,000 men in the following year, it shrank, for the first time, from fulfilling it. The general court at first resolved that it was impossible to raise more than 3,600 men, because of the efforts of the past three years, and of the numbers of its citizens who had enlisted in the royal provincial regiments or among the boatmen. On the urgent request of the governor, the number was increased to 4,000; and another session, two months later, finally raised this to 5,000, the number first called for. The encouragement afforded by the capture of Quebec made it easier to renew this effort the next year; and in 1761 it was called on for but two thirds the usual number. In 1762 the colony was called on for 1,000 men for the expedition to Havana. Lyman had command of all the provincial forces, 2,500 in all; and Putnam was now in command of Lyman's own regiment. In this, as in the expedition against Carthagena, there was a great deal of what was then known as "glory:" wounds, disease, and death for the many; booty, pleasure, and reputation for the few. Only a handful of the men who left Connecticut for the expedition ever returned; and this one event probably deprived the colony of the services of many an officer whose experience would have been invaluable twelve years later.

With the close of the French and Indian war, Connecticut was brought at last into close practical relations with her sister colonies: the union which she had rejected, through a somewhat extreme provincialism, in 1754, had been forced on her by circumstances, although it had not been put on paper, or definitely expressed in its terms; for that, a more severe exigency was necessary. But the pressure of well-understood common necessities had taught her people the duty of unselfish exertion for the common defense. She was now prepared, as she had never been prepared before, to take her place as a coördinated commonwealth in an American union. Before turning to the process by which this was accomplished, it is proper to notice the steps by which the colony, which was to extend from Narragansett Bay to the Pacific Ocean, was restricted to the limits with which she entered the Union under the Constitution.

CHAPTER XV.

COMMONWEALTH DEVELOPMENT. — WYOMING AND THE WESTERN RESERVE.

THE century following the grant and establishment of the charter was a period of quiet but almost uninterrupted growth for Connecticut. Comparatively undisturbed by wars or by the interference of the home government, with no royal agent within her borders to frame indictments against her policy and methods, and to press them upon the king's attention, she went steadily on her way to that which her people wanted most, — the undisturbed power of gaining a livelihood and of worshiping God under democratic government. Her charter had secured to them most of these objects; the obstacle to the attainment of the rest was the unkindly nature of her soil.

In 1680 the colonial government sent, in answer to a request of the board of trade for detailed information, a statement of the colony's condition. Its quaint and sometimes apparently guarded language carries in it many indications of the almost hopeless weakness of the colony, and of the stout hearts of the men who were maintaining it. The draft of the letter is from the hand of John Allyn. He estimates the fighting men, or "trained bands," of the colony, at 2,507, which might imply a population of between ten and twelve thousand, or about three persons to the square mile, — about half the proportion of Nebraska in 1880. The people had "little traffique abroad," and the bulk of their trade was in "sending what provissions we rays to Boston, where we buy goods with it, to cloath vs." The country was mountainous, full of rocks, swamps, hills and vales; most that was fit for planting had been taken up; "what remaynes must be subdued, and gained out of the fire as it were, by hard blowes and for smal recompence." The principal towns were Hartford, New London, New Haven, and Fairfield, with twenty-six smaller towns, in one of which "we have two churches." The buildings, however, were not so bad, "for a wilderness;" they were of wood, stone, and brick, many of them, says Allyn with pardonable pride, "40 foot long ånd 20 foot broad, and some larger: three and four stories high." On second thoughts, Allyn struck out these latter specifications, perhaps fearing that such a picture of opulence might excite the greed of the home government. The exports were farm products, boards, staves, and horses, mainly sent to Boston, but some small quantities to the West Indies, there to be bartered "for suger, cotton wool and rumme, and some money." Tobacco was grown for home consumption. There were but twenty merchants in the colony, and few of these had a foreign trade. There were very few servants, and only about thirty slaves, imported from Barbadoes at £22 each. The largest ship of the colony was one of ninety tons; twenty-eight others ranged from eight to eighty tons. Labor was scarce and dear; wages were 2s. and 2s. 6d. a day; and provisions were cheap, so that there was little necessity for poor relief. Beggars and vagabonds " were not suffered," but, when discovered, were bound out to service. There were no duties imposed by the colony on exports, and only a duty on imported wines, to be used as a school fund. The property of the colony was estimated for taxing purposes at about £110,000. But, in all such estimates, it should be remembered that about two fifths of it was more in the nature of a poll-tax, the tax being increased according to a somewhat arbitrary schedule of supposed wealth or position in the various trades and professions, so that it took the place, in part, of an income tax as well.

In spite of the poverty of the colony, its vitality was shown by the steady increase in the number of its towns. Allyn gives their number as twenty-six in 1680. Six of these, Lyme, Haddam, Simsbury, Wallingford, Derby, and Woodbury, had been incorporated since the union of the two colonies; and three more, Waterbury, Glastenbury, and Plainfield, were to become towns before the end of the century. In the development of these new towns there were two distinct processes, according to the nature of the case. A speculator or a company might buy lands from the Indians, with the approval of the general court, in some locality outside of the bounds of any town. As soon as the rates became sufficiently large to need the extension of the general court's taxing power over the little community, a committee was appointed by that body to bound out the town: it was then expected to choose constables, and send delegates to the general court. The other process continually tended to become the only one. A town, when first established, usually had extensive boundaries. Those persons who settled in the outflying districts of the township found it more and more troublesome, particularly in winter, to resort to the old church for preaching. When there were enough of such dissatisfied persons to support a minister of their own, they applied to the general court for permission to form a church. For the church was really a territorial term, quite as much so as the township; and the setting off of a new church meant the diminution of the area of the old church, and the inclusion of all persons within the new bounds in the new church. As this involved a diminution of the resources of the old church, it regularly met with strong opposition, and was only successful after several petitions. The erection into a town followed at the discretion of the general court. Plainfield may be taken as a combination of the two processes. Originally settled as "Quinnabaug plantation," it was important enough in 1700 to become a town. The general court therefore incorporated it, named it Plainfield, and gave it, as was an essential step, a special brand for its horses, in this case a triangle. In May, 1703, some discension having arisen, the court ordered the territory to be divided into two parts, the western settlers to pay their rates for the support of the eastern minister until they had "an approved minister" of their own. Their choice having been approved, the general court proceeded in October to constitute the people of the western half of Plainfield a distinct town, under the name of Canterbury, with a horse brand of its own.

The charter seems to have contemplated a general meeting of the governor, lieutenant governor, assistants, and deputies as the general assembly, still often called the general court; and this was the form which its meetings at first took. In 1678 the court ordered that the governor, lieutenant governor, and assistants should be a council to act for the commonwealth during the recesses of the court. This was the prelude to the inevitable introduction of a bi-cameral system. In 1698 the general court ordered that the council should sit as a separate house, and the deputies as the other, and that laws should be passed only by the assent of both houses; and the arrangement went into force the next year. This change was followed by the adoption of a double capital. Among the first measures of conciliation proposed by Connecticut to induce New Haven to accept the charter was that New Haven should be made a coördinate capital of the commonwealth, as well as county town of a distinct county. New Haven's rejection of the terms caused the former proposition to lapse for the time; but it was put into force in 1701. It was decided that the May session of the general court should be held hereafter at Hartford, and the October session at New Haven. This arrangement lasted until 1873, when Hartford was again made sole capital.

The long period of peace and comparative prosperity during the first half of the last century was prolific in new towns. From 1700 until 1745 thirty of them were incorporated, very nearly as many as were in existence in 1700. There was an equally steady growth in population, though all the figures for it must be mere estimates. It is estimated by Bancroft at 17,000 for the year 1688, and by Trumbull at the same figures for 1713. In 1755 the board of trade estimated it at 100,000; and Bancroft at 133,000, with 3,500 slaves. It is not possible to get nearer to the truth; but the constantly increasing quotas of Connecticut to New England armies during the years between 1690 and 1763 are enough to show the growing population of the colony. At the date last named, a comparison of Bancroft's estimate for Connecticut with that for Massachusetts (207,000), and for whites in Virginia (168,000), will show that the seed planted on the banks of the Connecticut had grown into one of the stateliest trees on the continent. It had grown so large as to feel the cramping influence of its surroundings.

In 1762 all the soil of the colony had been allotted to townships, and new towns formed after that year were carved out of townships already in existence. Long before that time, population had begun to show a disposition to swarm. The first effort in this direction was due to the boundary settlement of 1713–14 between Connecticut and Massachusetts. In consideration of certain concessions in straightening the line, Massachusetts gave Connecticut a parcel of her western lands. Some of these (60,000 acres, according to the New York attorney general's report in 1752), though then believed to be in Massachusetts, were really in the district to be known as Vermont. These lands were sold by Connecticut to private parties, and their purchases drew off the attention of a considerable number of her people to this territory. The erection of Fort Dummer in 1729 offered some promise of protection to settlers, and those who had long owned these wild lands began to think of settling upon them. At first, a few young men were sent thither in the summer to work the land, returning home for the winter. New York claimed jurisdiction over the whole territory, under the iniquitous grant to the duke, which had been extended up to the Connecticut River in defiance of the Massachusetts and Connecticut charters. So far as these two colonies were concerned, the claim had been given up; but New York still maintained it against New Hampshire. Governor Wentworth, of New Hampshire, insisted that the limits of his colony extended as far west as the two colonies to the south, though it is not easy to see on what ground. He proceeded to make grants of land in the disputed territory, very many of them to Connecticut settlers. He cared for little except the proceeds of the sales, and left civil organization to the settlers. The result was that the Connecticut town system was again transferred to a wilderness, there to begin a struggle with the centralized system of New York. The Vermont towns were even more independent than their prototypes; and their "independence and unbridled democracy" formed one of the arguments by which New York obtained a judgment in her favor from the home government. Connecticut blood and town and personal names were strongly represented in the " Hampshire Grants;" indeed, some of the towns in the grants held their first town meeting in Connecticut before the removal of their settlers. Ethan and Ira Allen, Warner, the Chipmans, Chittenden, and a host of other Connecticut men, took a leading place among those who resisted the authorities of New York, with, perhaps, a touch of hereditary bitterness; and when the territory erected itself into a State in 1777, it assumed the significant title of " New Connecticut," the more appropriate name of Vermont being substituted in the course of the year. The details of the struggle are not within our province. It need only be said that the New York authorities seem to have found most embarrassment in dealing with the new and vigorous form of local government which had become established in the territory, and that the final establishment of the State of Vermont may fairly be claimed as another success of the Connecticut town system.

Here dropping this extra-legal effort at commonwealth expansion, we come to the strictly legal attempt to enforce the charter boundaries, and its failure. The effort evidently arose from an instinctive perception that the practical bounds of the commonwealth would seriously cramp its growth, and reduce its rank among the States, as they have since done. The charter bounds extended west to the Pacific Ocean: this would have carried Connecticut over a strip covering the northern two fifths of the present State of Pennsylvania. Stuart faithlessness interfered with this doubly. Almost immediately after the grant of the charter, Charles granted to his brother James the Dutch colony of New Netherland, thus interrupting the continuity of Connecticut. Rather than resist the king's brother, Connecticut agreed and ratified the interruption. In 1681 a more serious interference took place. Charles granted to Penn the province of Pennsylvania, extending westward five degrees between the 40th and 43d parallels of north latitude. The width of the province would have been from the northern outskirts of Philadelphia to about the present city of Utica in New York, thus taking in five degrees of Connecticut's grant, and all western New York except the lake-shore. Geographical knowledge was not very profound; and Penn seems to have founded his capital city before discovering that he had unluckily placed it too far to the south, outside of his own province and in the Baltimore grant. What was to be done? The solution of the difficulty deserves more credit for its ingenuity than for its ingenuousness, and Bancroft absolves Penn from responsibility for it. The language of his grant was from "the beginning of the 40th parallel" to "the beginning of the 43d." What was "the beginning of the 40th parallel"? Evidently, said the Pennsylvania argument, the 39th. And "the beginning of the 43d"? As clearly, the 42d. Ergo, Pennsylvania extended south from its present northern boundary to Annapolis, taking in the city of Baltimore on the way. The war having thus been carried into Africa, the offer was made to compromise with the Baltimore family on the present boundaries, from about latitude 39° 45' to latitude 42°, and, after half a century's struggle, the compromise was adopted. New York was more than satisfied with the arrangement, as it carried her southern boundary a full degree to the south; and all the parties seem to have ignored Connecticut.

The territory taken from Connecticut by the Penn grant would be bounded southerly on the present map by a straight line entering Pennsylvania about Stroudsburg, just north of the Delaware Water Gap, and running west through Hazelton, Catawissa, Clearfield, and New Castle, taking in all the northern coal, iron, and oil fields. It was a royal heritage, but the Penns made no attempt to settle it, and Connecticut until the middle of the eighteenth century had no energy to spare from the task of winning her home territory "out of the fire, as it were, by hard blows and for small recompense." This task had been fairly well done by 1750, and in 1753 a movement to colonize in the Wyoming country was set on foot in Windham county. It spread by degrees until the Susquehanna Company was formed the next year, with nearly 700 members, of whom 638 were of Connecticut. Their agents made a treaty with the Five Nations July 11, 1754, by which they bought for £2,000 a tract of land beginning at the forty-first degree of latitude, the southerly boundary of Connecticut; thence running north, following the line of the Susquehanna at a distance of ten miles from it, to the present northern boundary of Pennsylvania; thence one hundred and twenty miles west; thence south to the forty-first degree and back to the point of beginning. In May, 1755, the Connecticut general assembly expressed its acquiescence in the scheme, if the king should approve it; and it approved also a plan of Samuel Hazard, of Philadelphia, for another colony, to be placed west of Pennsylvania, and within the chartered limits of Connecticut. The court might have taken stronger ground than this; for, at the meeting of commissioners from the various colonies at Albany, in 1754, the representatives of Pennsylvania being present, no opposition was made to a resolution that Connecticut and Massachusetts, by charter right, extended west to the South Sea. The formation of the Susquehanna Company brought out objections from Pennsylvania, but the company sent out surveyors and plotted its tract.

Settlement was begun on the Delaware River in 1757, and in the Susquehanna purchase in 1762. This was a temporary settlement, the settlers going home for the winter. A permanent venture was made the next year on the flats below Wilkes Barre, but it was destroyed by the Indians the same year. In 1768 the company marked out five townships, and sent out forty settlers for the first, Kingston. Most of them, including the famous Captain Zebulon Butler, had served in the French and Indian war; and their first step was to build the "Forty Fort." The Penns, after their usual policy, had refused to sell lands, but had leased plots to a number of men on condition of their "defending the lands from the Connecticut claimants." The forty Connecticut men found these in possession when they arrived in February, 1769, and a war of writs and arrests followed for the remainder of the year. The Pennsylvania men had one too powerful argument in the shape of a four-pounder gun, and they retained possession at the end of the year. Early in 1770 the forty reappeared, captured the four-pounder, and secured possession. For a time in 1771 the Pennsylvania men returned, put up a fort of their own, and engaged in a partisan warfare; but the numbers of the Connecticut men were rapidly increasing, and they remained masters until the opening of the Revolution, when they numbered some three thousand. The Connecticut general court passed a resolution in 1771, maintaining the claim of its colony to its charter limits west of the Delaware. In 1774 it erected the Susquehanna district into a town, under the name of Westmoreland, making it a part of Litchfield county, the farthest northwest of the original counties; and its deputies took their seats in the Connecticut legislature. In 1776, Westmoreland town was made a distinct county, and its civil organization was complete. Connecticut laws and taxes were enforced regularly; Connecticut courts alone were in session; and the levies from the district formed the twenty-fourth Connecticut regiment in the Continental armies. The sordid, grasping, long-leasing policy of the Penns had never been able to stand a moment before the oncoming wave of Connecticut democracy, with its individual land-ownership, its liberal local government, and the personal incentive offered to individuals by its town system. So far as the Penns were concerned, the Connecticut town system simply swept over them, and hardly thought of them as it went. But for the Revolution, the check occasioned by the massacre, and the appearance of a popular government in place of the Penns, nothing could have prevented the establishment of Connecticut's authority over all the regions embraced in her western claims.

In July, 1778, after the Continental Congress had refused to allow the temporary return of the able-bodied men whom the Westmoreland people had sent freely into the army, the Tories and Indians, under John Butler and Brandt, fell upon the almost defenseless settlement. They met no unresisting victims. The old men and boys, the town dignitaries who had been administering civil affairs, mustered into rank, and only yielded and fled after a loss of half their number. The women and children were spared for the greater horrors of the overland retreat to Connecticut; and the Connecticut possession vanished again into thin air. Detached parties returned from time to time, gathered scanty crops under constant danger from Indians, and kept alive the claims of individuals and of the commonwealth. But Westmoreland county, as it had been, was no more.

The articles of confederation went into force early in 1781. One of their provisions empowered congress to appoint courts of arbitration to decide disputes between States as to boundaries. Pennsylvania at once availed herself of this, and applied for a court to decide the Wyoming dispute. Connecticut asked for time, in order to get papers from England; but congress overruled the motion, and ordered the court to meet at Trenton in November, 1782. After forty-one days of argument, the court came to the unanimous conclusion that Wyoming, or the Susquehanna district, belonged to Pennsylvania and not to Connecticut. It came to light, more than ten years afterward, that the court had secretly agreed on two points for its guidance: (1) whatever its decision might be, it was to assign no reasons for it; and (2) the minority was to yield to the majority, in order to make the decision unanimous. The knowledge of these antecedent conditions takes away much of the force of the decision; but they were not known in 1782, and Connecticut yielded at once. For this yielding, however, there were probably reasons apart from the justice of the decision.

It was just at this time that the Western territory was the controlling question in politics. Virginia, under a strained and very dubious interpretation of her northern boundary, claimed the whole Northwest, in addition to Kentucky. The States whose western boundaries were fixed had two points of objection: Virginia would get none of this territory if the authority of the crown were reëstablished; and they did not intend to spend their blood and money in order to obtain the Northwest for Virginia. Connecticut's western claims, though based on a clear, not on a doubtful, charter statement, were too much on a par with those of Virginia to be easily separated from them. There was an instinctive sense, outside of Virginia, that the national existence of the United States was bound up with the jurisdiction over this Northwest territory; and Connecticut's share in the feeling was enough to balance even her selfish interests. She even imperiled the latter by yielding to the decision; for it is hardly possible to reconcile the decision of 1782, which ignored the charter, with the acceptance by congress of the Connecticut cession of 1786, which impliedly recognized the charter and the very claims which had been rejected in 1782. There was no bargain, for Pennsylvania in 1786 voted not to accept the cession, on the ground that it recognized the charter. Connecticut simply made way intelligently, if somewhat regretfully, for the coming nationality.

The cession of 1786 of course put an end to all Connecticut's ambitions of commonwealth expansion: she was to be forever restricted to the territory lying between Massachusetts and Long Island Sound, and between Rhode Island and New York. And yet the legal title of Connecticut to the territory which she gave up by this cession was beyond dispute. It has been suggested that the crown made the grant under ignorance, supposing that North America was far narrower than it proved to be. But the Plymouth council, when it gave up its charter in 1635, notified the king that their grant was "through all the main land, from sea to sea, *being near about three thousand miles in length.*" There was not a geographer in England but knew that the Connecticut grant, in its turn, was three thousand miles long. It was adduced as a prior grant by the English commissioners against the French in 1752, in order to assert title across the Mississippi. Its validity was recognized by the Albany congress of 1754, Pennsylvania being represented. The establishment of the Mississippi as a boundary line between the colonies and Spain was founded on these western charters of indefinite extent. The peace of 1783, which laid claim to the Mississippi as a western boundary for the United States, was a renewed affirmation of the charters which had carried the claims of the United States up to that river. Finally, the acceptance of the Connecticut cession by the United States in 1786 was a renewed confirmation of the charter's validity, on which the further claim of the United States was based. The fact that Connecticut had yielded to the erection of the new colony of New York was of interest only to the two colonies involved, — Connecticut and New York; no third party, as Pennsylvania, could gain or lose any rights thereby.

It would have been absurd to ask Connecticut to surrender a claim so sound in law, and so fortified by repeated recognitions, without any recompense. Her proposition, that she should reserve a tract of about the same length and width as the Wyoming grant, west of Pennsylvania, in northeastern Ohio, was accepted; and this was the tract known as the Western Reserve of Connecticut. It contained about three and a half millions of acres. In 1792 some five hundred thousand acres in the western part of the Reserve were devoted to the relief of those persons who had been burned out and plundered by the British: this was known as the "Fire Lands." The rest was sold under the direction of a legislative committee, and the proceeds were devoted to the school fund of the commonwealth. It was not very productive until Senator James Hillhouse was appointed sole commissioner in 1810. He held the position for some fifteen years, and increased the principal to nearly $2,000,000, with an annual income of over $50,000. This principal still remains intact.

The unfortunate Wyoming settlers, deserted by their own State, and left to the mercy of rival claimants, had a hard time of it for years. The militia of the neighboring counties of Pennsylvania was mustered to enforce the writs of Pennsylvania courts; the property of the Connecticut men was destroyed, their fences were cast down, and their rights ignored; and the " Pennamite and Yankee War " began. The Yankees were evidently getting the worse, and their friends at home were not deaf to their grievances. The old Susquehanna Company was reorganized in 1785-86, and made ready to support its settlers by force. New Yankee faces came crowding into the disputed territory. Among them was Ethan Allen, and with him came some Green Mountain Boys, the promise and potency of more, and pungent memories of the manner in which Vermont had solved a similar difficulty with New York. It was an open secret that the intention was to organize a new State, and weary Pennsylvania and congress into a recognition of it. Its constitution had been drafted, and its state officers tacitly agreed upon.

Pennsylvania in 1786 passed an accommodation

act, by which the lands of actual settlers were confirmed to them, and the district was erected into the county of Luzerne. Unfortunately, there were dissensions between the old settlers and the new-comers of the Wyoming district, and Pennsylvania suspended the accommodation act in 1788, and repealed it in 1790. There were renewed struggles, and in 1799 the act was substantially reënacted, and the controversy came to an end. The settlement had the result of carrying into Pennsylvania a large infusion of Connecticut blood, the source of the prevalence of Connecticut names in this part of Pennsylvania.

CHAPTER XVI.

THE STAMP ACT AND THE REVOLUTION.

THE close of the French and Indian war marks the period when Connecticut's democratic constitution began to influence other commonwealths. Her charter was an object-lesson to all of them. It was the standard to which their demands gradually came up; and their growing demands upon the crown caused an equally steady approximation toward the establishment of a local democracy like that which Connecticut had kept up for a hundred and fifty years.

The passage of the Stamp Act by the English Parliament was met at once by a protest from the Connecticut general assembly, followed by instructions to its agent in London to insist firmly on "the exclusive right of the colonies to tax themselves and on the privilege of trial by jury," as rights which "they never could recede from." It had good reason to speak plainly, for the principle of the act struck more heavily at Connecticut than at any other colony except Rhode Island. No other colonies had been so completely free from any appearance of royal interference as these; and Connecticut's lack of commerce had prevented it from feeling even those forms of royal interference which the commercial interests of Rhode Island had brought upon it. To Connecticut the act was simply intolerable, and she not only spoke but made ready for action.

Jared Ingersoll, of New Haven, was sent to London as special agent to remonstrate against the passage of the act. When his mission had failed, he accepted the office of stamp agent for Connecticut, by advice of Franklin, and set out for home. He found things there in a ferment. The governor and some of the leading men were willing to submit, rather than risk the loss of the charter, but the instinct of the democracy taught it that this was the time to put its charter privileges into security forever. The ministers were preaching against the act; the towns were ordering their officers to disregard it, promising to hold them harmless; Trumbull had become the head of a popular movement; and volunteer organizations, calling themselves "Sons of Liberty," were patrolling the country, overawing those who were inclined to support the home government, and making ready to resist the execution of the law. Ingersoll seems to have been sufficiently impressed with the strength of the home government to be willing to avoid a conflict; and he meant now to execute faithfully the office which he had accepted only to make its provisions more tolerable to his countrymen. The meeting between him and them was that of the flint and steel. The Sons of Liberty were out and in waiting for him as he rode from New Haven to Hartford; and he entered the capital under the escort of a thousand horsemen, farmers and freeholders, who had compelled him to resign his office. He had not lost his head or shown any craven frailty: he had simply made up his mind that he had gone far enough in an unpleasant duty, and that "the cause was not worth dying for." He had, however, carried his resistance up to the verge of temerity; and, as he rode on his white horse at the head of the triumphant mob, he said afterward that he realized at last what the book of Revelation meant by "Death on the pale horse, and hell following him."

Governor Fitch died in 1766, and, after a three years' service of William Pitkin, Jonathan Trumbull, the first "war governor" of Connecticut, succeeded him. He held the office until 1783; he was the trusted associate of Washington, and the latter's familiar way of addressing him when asking his advice or assistance is said to have been the origin of the popular phrase "Brother Jonathan." The family has been one of the most noted in the history of the commonwealth. It has included Governor Jonathan Trumbull, his sons John (the painter), Jonathan, governor from 1798 until 1809, and Joseph, commissary general of the Revolutionary army; John Trumbull, the author of "McFingal;" Benjamin Trumbull, the author of one of the standard histories of the State; James Hammond Trumbull, the recognized authority on the Indian languages and the history of the State; his brother, H. C. Trumbull, a leader in missionary and Sunday-school work; and ex-Senator Lyman Trumbull, of Illinois. The reign of the Trumbulls was ushered in brilliantly by the governor. In him the people had found the man they needed, and doubt and hesitation fled before him.

The rapid succession of events which followed the Boston Tea Party — the Boston Port Bill, the Massachusetts Act, and the preparations of Massachusetts for active resistance — met prompt sympathy and support in Connecticut. The non-importation agreement had been universally signed in 1768-69, and, if contemporary accounts are to be trusted, was kept far more faithfully in Connecticut than in some of her neighbor colonies. Unofficial preparations, with the quiet approval of the official authorities, were now made, so that, when hostilities began, Connecticut was the first colony to take her place abreast of Massachusetts. In all this there was not one iota of change in the traditional policy of the colony. In the proceedings which led to the loss or serious modification of the Massachusetts charter in 1691, Connecticut had taken no part with the attacked colony, partly because the latter had no intentions of real resistance, and partly because such resistance, under the circumstances into which Massachusetts had got herself, was evidently hopeless. In 1728 likewise, when Massachusetts was engaging in a war of annoyances with her royal governors, Connecticut had instructed her London agent to take no part with Massachusetts, but to secure the colony's maintenance of her charter quite independently of her. The Connecticut general assembly had a great trust confided to it, and it was not disposed to risk it in Quixotic enterprises of this sort. In 1769-70 Massachusetts had at last been wrought up to concert pitch: her people evidently meant to fight; there was a fair chance of success, since the other colonies showed their intention of supporting her; the enterprise was necessary, was no longer Quixotic, and Connecticut went into it heart and soul. Nothing in the history of this commonwealth is so noteworthy as the prevailing characteristic of its people, — their judicial power of estimating the chances of success, their self-restraint under every provocation until the chances seem to be reasonably good, and their unreserved abandonment to action when the time for action seems to have fully come. It is Connecticut tradition that the first step of the general assembly in 1763 was to appoint three of its ablest men to argue in favor of the right of parliament to tax the colonies, and three fairly matched opponents to argue against it; that the argument, consuming several days, took place before the assembly under a pledge of secrecy from all concerned; and that its result was the unanimous agreement of the members against the right of parliament, and in favor of the lawfulness of resistance. The story is fairly typical of the Connecticut way of looking at questions of the kind, its determination to anchor tenacity of purpose fast in legality of object, and to insist first on being right. One may well speculate as to the results on American history if such a people, instead of being cribbed into four thousand square miles of territory, had been able to impress their characteristics on the population of the magnificent domain which was theirs by charter.

At first, the preparations for resistance were made by the towns, which acted, in the traditional Connecticut fashion, as if they were little commonwealths in themselves. They met, voted solemn condemnation of the ministry, appointed committees of safety, and appropriated money to buy arms and powder. Every town sent its contribution to the poor of Boston, and every committee felt bound also to send a long letter of condolence. The general assembly then began preparations to direct the storm. In May and October, 1774, it appointed military officers where they were needed; directed every military company in the colony to be drilled, with fines for non-attendance; and sent delegates to the Continental Congress. The recommendations of that body against importing or exporting goods from or to Great Britain were endorsed by the general assembly, and were faithfully carried out. But it is, again, a curious survival of primitive conditions that the towns thought it necessary for them also to meet and endorse the action of congress and the assembly. The town republics, which had given birth to the commonwealth, were still conscious of an abundant vitality.

The battle of Lexington led to the first offensive movement by the Americans; and it is a singularly fitting testimony to Connecticut's readiness to help Massachusetts, that, while the latter was defending herself, this offensive movement for her relief, the capture of Ticonderoga and its stores, came from Connecticut. The general assembly refrained from officially sanctioning it; but it was undertaken with its approval, and it paid the bills for the expedition two years afterward. The opportunity for the venture was offered by the close connection which had so long existed between Connecticut and Vermont. Silas Deane and ten associates, having assurances of the assembly's approval, took the money, some £800, out of the treasury, giving their receipts therefor; took a party of Connecticut volunteers to Vermont; raised a force among the kindred spirits of that region; and made the capture which brought encouragement and relief to the blockading army before Boston.

Long before this, however, the men of Connecticut had been in motion for Boston. The first message from the governor to Putnam, announcing the fight at Concord and Lexington, found the veteran at work in his field. He left the plow in the furrow, galloped to the governor's residence, and received orders to go to Boston forthwith. He rode thither in eighteen hours, without dismounting, and was followed by the volunteers of his colony, many of whom had undergone training in the French and Indian war. With Putnam, as leading officers, were David Wooster and Joseph Spencer, also veterans; they were commissioned by congress as brigadier-generals, and Putnam as major-general. It is a little curious that Arnold, though a Connecticut man by birth, did not receive any special recognition from the colony, his commissions and employments being mainly from Massachusetts.

The general assembly ordered the emission of £100,000 in bills of credit, to provide for the equipment of eight regiments, which were ordered to be enlisted from the militia. One result of the far-sighted preparations of the commonwealth was, that, when the battle of Bunker Hill was fought, and the ammunition of the fort's defenders consisted of but sixty-three half-barrels of powder, thirty-six of them were a present from the colony of Connecticut. Like all the other New England colonies, she sent men who were unaccustomed to discipline, and were not easily brought under prompt military obedience; but Bunker Hill was enough to show that they could at least fight when placed before an enemy. If there was a flag in the line, it was theirs; they held the rail fence until the retreat was secured; and their leader, Putnam, put his own life at stake again and again in the effort to check the retreat at Bunker Hill, and at every step on the road off the peninsula. Indeed, it is a mooted question whether, in the general confusion of the day, Putnam should not be considered the commander of the American forces engaged.

The colony itself was comparatively safe from invasion except on the coast, where there was an attack on Stonington by a British vessel. Nevertheless, those who had not gone to the seat of war were not disposed to remain idle. Connecticut was practically unanimous on the great question; New York was badly divided, and the Tories there were men of influence and determination. The man of most influence among them was Rivington, the publisher of the "New York Gazette," the Tory newspaper organ. Early in September, 1775, Captain Isaac Sears, having raised a troop of Connecticut horsemen, rode into New York city, raided the "Gazette" office, and carried off the types and apparatus. Early in 1776 General Lee seized New York city with some 1,200 Connecticut troops, and held it until Washington's army was transferred thither after the evacuation of Boston. Then Putnam was put in command of the city and its environs, and drove off the English fleet. One of the ornaments of the city had been an equestrian statue of King George, cast in lead and gilt. Just a week after the adoption of the Declaration of Independence, this was carried off by night to the house of Oliver Wolcott, in Litchfield county, and there cast into bullets, making 42,088 cartridges.

While the zeal of the people thus outran official discretion, the Connecticut authorities also had all that they could attend to, though in a soberer way. Governor Trumbull's correspondence with Washington had already assumed that close and confidential cast which it maintained throughout the contest. The assembly was busily engaged in raising men, and providing for their support by the issue of bills and by taxation. It is not too much to say that for a time almost the entire burden of the struggle lay upon Connecticut; and the unflinching manner in which it was met and sustained is made more conspicuous by the fact that the colony was not individually menaced as were colonies which refused to bear any fair proportion of the burden. The Department of the North, in 1775, had 2,800 men in the field; 2,500 of these were Connecticut troops. When Washington's army settled down around New York, more than half of his force of 17,000 men had been contributed by Connecticut. It was not wonderful that Washington should write to the governor that he had "full confidence in your most ready assistance on every occasion, and that such measures as appear to you most likely to advance the public good, in this and every instance, will be most cheerfully adopted;" nor that he should speak of the assembly in such terms as these: " I have nothing to suggest for the consideration of your assembly; I am confident they will not be wanting in their exertions for supporting the just and constitutional rights of the colonies." Even Washington's emphasis had something of reserve and self-restraint about it; and his unreserve in this case derives additional force from his well-grounded complaints of the action of colonial authorities in general.

One of the captains of Knowlton's Connecticut regiment was Captain Nathan Hale, a graduate of Yale in 1773, a young man of fine personal presence and of high intelligence. His family was settled in Coventry, Conn.; and his ancestor had been the first minister of Beverly, Mass. While Washington was lying near Fort Washington, after the retreat from Long Island, it became imperatively necessary for him to obtain accurate intelligence from the British camp. He called for a volunteer from the younger officers of the army, and Hale was the only one who offered himself. His offer was accepted, and his mission had been accomplished with skill and success, when he was recognized by a Tory relative in the British lines, who sent word to headquarters that an American spy was at work in the camp. Advertised and described throughout the lines, he yet had sufficient address to make his way as far as the outposts before he was arrested. The testimony of his relative convicted him, and he was hanged on the following morning. Not so much his fate, as the manner of it, exasperated the people of the commonwealth. He was denied the company of a minister; the poor consolation of a written message home was refused; and it was the common report that the reason for this barbarity of punishment was that "the rebels might not know that they had a man in their army who could die with such firmness." In the traditional Connecticut spirit, having undertaken the work, he did not flinch from its consummation. His last words were: "If I had ten thousand lives, I would lay them down in defense of my country." The words meant something in his mouth.

On the coast, the preponderant navy of the king was very annoying, but principally in its attacks on chicken-roosts and sheepfolds. Yankee ingenuity exerted itself to get rid of the annoyance. David Bushnell, another young graduate of Yale, of the class of 1775, living at Saybrook, stimulated by the necessity of the case, brought out his " American Turtle," which was to anticipate the modern system of torpedoes, and blow the British fleet out of water. The Turtle contained a magazine of explosives, and a connected system of clock-work, and could be kept under the control of the operator on shore, so as to rise and fall at his will. The first attempt, made by a person unfamiliar with the mechanism, resulted in a tremendous explosion, not under the vessel aimed at, but near enough to put the naval officers into a terrible fright. Another attempt had better success, and this increased the terror. Still another, in 1777, gave rise to the panic among the British forces at Philadelphia which Hopkinson celebrated in his " Battle of the Kegs." Long afterward, in 1813, on a similar occasion, the too impertinent intrusion of the British fleet on the shores of Connecticut was rebuked and checked in the same fashion. A British vessel was allowed to capture a vessel in which explosives had been connected with a clock-work. The Ramillies barely escaped destruction, and her angry commander inflicted a bombardment on the offending town, Stonington, demanding as the price of exemption that the inhabitants should promise to set no more torpedoes afloat, a demand which was promptly refused.

The interior of the commonwealth, secure alike by its distance from the seat of war, by the universal loyalty of its population, and by the primitive simplicity of a people who knew all their neighbors for miles, and could detect any one attempting an escape, was a most excellent place for the detention of prisoners. The jails, the public buildings, and even the private houses of the northern townships, were made places of deposit for prisoners of war or for political prisoners. Hither came the Tory officials of New York, the prisoners from Long Island, and others; and the lenity of their treatment stood in strong contrast with the condition of the Americans who returned from the horrible prison-hulks of the British forces, starved, diseased, and treated with every shade of heathenish cruelty short of absolute cannibalism. Their return home is particularly creditable to the colonists in that it seems to have made no difference in their treatment of their own prisoners, or rather guests.

It must be acknowledged that the substantial unanimity of the people had been secured by strong, if unofficial, measures. The authorities winked assiduously at the operations of the town committees who made it their special business to see that Tories recanted, left the town, or were placed where they would do the least harm. We have no means of ascertaining exactly how far it was necessary for these committees to go. Terrible accounts of their doings, of their riotous proceedings, tarrings and featherings, etc., are given us by the Rev. Samuel Peters, a Tory clergyman of the Church of England, who was driven from the colony during the opening troubles, and afterwards took a terrible revenge by publishing a " History " of Connecticut in London. But Peters stands also as the only authority for the phenomena at Bellows' Falls, where the water of the Connecticut River runs so swiftly that an iron crowbar cannot be forced into it, but floats on the surface ; for the inhumanity, to give it no worse name, of Hooker, in giving to the Connecticut Indians Bibles infected with the smallpox, so as to put them out of the way of the rising young colony ; for the amusing manner in which the inhabitants of Windham, alarmed by the noise of an invading army, kept guard against it all night, finding in the morning that it was no more than a flying column of frogs on the way to water ; for those singular members of the Connecticut fauna, the " whapperknocker " and the " cuba," whose untamable ferocity, so well known to all naturalists, the veracious " Doctor " takes pleasure in describing from personal observation ; and for such a mass of other lies as Munchausen himself might have been proud to father. Unless this mass of fiction is also to be taken on Peters's authority, it is difficult to see how his authority is to count for much as to the asserted mistreatment of Connecticut Tories.

Outside of Peters's statements, and the vague newspaper stories current at that day, the strongest case made against the Connecticut fathers of the republic is in their use of the Simsbury copper-mines as a place of confinement for Tories "and other notorious offenders." The existence of copper at Simsbury was suspected as early as 1705; and the town leased the mines to various companies, who brought over miners from Germany and spent their money freely, but got little of it back. The ore contained from fifteen to twenty per cent. of copper, but was too refractory to do more than lure speculators into bankruptcy through assayers' reports. Governor Belcher wrote in 1735 that he had spent $75,000 there since 1721. Coins, called "Granby coppers," from the residence of the coiner in the neighboring town of Granby, were made from the metal in 1737–39; but the copper was so nearly pure, and so much in demand for jewelers' alloy, that they have almost disappeared. In 1773 mining ceased, and the colony spent about $375 in fitting up the mine as a prison. The main shaft was near the top of a small hill; and the buildings at the mouth, the wall surrounding them, and the naked hill sloping down in front of it, must have added a shade of horror to the unknown future in the mind of the Tory who was approaching it. Certain it is that hardly anything was so dreadful to the Tory mind as the prospect of incarceration at Simsbury. In 1781 congress applied for permission to use it as a prison for state offenders; but the almost immediate cessation of hostilities relieved the national authority from any such necessity.

The number confined here, both of ordinary offenders and of Tories, probably never exceeded thirty at any one time; but the number of insurrections and escapes was disproportionately great, showing that even copper-mines will not a prison make. The shaft was nearly a hundred feet deep; but the cells were in the galleries, none of them more than sixty feet below the surface. In spite of the frequent escapes, public confidence in the security of the place was unimpaired, and it was the ordinary state prison from 1790 until 1827, when the new prison at Wethersfield took its place. In defense of the establishment of the prison in such a location, it may be urged that such a step was not considered improper anywhere at the time; that the terrors of the place were more in imagination than in reality; that the health of the prisoners was good and was not affected unfavorably by their location; and that special practices of that time must not be judged by the more civilized theory of a later era. So late as 1807, a traveler who visited it could go no further in reprehension than to say: " For myself, I cannot get rid of the impression that, without any extraordinary cruelty in its actual operation, there is something very like cruelty in the device and design." How much more lenient must have been the judgment of a sound Whig of 1775 when he saw a Tory consigned to the Simsbury Newgate!

Patriotic solicitude must have been reinforced by religious intolerance. The Episcopal Church had always been an alien in Connecticut. Its founders had broken away from the Established or Congregational Church; their success had diminished the resources of the latter; their ministers had to cross the ocean to be ordained, and to take a special oath of allegiance to the crown; they were his majesty's opposition in a colony which liked neither majesty nor opposition; and they were strongly suspected of a design to reduce this, with the other colonies, to some form of episcopacy. The latter belief, which had a special weight in bringing about the final revolution, was increased in Connecticut by the fact that, whenever the Episcopal Church had come into collision with the colonial authorities, its first and most effective weapon had always been a threat of appeal to the home government. There was probably hardly a man in Connecticut who, being a Whig and a Congregationalist, did not believe that every Episcopalian was either an open or a secret Tory, and that the Episcopalian ministers were their leaders and guides. The Episcopal churches in the colony were shut, and the ministers were silenced, except Rev. John Beach, an Episcopalian missionary at Reading and Newtown, who persisted in praying for the king as usual, in spite of rough treatment at the hands of the Whigs. For the time, the Episcopal Church in Connecticut was suspended, and its members were almost outlawed, for the colonial authorities would give them only a grudging protection. The reëstablishment of peace brought the reëstablishment of the Church; and, thirty years later, the sons of its members had the pious satisfaction of disestablishing the Church which had persecuted their fathers.

The connection between the Episcopalians of Connecticut and of New York city had always been close, and it cannot be supposed that the sufferings of the Connecticut Tories had been looked at with indifference in New York. As the tide of war rolled off through the Jerseys toward Philadelphia, stripping Connecticut of a large portion of its able-bodied men, the time seemed to have come for a blow that should teach the Congregational colony that its enemies had still some of the terrors of war at their command. Tryon, the royalist governor of New York, with a force of two thousand men and twenty-five vessels, sailed eastward through Long Island Sound, and landed at Saugatuck, about twenty miles from Danbury, where a considerable amount of Continental and State stores had been gathered. A hasty march overland brought them to Danbury, April 26, 1777, where they destroyed not only the stores, but the bulk of the town, carefully sparing Tory property. There were some Continental soldiers in the neighborhood, and two officers of rank, Wooster and Arnold. The latter rallied all the men available, regulars and militia, and headed Tryon on his retreat, at Ridgefield. In the battle, Wooster was mortally wounded, and Tryon broke through and resumed his way to the Sound. Arnold kept up the pursuit until the British took refuge on the shipping and sailed away. The expedition was followed by one from New Haven in retaliation. Colonel Meigs crossed the Sound with nearly two hundred men in whaleboats to Sag Harbor, attacked the place a little after midnight, captured it, and burned twelve vessels, with a large amount of stores. He then recrossed the Sound with ninety prisoners, and without losing a man.

In the mean time Connecticut had become a State. In May, 1776, the people had been formally released from their allegiance to the crown; and in October the general assembly passed an act assuming the functions of a State. The important section of the act was the first, as follows: " That the ancient form of civil government, contained in the charter from Charles the Second, King of England, and adopted by the people of this State, shall be and remain the civil Constitution of this State, under the sole authority of the people thereof, independent of any King or Prince whatever. And that this Republic is, and shall forever be and remain, a free, sovereign, and independent State, by the name of the State of Connecticut." The form of the act speaks what was doubtless always the belief of the people, that their charter derived its validity, not from the will of the crown, but from the assent of the people. And the curious language of the last sentence, in which " this Republic " declares itself to be " a free, sovereign, and independent State," may serve to indicate something of the appearance which state sovereignty doubtless presented to the American of 1776-89. It is not safe to take " the United States " of 1887 as exactly equivalent, in the eyes of the people, to " the United States " of 1776-89. The nation was born; but its constituent units were often painfully unconscious of the birth.

The main theatre of war continued to be outside of the State; but her troops shared in all its dangers and hardships. The one great business of the State authorities was to fill up the State's quota of men and provide for their maintenance; that of the towns was to fill up their quotas, and to follow the ever-shifting continental currency by changing the necessary salaries as it changed. No one can follow the town records without receiving an increased respect for the persistent devotion of the people to the common cause. There seems to have been little attempt to shift burdens to the shoulders of others; but each town accepted its share as a necessary fact, and strained every energy to meet it. It would have been hardly possible that such devotion should have been purely unselfish; the fact was that, safe as the State was in general, there was hardly a moment when it was not exposed to the possibility of harassing partisan warfare. The British headquarters in New York city were so near, and transportation by ship was so easy, that the whole coast of the State was exposed. In addition to the services of her regular levies, the purely State troops were compelled to serve tours of duty on the coast; and detachments were posted in the various exposed towns. Putnam had been in command of the American forces, and his headquarters had been at Peekskill, within supporting distance of the new post at West Point, whose importance he had been the first to see and secure. He removed his headquarters to Reading in 1778, and from that place fulfilled his old duty, while aiding in the defense of the exposed portions of his own State. It was during this period of service that he met with the adventure at Horse Neck, which is one of the best known of his eventful life, though it was probably one of which he thought the least. One of the most urgent needs of the "rebels" was salt. It was made roughly at various places on the coast, and, with all its inevitable impurities, was grateful enough to the people. One of these salt-works was at Horse Neck, and a British force came up from New York to destroy it. Putnam delayed so long in providing for his men's retreat that his only way of escape was to plunge on horseback down a long flight of stone steps, his baffled pursuers reining in at the top and contenting themselves with firing ineffectually at him as he went.

Early in the winter of 1779–80, Putnam undertook a visit to his home in Pomfret, but was struck with partial paralysis on his journey. He never recovered from it, but was disabled until his death in 1790. Washington thus lost the services of one on whom he had always leaned largely. He was perhaps the most uneducated officer in the army; his name was synonymous in the British view with bad manners and coarseness; his portrait is that of a gross, heavy man, as far removed as possible from the popular notion of the Connecticut Yankee; but his prompt decision, natural intelligence, and unswerving determination were just the qualities that would recommend him equally to his men and to the commander-in-chief. They are shown in his letter of the previous year to Tryon, in a case in which the latter had threatened retaliation. If it is not genuine, it is a most skillful forgery, for it speaks the voice of Putnam in every line. It is as follows: —

"SIR: Nathan Palmer, a lieutenant in your King's service, was taken in my camp as a spy. He was tried as a spy; he was condemned as a spy; and you may rest assured, sir, he shall be hanged as a spy. I have the honor to be, &c.

ISRAEL PUTNAM.

His Excellency, GOVERNOR TRYON.

P. S. Afternoon. *He is hanged.*"

The Fourth of July in 1779 fell on Sunday, and the people of New Haven had made arrangements to celebrate the Declaration of American Independence on the day after. Before the exercises had fairly begun, the town was thrown into consternation by the news that Tryon's fleet and forces, numbering 3,000 men in some forty-eight vessels, had dropped anchor near West Haven at five o'clock that morning, and were on the march for New Haven. They came in two detachments, of 1,500 men each, one marching from West Haven, the other attacking and capturing a small fort at Black Rock on its way. The first detachment met some resistance, and entered the town by the Derby Road. By one o'clock in the afternoon all resistance had been overcome, and the invaders had met at the green, then an unsightly common. The town was given up to plunder until the following morning, when the British retired as suddenly as they had come. They had been guilty of many acts of the most barbarous cruelty, the accounts of which are preserved in tradition or print; they had inflicted a money loss of some £25,000, but the buildings of the college and the other public edifices were undamaged.

Sailing along the coast, Tryon landed at Fairfield, July 8, and destroyed that place. Here public and private buildings alike were fired. The same was the case at the village of Green's Farms the next morning; and then the British commander called off his dogs for a little space. They crossed the Sound to Huntington Bay, and remained there until July 11. Recrossing the Sound to Norwalk, they spent the day in the work of destruction. When they took their departure, the quiet little town had disappeared but for the smoke of its torment, which hung over the spot where it had been. By this time the population of the interior was mustering to meet Tryon at his next landing, and he prudently retired to headquarters. He had inflicted upon Connecticut a loss of about £250,000, as appeared by the proven claims for which the general assembly, as before stated, allotted 500,000 acres of northwestern lands in 1792. But he had not broken the spirit of the people; and his own loss in men, nearly three hundred, was enough to convince him that such attacks were no longer to take rank as purely plundering expeditions, but were to be attended with some danger to life and limb. Such knowledge was sufficient to appease his martial ardor, and he vexed Connecticut very little more.

Tryon had been so injudicious as to give special protection to the property of Tories in his work; and the Tories had been so imprudent as not only to receive the protection but to exult in it. A few of them had taken the inevitable next step, by retiring with Tryon's fleet; but others had the weakness or folly to remain. In May, 1778, the general assembly had begun the process of confiscation against avowed or absconding Tories, under the euphemism of "settling their estates;" the Tryon episode naturally had the effect of stimulating the energy of the State authorities in enforcing the process, and of provoking even a more bitter feeling of the Whigs against those Tories who retained their former dwelling-places. Some of the names which had been most influential in the history of the colony disappeared at this time from the records of the State, and their property passed into other hands. But some of the former holders remained, and their influence in subsequent politics is a fair witness to the clemency of Connecticut. Dr. Peters himself returned to his former parish in 1806, for a visit, and found that even his "History" had been condoned. He died at New York in 1826; and his nephew was governor of Connecticut in 1831-32.

The Connecticut authorities had been indefatigable in raising and provisioning troops, and her people had been equally earnest in offering their services. In the number of men contributed she stood second of the States with 31,939 men, Massachusetts being first with 67,907. Considering differences of population, and more especially differences in immediate danger, Connecticut's quota stands out well beside the 25,678 of Pennsylvania, the 17,781 of New York, the 6,417 of South Carolina, or the 2,679 of Georgia. In general orders of June 16, 1782, Washington spoke of the Connecticut Brigade as " composed of as fine a body of men as any in the army ; " and he expressed a wish for a general review of the men, to decide the relative proficiency of the Connecticut men. In another order, issued two days afterward, he thus expressed his high opinion of the State's line : " The General informs the Army he had great occasion to be satisfied at the review of the Second Connecticut Brigade yesterday, especially with the soldier-like and veteran appearance of the men, and the exactness with which the firings were performed. He felt particular pleasure in observing the cleanliness and steadiness of the second Regiment under arms." And the historian of the commonwealth may be pardoned for taking a "particular pleasure " in noting the fact, that, with the exception of a briefer compliment to a Massachusetts brigade, this is the only instance in Washington's Revolutionary orders of such public commendation of any State's quota. In almost all cases Connecticut men were drafted into service outside of the State, to make good the deficiencies of less zealous States. She had, in addition, to maintain almost all the defense of her own borders, and that while Long Island Sound was under complete control of the enemy's ships. Her success in so doing almost stopped civilized life around the Sound. The Connecticut Tories were driven to Long Island, while the Long Island Whigs crossed into Connecticut; and the waters of the Sound were harassed by almost continual skirmishing. When the French forces were quartered within the State, her people enjoyed a season of comparative tranquillity. When they were withdrawn for the march on Yorktown, which was planned by Washington and the French leaders in a meeting at Wethersfield, Arnold, now in the British service, made his raid on New London, and the State, as usual, was compelled to meet the shock almost unsupported.

Arnold, a native of Norwich, knew the country around New London well, and its defenseless condition was no secret to him. Two small works had been thrown up, forts Trumbull and Griswold; but the former was open at the rear, and had a garrison of but twenty-three men, who were ordered to retreat to the other fort at the approach of danger. Colonel William Ledyard was in command of both forts. Arnold's landing on the morning of September 6, 1781, seems to have been a surprise to every one in the town; and his 1,700 men were at work on both sides of the river before any effective preparations could be made to meet him. Indeed, no such preparations could have been made, even with a day's notice; there were no troops to draw upon. Fort Trumbull was taken with a rush: Ledyard drew in his men to Fort Griswold; and while Arnold reserved to himself the congenial task of burning the town, its dwellings, warehouses, and shipping, the next in command, on the other side of the river, was directed to storm Fort Griswold.

The British soldier is a noble animal; but the notion that he will not strike an enemy who is "down" should be relegated to the ante-Buffonian period of natural history. Badajos was neither the first nor the last witness to the contrary; and too many British officers have put on record their impressions of the British soldier in the moment of victory for us to be surprised at such a little matter as happened at Fort Griswold. The unusual circumstance in this case was that the officer in command was the greatest brute, apparently, of the storming party. After an obstinate resistance, in which Ledyard exhausted every means of defense, and all the British officers of high rank had been carried off dead or dying, the storming party, of which a Major Bromfield was now left in command, poured in. "Who commands this fort?" called Bromfield. "I did, sir; but you do now," said Ledyard, offering his sword. Bromfield, infuriated by the unexpected slaughter, seized the sword and plunged it into Ledyard's breast. With such an example from one in authority, the soldiers' instincts came out at their worst; the defenders were bayoneted whereever they sought refuge, until all but about twenty-five of the one hundred and fifty men in the fort were killed or desperately wounded. The fire of rage dying out for want of sound material, was revived by the collection of the wounded; and thirty-five of these were placed in a cart and rolled down the slope, among rocks and stumps, to be dashed to pieces at the bottom for the amusement of the soldiers. The plea has been offered that the laws of war allowed military execution of the sort upon a fort which persisted in a hopeless defense; but this point of the laws of war has probably never been so strained before as in this case, and, in any event, the wounded have commonly been held exempt.

As Arnold passed out of New London harbor, the Revolutionary struggle passed away with him. It had been a time of sudden and tremendous growth, this transformation of the colony into a State, of the disappearance of old ideas and of old loyalty, of burnings and plunderings, of life-long separations through the fortune of war, of family and social disintegration, of heavy taxation amid stringent poverty, of great burdens manfully borne; but the fancy is almost forced to picture, as the crowning episode of the war, the old commonwealth sitting among the ruins which her recreant son had wrought, and watching him as he sailed away to be worse and less than a foreigner to her forevermore. It may be only a natural shrinking from an unnatural crime, or it may be a remnant of ancient controversies, which has made the historians of Connecticut so careful to note the fact that Arnold was by blood a Rhode Island man.

CHAPTER XVII.

THE ADOPTION OF THE FEDERAL CONSTITUTION.

THE relations of Connecticut to the articles of confederation were peculiar. For a century and a half, the full energy of the commonwealth had been at work to maintain the autonomy secured by the charter, and to exclude from the soil of Connecticut every vestige of authority not owning the people of Connecticut as its legitimate source. From this standpoint, the articles, with their express and tacit attempts to reserve and strengthen state sovereignty, were the exact representatives of Connecticut feeling. The vote in favor of them would have been practically unanimous in 1781, the year in which they went into effect.

Other considerations soon compelled attention. One of the first results of the adoption of the articles, as has been stated, was the ousting of Connecticut from her western claims, with the exception of a reservation which seemed pitiful alongside of Virginia's royal reservation for the satisfaction of her debts and obligations. Instead of the maintenance of vast claims in the Northwest, her business was now to secure her independence of her nearer neighbors : and this was difficult enough. The desolation wrought by the Revolutionary conflict, with the features peculiar to it in this quarter of America, was of continuing effect: the towns of the Connecticut coast were poverty-stricken, their merchants were bankrupt; there was no energy to spare among the people for the revival of foreign commerce, and the imports of the State were of necessity made through Boston or New York. Here they found no amicable treatment, under the provisions of the articles of confederation which allowed each State to levy taxes on imports. Something like one third of the expenses of the New York government were paid by taxation levied so as to be borne by imports into Connecticut; even this burden was not enough to develop a domestic commerce in the subordinate State; and the only resource available was the poor one of turning to pay, in like manner, one third of the expenses of the Massachusetts government. State sovereignty was very fine in theory; but a state sovereignty bottomed on the sole power of the State was found by Connecticut to be a very poor resource for her. It was not long before the leading minds of Connecticut were ready to give up this naked and deceptive state sovereignty for state rights, bottomed on the guaranty of a national power.

In February, 1781, just before the articles actually went into effect, congress notified the States that it would be absolutely necessary for them to surrender to congress a limited power to levy taxes on imports, in order to satisfy the public debt. It was essential that every state legislature should agree to this, and the assent of Connecticut, with all but one of the other States, was balked by the veto of the smallest of the States, Rhode Island. Before Rhode Island could be reasoned with, Virginia repealed her assenting act, and the veto was made more positive. For the next half-dozen years the position of Connecticut was unchanged: her people, instinctively willing for national taxation, were moved by what may seem an unreasonable jealousy of the Society of the Cincinnati, and were unwilling to see a national taxing power under its control or in its interest. For this, however, there was some excuse. The feeling of the military authorities toward the privates of the Revolutionary armies would seem odd to men of the present day. To Washington, for example, it was always the officers who were the "gentlemen of the army;" the privates were food for powder, well enough off with rations, clothes, and glory. When "half-pay for the army" was proposed by congress in 1778, it was only for the commissioned officers; $80 apiece in continental money at the end of the war was thought a quite liberal provision for the insignificant privates. It may very easily be seen that such notions as these were not likely to be popular in an ultra-democratic State like Connecticut; and it is probable that her Revolutionary privates were as bitter in their opposition to the Society of the Cincinnati as those who had not entered the army at all. It was not "the old leaven of Silas Deane," as Hamilton thought, but the instincts of democracy, that fought against caste distinctions in the army, as elsewhere.

In April, 1783, a still more limited proposition to grant taxing powers to congress, with a recommendation to change the basis of contribution from land to number of inhabitants, was sent out to the States. Connecticut assented at once, with New Jersey, New Hampshire, Massachusetts, Virginia, North and South Carolina; but the other States assented so slowly or so grudgingly that the proposition hung fire. When New York gave it the *coup de grace* in 1786, Connecticut had been on the side of the proposed reformation in every vote. She sent no representatives to the Annapolis Convention of 1786; and Knox attributes her neglect or refusal to "jealousy." With all respect to his judgment, it must be noted that the meeting of that body took place in the height of the anti-Cincinnati excitement; that this seed of discontent was removed before the Philadelphia Convention met; and that Connecticut's delegates to that body showed that her previous "jealousy" had been of a nature to which neither Knox nor any other typical Revolutionary officer could do substantial justice, much less deal kindly with it.

ADOPTION OF THE FEDERAL CONSTITUTION. 319

In May, 1787, the general assembly of Connecticut appointed William Samuel Johnson, Roger Sherman, and Oliver Ellsworth delegates to the federal convention at Philadelphia, with instructions to meet the delegates of the other States, and "to discuss upon such alterations and provisions, agreeably to the general principles of republican government, as they shall think proper to render the Federal Constitution adequate to the exigencies of government and the preservation of the Union." The convention met May 14; a majority of the States were ready for business May 25; and Ellsworth attended May 28, Sherman May 30, and Johnson June 2. From the first appearance of Ellsworth the Connecticut delegation was in the thick of every struggle. It has been said that its members "aspired to act as mediators" in the convention; if so, the aspiration was justified by its fruits, for the ability of the delegates was reinforced by the peculiar position of their State. Sherman, though of Massachusetts by birth, was of that family which has always been strong in the Connecticut Valley, and has since blossomed into new power in Ohio. Johnson, of the Stratford blood which had introduced Episcopacy into Connecticut, was yet a devoted and trusted Whig throughout the Revolution. Ellsworth, subsequently chief justice of the United States and of his State, was of a Windsor family. The three were probably the ablest lawyers in the State, represented all shades of opinion in it, and all its territorial divisions, and were united only in the desire for a good national government. No interest in the State could claim more than one of them; they belonged to the whole State and to the Union.

The attitude of Connecticut has been represented as that of a "small State," intent only on obtaining every possible reservation of state sovereignty. Such a representation is grossly unfair. There was no reason for it *a priori*. The State had nothing to gain by it. Her territorial limits were distinctly closed for the future; and she was wisely and justly determined that the new government should not take the form proposed by Virginia, a congress of two houses, both chosen by the States in direct proportion to population, with a president and judiciary appointed by this congress, so that a caucus, or "deal," by a few large States would give them absolute control of the government in *all* its branches. This latter proposition would in reality have been the greatest of calamities for a real development of national spirit and power. Connecticut desired a sound and practical national government, and the path to it was marked out for her delegates by their own commonwealth's development and history for one hundred and fifty years.

Through this long period, Connecticut had been the only colony, with the exception of Rhode Island (unrepresented in this convention), which had had a governor and council, chosen by majority vote and by almost universal suffrage; her delegates were therefore quite prepared for the proposition that at least a part of the new federal government should be chosen in much the same way. On the other hand, in the development of new towns, Connecticut had always been careful to maintain the substantial equality of each township in at least one branch of her government; her delegates were therefore quite prepared for the proposition that at least a part of the new federal government should similarly recognize the equality of the States. Her combination of commonwealth and town rights had worked so simply and naturally that her delegates were quite prepared to suggest a similar combination of national and state rights as the foundation of the new government. The circumstances were enough to clear their mental vision, to enable them to look calmly and judiciously at every new proposition, and to make them real "mediators." This is the crowning glory of the system which Hooker inaugurated in the wilderness, and of the commonwealth of Connecticut. For a century and a half, she had been maintaining the rudimentary form of that mixture of the national and federal elements which are now united in our federal government and give it its strength. This system had bred up a race of public men who were accustomed to it. Their chosen men went as delegates to the convention, and were urged at every step in the line which Hooker had marked out for them, and which their commonwealth had been making straight for them for a hundred and fifty years. It is hardly too much to say that the birth of the constitution was merely the grafting of the Connecticut system on the stock of the old confederation, where it has grown into richer luxuriance than Hooker could ever have dreamed of.

The proceedings of the convention, in dealing with the legislative, executive, and judicial elements of the constitution, are so voluminous and complicated, and Sherman, Ellsworth, and Johnson made up so large a part of almost every debate, that the reader of the convention's proceedings may easily become confused, and will be apt to conclude that, able as these men were, they simply contributed detached portions of the work; and thus the essential service of the Connecticut commonwealth may be altogether lost sight of. It is far better to fix the attention on one point of time, the most critical, perhaps, of the convention, and thus to see how the whole force which had been accumulating for one hundred and fifty years came in at the right time to turn the convention into the exact track which made permanent success possible, against the desires of the mass of the members. It should be remembered, also, that Connecticut delegates had strong grounds of appeal to the confidence of their fellows through the course

of the commonwealth in the public affairs of the
previous half-dozen years. She was evidently disinterested, with no selfish schemes to work for and
no selfish object to gain. Her population gave
her respect in the eyes of the large States. Her
democracy gave the small States confidence in her.
Her position was one of unusual advantage; but
it would have been worthless but for the long years
of preparation which had been begun in the three
little towns on the banks of the Connecticut.

The two plans which came to the front in the
opening hours of the convention — the "Virginia
Plan," presented by Randolph, and the "Jersey
Plan," presented by Patterson — are usually described as respectively the "National" and the
"State Sovereignty" plans. Nothing could be
more misleading than such a classification; neither
had anything of the spirit of nationality in it. The
Virginia plan, giving control of both houses of
congress to numbers, and control of the executive
and judiciary to the two houses, was merely a
scheme to secure the bulk of the spoils to the combination of a few large States; the Jersey plan,
continuing the articles of confederation, with the
power of coercing insubordinate States, was a
counter-scheme to insure the safety of the small
States against the large ones. The futility of the
appellation "national" may be seen in the disgust
with which the large-State men looked at their own
plan when Connecticut had forced a really national

element into it. They no longer loved their offspring.

The discussion of the two plans ran on through the month of June. Between the two parties, and belonging to neither, was Connecticut, and her unswerving position was first made public on the 11th of June. Here were two sets of States: one voting steadily for proportional representation in both of two houses, the other voting as steadily for a single house and absolute State equality in that. In the first class were usually Massachusetts, Pennsylvania, Virginia, North Carolina, South Carolina, and Georgia; in the second, New York, New Jersey, Delaware, and Maryland. It is odd that great expectations of coming immigration kept the Southern States in the column of "large" States, while New York, without a thought of her coming western expansion, posed contentedly as a "small" State. The discussions of the successive items of the rival plans were conducted daily in committee of the whole house, and Connecticut seized the opportunity to declare her position, June 11. On motion of Sherman, slightly amended by King, it was voted that representation in the first branch of the national legislature should be proportional, not equal. This was a "large State" proposition, but Connecticut voted for it, placing herself in the large-State column, and making the vote seven in favor, three against, and one (Maryland) divided. Then Sherman, seconded by his own colleague Ellsworth, as if to make the attitude of their State more pronounced, moved that each State have a vote in the second branch (the senate). This was a practical incorporation of the small-State proposition, and the large States voted it down, six to five. From this time on, the proposition of State equality in the upper, and proportionate representation in the lower house of congress was renewed again and again by the Connecticut delegates, was commonly cited as "the Connecticut proposal," and was regularly voted down by six to five until July 2. This steady vote of Connecticut with the small States made that a minority not to be disregarded; and, as passion rose higher until a public threat was made that the small States would confederate and find a foreign power which would take them by the hand for their protection, the cool, deliberate, and persistently offered compromise of Connecticut became harder to resist. On the 2d of July, the large-State delegates showed the first symptoms of breaking, by referring the Connecticut proposal to a committee of one from each State. We have no means of knowing the proceedings of the committee, but they must have been interesting. It is only known that Franklin's influence was cast for the Connecticut proposal; and that it was reported favorably, July 5. The report met a storm of opposition. Madison "only restrained himself from animadverting on the report from the respect he bore to the members of the committee." Wilson angrily exclaimed that the committee had exceeded their powers. On the 7th of July, North Carolina came over to the Connecticut proposal, and the report of the committee was at last adopted by a vote of six States for it, Pennsylvania, Virginia, and South Carolina against it, and Massachusetts and Georgia divided. The great question was settled, and the Connecticut proposal went on the 26th of July to a committee of detail, which reported the constitution of the senate, much as it was finally adopted.

With this achievement, Connecticut's work in the convention was really finished. Her delegates constantly lent the great weight of their legal ability and strong common sense, reinforced by the general confidence in them, to the subsequent debates; but their leadership, assumed unwillingly and only from a sense of duty, was dropped as soon as the occasion which called for it was over. The system of complete local liberty, with a limited but concentrated central power, under which the Connecticut river towns had filled out their boundaries and had struggled desperately but vainly for expansion abroad, had passed into a wider field, where it was to have a wider success. Governor Huntington was a hearty supporter of the proposed constitution; the assembly unanimously called a convention to consider it; and that body met at Hartford, and ratified the constitution, January 9, 1788, by a vote of one hundred and twenty-eight to forty. Ellsworth and Johnson received the deserved honor of being chosen as the State's first representatives in the senate of the United States; and the commonwealth of Connecticut became merged in the greater commonwealth of the United States, its own lineal successor.

CHAPTER XVIII.

INDUSTRIAL DEVELOPMENT.

The development of Connecticut under the constitution has been a curious but natural consequence of her preceding history. All her institutions had tended to the development of an abounding individualism among her people. Thrown into any situation, a Connecticut party set at once about organizing civil government, and the individual began the promptest and most efficient preparations for taking care of himself. It was the institutions of the commonwealth, not any wonderful or elaborate system of common schools, that made the people of Connecticut what they were; for the hopes of early years, for a thorough common-school system, have only been realized in recent times. Until the new era in popular education came in, the ordinary Connecticut citizen had what would now be considered a very meagre education; but he had something much better in the thoroughly learned lesson of looking out for himself. Further, the constant application of this lesson, under the necessities of the people, had developed the class of what are often called "household industries " very considerably before the close of the last century. Farmers and their sons did not lose the evenings or rainy days: these were spent in making nails and other iron products, or anything which would sell. All this, continued through generations, took the place of the technical education which is now finding its way into our school systems. The consequence has been, during the last seventy years, the development of the modern Connecticut mechanic out of the Connecticut agriculturist of the last century, and the transformation of the commonwealth into a great industrial community.

The devastation of the Revolution had rather checked than stopped the internal development of the commonwealth. New towns were erected even during the heat of the war, and while so many of the old towns were under plunder and fire; and the attainment of peace was like the throwing down of a dam — the new towns numbering two in 1784, five in 1785, thirteen in 1786, and ten between that year and the close of the century. It was estimated by the convention of 1787 that the State then had a population of 202,000, exceeded only by Virginia (600,000), Massachusetts (352,000), Pennsylvania (341,000), Maryland, (254,000), and New York (238,000). In the assignment of representatives in congress before the first census, ten were given to Virginia, eight each to Massachusetts and Pennsylvania, six to New

York and Maryland, and Connecticut, North Carolina, and South Carolina were put on a level with five each. When the first census was taken it was found that the population of the State was 237,946, making its rank eighth among the States. The second census, in 1800, gave it the same relative rank with a population of 251,002.

Almost all the interests of this population were agricultural. The commonwealth was not that scene of busy activity which it is to-day, with streams of raw material pouring into it from every side, springs of manufactured product bubbling up in every acre, and outflowing in freight bound to every part of the world. In 1790, the activity was altogether local. The whole commonwealth was dotted with towns; but these were the little centres of small agricultural circles, with very little surplus for exportation beyond that which was necessary for the support of their own people. The green in the heart of the town had its church, and leading to it was a street, with wooden houses, usually comfortable, but often unpainted, and seldom representing any great amount of luxury. Each local circle was able to raise most of what was needed for its people; exchanges among the people made up special deficiencies; and the peripatetic tailor, shoemaker, or other workmen completed whatever was lacking in the simple life of a simple people. Pay was still usually in kind, so that each little circle was able to keep its own affairs in motion without much reference to its neighbors. When any unusual surplus was to be exported, it was put into some shape, such as cattle, which could be most easily transported. Mules for the Southern or West Indian market were a common form; and a drove of mules on its journey was very likely to be a Connecticut product. The story is told of John Randolph, that, seeing a drove of mules passing through Washington, he pointed it out to Tracy, one of the Connecticut senators, and said, in his genial way, "Tracy, there go a lot of your constituents." "Ye-es," said Tracy, "going down to Virginia to teach school."

If the occupations of the people were agricultural, their institutions went far to insure them against any of that tendency toward stagnation which had long been associated with the common notion of purely agricultural peoples. The Connecticut citizen of the early years of this century was a busy man, in some respects, for the commonwealth or the town was continually calling on him to take part in political life. Let us try to follow out the political relations of the citizen before the adoption of the constitution of 1818. Most of his public concerns were with the town. He had gained a legal residence there by being born in it, by being received by a vote of some town meeting, by the approval of the selectmen, the town's executive committee, or by being chosen to some office by the town. Unless having thus acquired residence, he was in the town only on sufferance. If there had been any reason to apprehend that he would become a charge on the town, it would have been the duty of the selectmen to send him to his own town if he had one in the State, to send him out of the State if he belonged to another State, or to hold his entertainer responsible for him. Supposing him to have acquired residence, he had become a voter, on arriving at the age of twenty-one, by reason of having a freehold estate of an annual value of $7, or a personal estate on the tax list of $134, by being approved by the selectmen as a person of good moral character, and by taking the freeman's oath. Twice a year, as a voter, he attended the town elections for representatives in the general assembly, at which also the new voters formally took the freeman's oath. At the September meeting, he, with all the other freemen of the State, voted for twenty names, as candidates for the council or upper house of the assembly, at the election to follow in April. The total number of votes cast for all persons was transmitted by the town officers to the assembly; that body counted them and published the twenty names which stood highest on the whole vote of the State; and at the election in April, when the freemen came to vote for representatives again, he voted for twelve of the published list to be of the council for the following year. In May, the general assembly counted the April vote from all the towns, and announced the names of the fortunate twelve who stood highest and were elected. After casting his votes for the council, the freeman voted for governor, lieutenant-governor, secretary, and treasurer; and the votes were sent in like manner to Hartford, to be counted in May under direction of the assembly. Members of congress were chosen in the same way as councilors. The freemen voted for eighteen names in April; the assembly counted the votes in May, and declared the eighteen names which stood highest; the freemen voted for seven of these eighteen in September; and the assembly declared the seven elect in the following month. Such were the limitations which the popular vote had imposed upon itself under the charter.

The occasion of counting the votes was still known by its primitive name of the general election, though it had long ceased to be anything more than a canvass of votes already cast, and now returned to the general assembly as a canvassing body. Until about 1836 it was an occasion of solemn import and unusual magnificence. The governor, if he was not a Hartford man, was met on the outskirts of the capital, the day before that of the great ceremonial, by a company of cavalry, and escorted to his lodgings. When he was notified, on the next morning, that the representatives had organized and chosen their speaker, he and they, with the council, the sheriffs of the whole commonwealth with white staves, and the clergy, marched in procession to the first church, escorted by the governor's foot-guards and horse-guards. At the church, the election sermon was delivered by the preacher appointed for that service. It was no brief or trivial performance. The election sermon of President Stiles, in 1783, made up 120 pages of about 300 words each, though he certainly added matter before publication. At the end of the church services the procession returned to the state house; the votes were counted by a committee of the assembly; the governor, lieutenant-governor, secretary, treasurer, and council for the year were announced, and the general election was over. An election ball occupied the evening. The theory of the commonwealth still was, until 1818, that our supposititious voter was present and voting for commonwealth officers; but it had long since ceased to be the case. He made one of the spectators occasionally; but, as a rule, he heard of the festivities from others.

The town was the political body which came nearest him. Its annual meeting fell in December, when town officers were chosen; and a formidable list it was and still is. There were selectmen not more than seven in number, a town clerk, a town treasurer, constables, surveyors of highways, fence-viewers, listers, collectors, leather-sealers, grand jurors, tithing-men, hay-wards, chimney-viewers, gaugers, packers, and sealers of weights and measures, besides any other officers whom the peculiar circumstances of the town required. Many of these offices have since fallen from their once high estate, and combinations of voters are sometimes formed with the improper purpose of choosing unseemly persons to fill them; but in their time they were both ancient and honorable. At all events, the multitude of offices and the annual term of office together made the opportunities of public service exceedingly numerous, and the prohibition against refusing office under penalty of fine in default of good excuse, brought all citizens into the supply of available material for public service. One consequence was, that there were few freemen of Connecticut who passed through life without at some time filling an office on the summons of their fellows. The town meeting, properly warned and limited in its action to the subjects specified in the warning, was a political school in which the freeman received his training; the multitude of minor offices provided higher courses for almost all the freemen; and from the two together the people received an uncommonly good political education and a sense of personal interest in public affairs.

After all, the main features of the system were the town meeting, the constables, and the selectmen. The democratic element was supplied by the town meeting; the element of dictatorship, which seems to lurk somewhere in democracy, was in the selectmen; and the constables represented the commonwealth. The powers of the town meeting were rather more clearly defined than those of the selectmen, probably for the reason that the latter could be held to a stricter personal responsibility. The town meeting represented the popular force; when it adjourned, the selectmen were almost the autocrats of the town until the next town meeting. It is worthy of note that such powers have so seldom been abused or betrayed, and that men, often active business men, could have been found for more than two centuries, as they still are found, to manage without fee or reward the complicated, difficult, and sometimes dangerous affairs of a Connecticut town.

The registration of births, marriages, and deaths was with the town clerk; licenses to marry came from him; and deeds and leases of lands within the township were registered with him. The probate judge was a town officer; and the mass of business of this nature, a county affair outside of the influence of the New England system, was here purely a town matter. Indeed, it may quite safely be said that about all the relations which the citizen holds to the county in other States than those of New England, and very many of the relations which he holds to the State itself, he held in Connecticut to the town only. His little town republic hemmed him and his interests in on every side, and it was but seldom that he became conscious that there was a larger and a still larger republic which also claimed his allegiance and interest.

It must not be supposed that the description of the Connecticut freeman's political position in 1810 is vitally incorrect for his successor of 1887. It has been altered mainly by the increase in the number of cities, — New Haven, Hartford, Bridgeport, Norwich, Waterbury, Middletown, Meriden, New London, and South Norwalk, — with their introduction of stronger municipal powers, and by the erection of " boroughs," or semi-cities, in the more thickly settled portions of the townships. All these steps are detractions from the original powers of the towns, and are a tendency to diminish the citizen's dependence on the township. They have not yet been very serious, though attempts to extend the drift in this direction are often renewed. The essential thing to be remembered is, that changes in the commonwealth's constitution have affected the status of the towns very little. The original constitution was changed into the charter, and this into the constitution of 1818; but these changes were mainly of the commonwealth, and the relative position or the absolute powers of the towns were hardly changed by any of them. To a remarkable degree the relations of the Connecticut citizen to his town are the same as those of his forefather when the first towns were planted. More than in any other New England State, the original vigor of the Connecticut town has enabled it to keep pace with the growing power of the commonwealth.

Hartford and New Haven were cities at the beginning of the century, having been incorporated in 1784, but both were very far from our notions of a city. They were little centres of less than 4,000 population, and the communication between them for passengers, mails, and traffic was supplied by two stages a week, leaving on Wednesdays and Saturdays. Each had a few weekly newspapers, some shops with a very miscellaneous stock in trade, and hardly any other evidence of city life. Incomes were derived, even in the cities, directly or mediately, from agriculture for the most part, and they were not large: it was rumored, with some natural hesitation, that Pierpont Edwards, the commonwealth's leading lawyer, enjoyed a revenue of $2,000 per annum from his practice, but this could not be taken as a standard. There were few who were very rich, and few who were very poor; and the life of the whole commonwealth was a little fuller than, but almost as equable and placid as when there were but three towns in it. Banks and insurance companies came into existence only during the twenty years 1790–1810.

New Haven had an advantage over Hartford in

its foreign commerce, which had begun to revive before the Revolutionary war, and had received a further impetus from the peace. Its "Long Wharf," 3,500 feet in length, whose greedy maw had swallowed all that private enterprise, lotteries, and commonwealth aid could offer it, was not finished until after 1802; but it was in active use long before it could be called finished, and it was the headquarters of foreign trade. Its merchants had their own local spirit, and their "wharf law" for the punishment of local offenses; and their ships went all over the world, hardly any of them returning without a contribution of material for the wharf. Thence sailed Isaac Hull, as the captain of a New Haven West Indiaman, long before he thought of meeting the Guerrière. Thither came the Neptune in 1799, with the richest cargo yet imported, its profits being a quarter of a million, and the duties on the cargo being nearly $70,000. And here came out again the old feeling of the "town-born" against the "interlopers," who had come into the town to share in its prosperity. It is said that one of the town-born New Haven captains, being forced to a jetson during a storm at sea, cautioned his men to throw over only the goods of "interlopers." But the influence of the college, with that of foreign commerce and resulting wealth, did much to raise New Haven above the general level of the commonwealth; and city life in the modern sense had its closest approximation here. The town poor were no longer sold at auction. Geese and cattle were banished from the Green, and that part of the city began to take on some of the beauty which has since made it so notable a spot. The city went a step beyond its contemporaries in beginning a cemetery on modern lines, abandoning the nakedly ugly New England burying-ground. There was even an earnest but vain effort to obtain a permanent supply of water in 1804.

While Hartford was in most respects more provincial than its rival, having only a small trade in West India rum and molasses, its atmosphere was for some reasons much more literary. Perhaps some of this tendency came from its more frequent communication with the outside world, through its natural position as a stopping-place on the road from New York to Boston. Since 1772, a stage passed each way once a week. Here were the writers so long known collectively as "the Hartford wits," Lemuel Hopkins, Humphreys, Alsop, Trumbull, the author of "McFingal," and Theodore Dwight, a younger brother of Dr. Dwight; here they were succeeded by Percival, Brainard, and Mrs. Sigourney, followed by the more recent writers who have maintained Hartford's position in the world of secular literature; and here were always strong ministers, able successors of the leaders of the first migration. Noah Webster was as yet known rather as a grammarian than as a lexicographer. Connecticut society, however, was strongly tinged with a curious provincialism in the times about 1800. Things were done and said without special criticism which would nowadays be thought unpardonable. The pastor of the First Church was Nathan Strong, the writer of the hymn so familiar in our hymn-books, "Swell the anthem, raise the song." In 1790 he and one of the leading members of his flock entered into partnership for the purpose of managing a distillery. The enterprise was a failure; and, as imprisonment for debt was still the law, the junior partner prudently sought refuge outside of the commonwealth's jurisdiction. The ministerial partner, however, stood his ground, remaining within doors on week-days, and appearing on Sundays, when the writ did not run, to minister to his indulgent parishioners. When the financial difficulty had been settled, the pastor's troubles were over. He continued his ministry until his death in 1816, and was made a doctor of divinity by the College of New Jersey in 1801. And the poems of the Hartford wits, largely devoted to political struggles, have in them a great deal more of the bludgeon than of the rapier. One must speculate on the mental constitutions of the audience which could cut out a high niche for the author of such poetry as this, which was to be sung to a familiar hymn-tune, as the first of a dozen similar stanzas, describing a Democratic meeting: —

> Ye tribes of Faction, join —
>   Your daughters and your wives;
> Moll Cary's come to dine,
>   And dance with Deacon Ives.
>   Ye ragged throng
>   Of Democrats,
>   As thick as rats,
>   Come join the song.

Sporadic efforts had been made in the agricultural districts of the State to introduce some products which should be more profitable than the cereals which were the staple. The silk-culture had been introduced about 1732, and in 1747 Governor Law wore the first coat and stockings made of New England silk. In 1758 the work was taken up by President Stiles of Yale, and by Dr. Aspinwall of Mansfield. The former wrote up the industry, and wore gowns of Connecticut silk at Commencement; the latter put the industry at Mansfield and its neighborhood on a foundation which has not since been lost. One of its outgrowths has been the silk-works developed by the mechanical and artistic genius of the brothers Cheney, at Manchester, near Hartford, beginning in a modest attempt to make the lower grades of silk, and rising to higher grades through the invention of improved machinery.

Attempts had been made since about 1736 to introduce woolen manufactures as a development of sheep-raising, and these were revived after the Revolution. With help from the general assembly, a manufactory of woolens was established at Hartford after the peace. Its product was mainly of the pepper-and-salt variety, but it was good and popular; and a suit of the factory's broadcloth was worn by President Washington at the opening of Congress in 1790. In 1802 a long step was taken in advance. David Humphreys, of Derby, formerly Washington's aide, now American minister to Spain, sent home a flock of one hundred merino sheep. The improved wool soon built up a manufactory at Humphreysville, near Derby; and a suit of broadcloth from it was worn by President Madison at his inauguration in 1809. From this beginning, the industry has grown and flourished in the State; and it had not gone far before its influence was felt in politics.

The Connecticut delegates in the Convention of 1787 had claimed that theirs was even then a manufacturing State. This was rather a desire than a fact. Since the time of Winthrop, whose attainments in natural science had led him all over the commonwealth in the effort to establish an iron-manufacture, this branch of industry had been carried on with more or less success. One of the first ventures at New Haven had been the establishment of the " iron workes; " and the erection of furnaces was encouraged by the assembly and by towns, through remission of taxes and otherwise, all through the eighteenth century. In 1716 the State encouraged the erection of a slitting-mill by Fitch & Co. by giving it a legal monopoly of the business for fifteen years. But, after all, the normal condition of iron production was that of a household industry. Each furnace was meant to furnish enough iron for a neighborhood; and the people of the neighborhood, using the intervals from agricultural employment in winter or at night, converted the iron into articles for domestic use, with a surplus of such things as nails for exportation. There was not yet enough stimulus in the industry to affect the purely agricultural character of the community seriously, but it was a preparation for the future.

The development of the iron district of the northwestern part of Connecticut, about 1730, had been carried to a considerable extent before the Revolution, and it seemed likely to make the commonwealth a mining and manufacturing community. The deposits in Salisbury and its vicinity were abundant, and the supply of wood, then the universal fuel, was plentiful. Encouraged by the Revolution, the production became of great importance. The cannon for the army and navy, the heavy chains which barred the rivers, the materials for gun-barrels and other military equipments for the Revolutionary armies, came from the works at Salisbury, which were never reached by the enemy. The workmen considered the Salisbury iron superior to anything else which could be obtained, at home or from abroad, and its reputation seems to have been deserved. It is still highly valued, and 38,000 tons of it were produced in 1880. Valuable as was the supply, it was not destined to work a revolution in the economic life of the people. When the time came for the real race, it was found that other States had a superior advantage in the bounty of nature, which had combined their iron-beds with adjacent beds of coal; and Connecticut was compelled to yield to circumstances and turn to other industries.

Before the final industrial revolution came on, the commonwealth was convulsed by a political revolution, caused partially by the first movements of manufactures, and in its turn a moving cause of subsequent developments. Connecticut had been Federalist from the first, and the Connecticut Federalist had become almost a peculiar type. Many influences aided the development. The almost exclusively agricultural employment of the people rendered them very susceptible to the personal influence of leading men, and community of religious belief strengthened this influence. The leading men were often connected directly or indirectly with commercial interests, which were patronized by the Federal party; or they were leaders in the Congregational Established Church, the natural enemy of Jeffersonian doctrine and prejudices. The new Democratic party therefore found in Connecticut a phalanx impenetrable to all its efforts to move it. Jefferson's attempt to establish a governmental influence in the State in 1801, by removing Elizur Goodrich, the Federalist collector of the port of New Haven, and appointing in his place Samuel Bishop, the venerable father of a rising young Democratic politician, merely made the Connecticut Federalists furious without converting them; and their feeling was increased by the embargo, which shut up eighty vessels in the harbor of New Haven alone, and nearly ruined the commerce of the port. Even after the national downfall of the Federal party in 1800, when other States yielded and chose Democratic electors, Connecticut and Delaware were the only States which chose Federal electors at every presidential election, so long as there were Federalists to vote for.

The Episcopal Church had begun to raise its head again after the Revolution, though it was still feeble. Every such symptom of revival, of course, seemed to the Congregationalist Whig simply a revival of Toryism. When the Episcopalians and other dissatisfied elements in New Haven won a substantial victory at the first city election in 1784, Dr. Stiles's diary takes it as a victory of the Tories, and adds, as a natural result the next month, " this day town-meeting voted to re-admit the Tories." The connection with Toryism became dimmed in time; but the grievances of the dissatisfied element, the Episcopalians, the " New Lights," the Sandemanians, and other sectaries, remained unabated. In 1791, the act which seemed to Congregationalists the summit of religious freedom was passed: it allowed any dissenting society to tax for the support of its own minister, and remitted the town tax to such as should lodge a certificate of their dissenting membership with the clerk of an Established Church. This was far from satisfactory to the dissenters. They were discontented that all persons not members of any church were still subject to taxation for the exclusive benefit of the Established Church; they asserted that the privilege of certificate was thwarted by the authorities on little or no legal pretext; and they complained that the treasury of the commonwealth was still put by the assembly at the service of Yale College, to the exclusion of any other denominational interest.

Finding that the dissenters were not content with what had no doubt seemed large concessions, and welded together more strongly by the national supremacy of their opponents and the ruinous embargo policy, the dominant party of Connecticut redoubled its resistance to change. The Connecticut Democrats considered the charter, readopted in 1776 by the assembly, as the cornerstone of their opponents' power. It had, they said, left the powers of government so undefined that the upper house, or council, consisting of but twelve members, had gained an extreme influence; that seven of the council, a majority, were lawyers, able to "appoint all the judges, plead before those judges, and constitute themselves a supreme court of errors to decide in the last resort on the laws of their own making;" and that these same men had complete control of the election machinery of the State. They demanded a constitution under which the legislative, judicial, and executive powers should be separated. In August, 1804, a convention of Democrats, or Republicans, was held at New Haven, and endorsed the programme for the autumn elections. The Federal majority rose higher than ever, and the assembly at its first meeting took steps to punish those malcontents whom it could reach. It deprived of their commissions five justices of the peace who had been delegates to the New Haven Convention, and censured one of its own members who had spoken too warmly in their behalf. The offending member, when called upon to rise and receive his reprimand from the speaker, interposed the ingenious point of order that there was no rule to prevent his receiving it seated; and the evident embarrassment of the speaker and assembly in dealing with the point took away much of the dignity of the punishment.

The rapid passage of the embargo difficulties into open war with Great Britain brought Connecticut Federalism into the broader field of New England Federalism. The first conflict with the general government came on the employment of the militia of the State. The Constitution gives congress, and an act of congress gave the President, the power to call out the militia of the States in three distinctly defined emergencies, — to execute the laws of the Union, to suppress insurrections, or to repel invasions. As the regular army was drawn off to invade Canada, the President called on the States for militia to do garrison duty in its place. The Connecticut governor, Griswold, asked in reply for a specification of the reason for the call, for the law that was to be executed, the insurrection that was to be suppressed, or the invasion that was to be repelled; and it is not easy to see how his question was to be answered or evaded. At all events, no effective answer was made. Connecticut provided a special force of 2,600 men for her own defense, but entered her protest, through the assembly, that " the war was unnecessary." The incidents of the war had little to do with Connecticut, with the exception of the blockade of New London by British vessels, and the constant danger of attack there or elsewhere, against which the State was compelled to defend herself, as the general government seemed unable or unwilling to do so. In April, 1814, a British force landed at Saybrook and destroyed some stores; and in August the Stonington militia beat off a squadron which attempted to land there, killing and wounding seventy-five men, with the loss of but a few wounded of their own number. All the credit due to the State's persistent defense of her own borders was taken away, however, by a charge which Decatur made without even offering evidence for it. Having been foiled several times in attempting to put to sea, he declared that warning of his attempts had been given from the shore by blue-lights; and the name "Blue-light Federalist" was at once used by the administration party as a good title for the dominant party of Connecticut. It was shown, on the other hand, that blue-lights were entirely unnecessary, since Decatur had never taken proper care to keep British emissaries out of his district; but he seems to have gone on the assumption that a failure by Decatur necessarily implied treachery on the part of somebody else.

It is unnecessary to go very far into the origin and history of the Hartford Convention, for Connecticut had no more special connection with that body than to furnish a meeting-place for it. The grievances which led to it, the neglect of the defense of the coast by the general government, and the preponderance of Southern interest in the government, were common to Connecticut with the other New England States; but there may have been a reason for the selection of the place. Nearly twenty years before, in 1796, there appeared in the "Connecticut Courant," at Hartford, a series of articles signed "Pelham." Written with consummate ability, and apparently from a profound prescience of the difficulties which the Union was to encounter, the articles attempted to show that the Southern slave-system made a permanent Union impossible, and that the Northern States should prepare for separate national existence. The tone of the Hartford Convention's recommendations for constitutional changes have so much of the spirit of these articles that one is disposed to think that, if "Pelham" was not a delegate, he was at least a close adviser, and that the desire for his advice was one reason for the selection of the place.

Connecticut's delegates to the convention were Chauncey Goodrich, James Hillhouse, John Treadwell, Zephaniah Swift, Calvin Goddard, Nathaniel Smith, and Roger Minot Sherman, the ablest men of the dominant party. The convention met with closed doors in the building in which the council of the commonwealth had been accustomed to meet, and Democratic leaders at Hartford and Washington looked for the outcome with apprehension. The Episcopal rector (afterward bishop), Chase, declined to offer prayer at its morning session, explaining that he knew of no form of prayer for rebellion. A fussy Federal officer contributed much to the excitement at first; but the substitution of Colonel Jesup preserved the peace, except that a squad of soldiers would now and then march around the building during the sessions, their fifes playing the "Rogue's March." With the exception of such little touches of nature as this, the proceedings of the convention are rather a part of national than of local history.

The endorsement of the convention's recommendations by the general assembly apparently left the Federalist control of the State complete. In reality, it was at death's door. The Methodist Church had been established in the State in 1789, and had extended with rapidity. It shared in the grievances of the dissenting sects, and reinforced their demands for abatement. Finally, the Democratic party of the State came to the decision to make common cause with the dissenters of all sects, and to fight the political battle on that ground. In January, 1816, a convention at New Haven nominated Oliver Wolcott for governor, and Jared Ingersoll for lieutenant-governor. Wolcott had been a Federalist, Adams's secretary of the treasury, and had been accused by the Democratic newspapers of resorting to arson to cover up frauds in his office. He had since been engaged in business in New York city. The adoption of his name indicates another element in the alliance. The manufactures of the State, particularly in wool, demanded protection by tariff, and had only a Democratic congress to look to for it. Wolcott's nomination was to give them confidence. Ingersoll was the Episcopal end of the ticket. Thus prepared, the "toleration party," as it called itself, went into the election. The dominant party, alarmed by the prospect, hurried to make concessions, but it was too late. Ingersoll was elected, and Wolcott barely defeated. In 1817 both were elected, with a two-thirds majority of the assembly. The first step was to put all sects on an equality as to taxation; the next, to repeal the "Stand-up Law," passed by the Federalists in 1801, by which votes were to be cast in town-meeting by rising, not by secret ballot; and the next, in June, 1818, to call a State convention to frame a constitution. The convention met August 26, at Hartford, with a Democratic majority of only ten out of two hundred members, just enough to compel mature deliberation and wise decision. It adopted the present constitution September 15, which was ratified by a slender majority October 5. The Democrats were rather more dissatisfied with it than the Federalists, and many of them voted against it.

The constitution provided for a government to consist of a governor, lieutenant-governor, treasurer, secretary, and comptroller, as State officers, and a general assembly composed of a senate and a house of representatives. The State officers were to be chosen annually by ballot, the general assembly to choose when no candidate should receive a majority vote. The representatives were to be chosen by the towns, the proportion of each town to be "as at present practiced and allowed." The erection of a new town was not to reduce the representation of the town or towns from which it was formed, without the consent of the old towns, and new towns were to have one representative only. The senate was to be chosen by districts, the districts at first numbering twelve, and, since 1828, not less than eighteen or more than twenty-four. The meetings of the general assembly were to be annual, and held alternately at Hartford and New Haven. Since 1873, Hartford has been the sole capital; and, since 1875, the State officers and senators hold office for two years, though sessions of the assembly and elections for representatives and half of the senate are still annual. The courts were to be a supreme court of errors, a superior court, and inferior courts to be constituted by the assembly. The supreme and superior court justices were to hold office during good behavior; their term of office was limited to eight years in 1856. Voters were to be white males of twenty-one years or over, and, as the conditions were simplified in 1845 and 1855, were to have resided in the State for one year and in the town for six months, were to have sustained a good moral character, and to be able to read. The selectmen of each town were to enforce the suffrage and election laws of the State.

Religious profession and worship were to be free to all, and no sect was to be preferred by law. No person was to be compelled to join, associate with, support, or remain a member of, any religious

INDUSTRIAL DEVELOPMENT. 355

body; and all religious bodies were to be entirely equal before the law. Thus ended the connection of church and state in Connecticut.

One consequence of the establishment of the constitution was the founding of two new colleges. An Episcopal academy had been incorporated at Cheshire in 1801, but it had been impossible to obtain for it a college charter from the general assembly. In 1823 the assembly chartered it as Washington College, locating it at Hartford. Its first commencement was held in 1827, with ten graduates. Its connection with its church has become closer during the intervening years, and its work, in conjunction with the related Theological Seminary until 1851, has been of the greatest service in the training of clergymen. In 1845 its name was changed to Trinity College. Its property is now valued at over a million dollars, and its buildings are among the finest in Hartford. Its presidents have been: Bishop Brownell, 1823–31; Dr. Wheaton, 1831–37; Dr. Silas Totten, 1837–48; Dr. John Williams, 1848–53; Dr. D. R. Goodwin, 1853–60; Dr. Samuel Eliot, 1860–64; Dr. J. B. Kerfoot, 1864–66; Dr. Abner Jackson, 1867–74; Dr. T. R. Pynchon, 1874–83; and Dr. George W. Smith, 1883. The Methodist Episcopal Church in the State also desired an institution for higher education, and it obtained a charter for Wesleyan University without difficulty in 1829, placing it at Middletown. Its presidents have been: Dr. Wilbur Fisk, 1831–39; Dr. Stephen Olin, 1839–41; Dr. Nathan Bangs, 1841–42; Dr. Stephen Olin, 1842–51; Dr. A. W. Smith, 1851–57; Dr. Joseph Cummings, 1857–75; Dr. Cyrus D. Foss, 1875–80; and Dr. John W. Beach, 1880. Its work and resources have increased until its productive funds are now about $700,000, and the annual income from them about $40,000.

The constitution has remained fairly satisfactory during the subsequent growth of the State, except that the representation of the towns has frequently given control of the general assembly to a minority of the popular vote; and efforts have been made, though as yet without success, to equalize representation. Whatever may be the present defects of the constitution, it certainly was a great advance on the charter. It seems to have lifted from the shoulders of the people a load which, however slight, had been sufficient to hamper them in their course up to that time. The original organization of society and government had been exceedingly democratic in 1637 and 1662; and the constitution of 1818 had only brought it into line with the development of democracy, which had passed beyond the charter. Labor had never been disregarded or degraded, but mechanical labor had never been considered as quite on a level with agricultural. The diary of John Cotton Smith, the last Federalist governor, is sprinkled with notes of his labor among his men in the harvest field and in the other departments of farm work; and he was but a representative of his class. On the other hand, there are such cases as that of Roger Sherman, who came into New Milford a shoemaker, and lived to be a senator of the United States; but they were as uncommon in Connecticut before 1818 as that of Smith was common. The mechanic was *primâ facie* vulgar, and his ability was shown by getting out of his class into law or into agriculture, not by increasing his wealth in it. There were mechanics, and good ones, in Connecticut before 1818; but the State only began to be a distinctly mechanical commonwealth when the constitution of 1818 had lifted all men into equality, and the mechanic was for the first time on an equality with the Congregational farm-owner.

Even under colonial conditions the mechanical genius of Connecticut had begun to develop the manufacture of the easier forms of hardware; and with this development came the first appearance of the peddler with his wagon. About 1770 the manufacture of tinware was begun in Berlin, eleven miles south of Hartford. This was the beginning of the industry with which the name of Connecticut was to be so closely associated, — the production of "Yankee notions." The peddlers carried the manufactures of this and neighboring towns over the country in wagons, exchanging them for local products and reaping a double profit on the exchange. Transactions of a darker dye than any legitimate profit were also laid to the account of these peddlers: their malignant ingenuity was debited with the introduction of wooden nutmegs, bass-wood hams, oak-leaf cigars, and similar frauds. Undoubtedly there was much fraudulent work: the loose conditions of such a trade, when ignorance on one side was always tempting any latent dishonesty on the other, would make some fraud inevitable. But the essence of the accusation was in the rivalry of local trade, in the jealousy of unsuccessful competitors, provoked by the sudden success of Connecticut workmen in their new field. They had found a sphere in which the niggardliness of nature could not check them. The lack of coal as fuel might weigh heavily against the value of their iron-mines, but the ingenuity of the workmen was a possession which could not be taken from the commonwealth. From the little beginning at Berlin has grown up a great system of towns, in the district along the Naugatuck and Connecticut rivers, devoted to the manufacture of hardware, of brass goods, of anything and everything in which the accuracy, skill, and ingenuity of the workman can make up for the distance of the place of manufacture from the source of the raw material and from the places of sale. Here are Ansonia, Waterbury, New Britain, Meriden, and a bewildering maze of other towns, all of which have been developed by water-power and human ingenuity; older places like Hartford, New Haven, and Norwich have felt the reflex influence and joined in the race; and quite new places, like Bridgeport, have sprung to life and activity under the impulse derived from the first tin pail made at Berlin. Before that time, every enterprising man kept his eyes keenly on the benevolence of Nature, and looked to the use of something produced in the commonwealth which he could improve for sale; since that time, such men, no longer heeding local resources, have scoured the world for materials, have brought them to Connecticut and passed them through the crucible of Connecticut ingenuity, and have found in the results a mine richer than the Spaniard's longings could compass.

The clock manufacture in Connecticut, with its adjuncts or derivatives, is an excellent example of the manner in which the mechanics of the commonwealth have made their ingenuity of public service. Wooden clocks, of the old high pattern, were made at Waterbury as long ago as 1790. About 1793 Eli Terry went thence to Plymouth and began a manufacture of his own by water-power, his first patent of improvements being taken out in 1797. About 1814 he introduced the new and far more convenient pattern of smaller mantel clocks. Chauncey Jerome began the manufacture of brass clocks about 1821, and with this the modern field of Connecticut ingenuity was opened.

The parts of the clocks were soon made interchangeable, so that one workman could give his entire time to the production of each part, while increased production made the whole clock far cheaper; and the application of machinery to the production of the parts soon made prices still cheaper. In 1840 the value of the clocks produced in the State, almost entirely for home consumption, was over a million dollars, and the manufacturers were ready to reach out after foreign trade. So low had they driven cost and prices that their first exports paid more than 2000% profit. The story goes that the first cargo of Connecticut clocks for the English market was invoiced so low, in spite of this abnormal profit, that the custom-house officers, suspecting undervaluation, enforced their right to take the cargo at its invoice value. This suited the exporters so well that they immediately shipped another cargo, which met the same fate. A third cargo staggered the custom house, and it went out of the clock business. Since that time the world has been supplied with machine-made Connecticut clocks and watches.

The little streams which fall into Long Island Sound are easily dammed, have abundance of water, and have been utilized from the first as a source of power. When Dr. Howe, of New York, invented his machine for making pins at one operation, his most urgent need was for competent mechanics. These could be found only among

INDUSTRIAL DEVELOPMENT. 361

the Connecticut men who had been working on brass clocks, and the manufacture of pins was established at Derby and Birmingham in 1835 and 1838. The making of pins brought with it the establishment of brass-mills for the production of the necessary wire; and the surplus of this production added the manufacture of about everything into which brass plate and wire could be stamped or twisted. Thus a constantly widening field has been offered for the peculiar talents of the Connecticut workman. "He is usually a Yankee of Yankees by birth, and of a temperament thoughtful to dreaminess. His natural bent is strongly towards mechanical pursuits, and he finds his way very early in life into the workshop. Impatient of the fetters which trade societies forge for less independent minds, he delights to make his own bargain with his employer, and, whatever be the work on which he is engaged, bends the whole force of an acute but narrow intelligence to scheming means for accomplishing it easily. Unlike the English mechanic, whom a different education and different circumstances have taught to believe his own interest ill served by facilitating the operations of the workshop, the Connecticut man is profoundly convinced to the contrary. He cherishes a fixed idea of creating a monopoly in some branch of manufacture by establishing an overwhelming superiority over the methods of production already existing in that branch. To 'get up' a machine, or a series of machines, for this purpose, is his one aim and ambition. If he succeeds, supported by patents and the ready aid which capital gives to promising novelties in the States, he may revolutionize an industry, forcing opponents who produce in the old way altogether out of the market, while benefiting the consumer and making his own fortune at the same time. The workshops of Massachusetts, Rhode Island, and especially of Connecticut, are full of such men. Usually tall, thin, reflective, and taciturn, but clever, and, above all things, free, — the equals, although mechanics, of the capitalist upon whose ready alliance they can count, — they are an element of incalculable value to American industry. Their method of attacking manufacturing problems is one which, intelligently handled, must command markets by simultaneously improving qualities and cheapening prices. We ourselves certainly aim, as they do, at the specialization of manufacture, but one scarcely treads upon the threshold of clock-land before feeling how much more universally the system is being applied in the States than here [in England]. Tools and processes which we are inclined to consider as exceptionally clever are the commonplaces of American shops; and the determination to do nothing by hand which can be done by a machine is a marked characteristic of the workmen there, while it scarcely exists among operatives here."

This description, by a competent English observer (Mr. Daniel Pigeon), has been extracted and inserted in spite of the unjust characterization of the workman's intelligence as "narrow," for the sake of the clearer view which is always gained by an observation from the outside. The characteristics which he notes are not at all confined to the clock and brass industries: wherever human ingenuity, in the peculiar form it has taken in Connecticut, can enable a manufactory to compete successfully with its more favorably situated rivals, the attempt has been made to localize it in the commonwealth. When Eli Whitney, of New Haven, had been robbed of the profits of his wonderfully simple invention of the cotton-gin, he turned his attention to the manufacture of arms. The United States government wanted a supply of firearms, and Whitney, without any facilities for making them, took the contract for the work, relying justly on Connecticut ingenuity to find a way. Everything had to be created; but the means on which he relied and with which he succeeded were the persistent substitution of machinery for handwork, the encouragement of invention, and the use of equivalent parts, so that each part could be made by the thousand and yet any part would fit the others. The completion of the contract established a successful arms-factory at Whitneyville, near New Haven. Here, in 1848, Samuel Colt began the manufacture of his revolver, which he had invented while a boy of fifteen, during a voyage to India, and had patented in 1836. In 1850 he removed to Hartford, and the Sharp's Rifle Company followed him the next year. The Winchester Arms Company of New Haven has since taken another variety of work. There have been times when contending armies have both been armed from the little State of Connecticut; and yet the State itself has furnished hardly a particle of the raw material, its entire contribution being the ingenuity of its workmen and the mechanical genius of its inventors.

It would be unjust to leave it to be inferred that this mechanical ingenuity has been narrow in its scope or narrowing in its results. Putting aside such cases as those of Whitney and Goodyear, in which invention has been applied to the broadest and most useful fields, the later records of the commonwealth have been crowded with the names of men who have owed their rise to genius of this type, and have done no discredit to any employment to which the commonwealth has seen fit to call them. To specify would necessarily be to do injustice to those whose names would have to be omitted. One must hold to the general statement that many of the best public servants of the commonwealth, since its great industrial revolution began, have owed their rise to their success in some branch of mechanical industry. Connecticut manufacturers have regularly risen from the ranks, and when they have been transferred from private to public business, they have held their own well in the inevitable comparison with their professional rivals.

The character of the Connecticut workman has led to a peculiar kindness of relations between himself and his employer. It would be impossible to go into particulars of the thoughtfulness of Connecticut employers for their employees, of the well-understood equality of relations between them, and of the consideration of employees for the necessities of employers, without seeming to advertise those few establishments that must be selected for illustration. Any one who will take the trouble to examine for himself into the relations between the real Connecticut workman and his employers need not go far into the State before being satisfied. The institutions which Hooker founded still retain their influence over the descendants of the first settlers.

And yet one cannot but feel some fear for the future of the Connecticut mechanic, and, with him, of Connecticut industries. The tendency of the organization of industry is so strongly toward forms of combination of labor which cannot but be a drawback upon complete individual initiative, that it must be reflected in Connecticut. Indeed, it has already begun to affect the relations between employer and employed. The report of the Connecticut Labor Bureau for 1885 shows, in its accounts of the grievances alleged by employees, and of the remedies which they suggest, a spirit which has not been common in the State heretofore. Whether it is justified or not, is not the question: the main fact is that it exists, and that there is danger that it may result in forms of labor which would be fatal to individualized production. Other commonwealths, more favored by nature, may continue to produce with success under systems which substitute combined for individualized labor. But Connecticut has no such advantage; her long lead in the industrial race has come purely from the high individual ability of her workmen, and any tendency which operates against this element of prosperity cannot but affect the welfare of the commonwealth.

The reputation of the Connecticut workman has been so long established that one is apt to think of the commonwealth of the last century as only a smaller edition of the Connecticut of the present. It has seemed advisable, therefore, to lay stress upon the fact that the Connecticut of the present is the creation of this century; that Connecticut was almost as much an agricultural commonwealth in 1810 as she is now a mechanical and manufacturing commonwealth. How far the forward step which democracy in the State took in 1818 was a cause or only a symptom of the revolution which followed so rapidly, is more than any one can say; but it is difficult to resist the conviction that the relation between them was an intimate one.

Apart from the peculiarly State features of the industrial development, at least one feature of it has had a national and international influence, as Mr. E. E. Hale has pointed out. The Connecticut Joint Stock Act of 1837, framed by Mr. Theodore Hinsdale, a manufacturer of the commonwealth, introduced the corporation in the form under which we now generally know it. Its principle was copied by almost every State of the Union, and by the English Limited Liability Act of 1855; and the effects of its simple principle upon the industrial development of the whole modern world are quite beyond calculation. All that can be done here is to notice the wide influence of a single Connecticut manufacturer's idea, and to call attention to this as another instance of the close connection of democracy with modern industrial development.

The census of 1880 showed that the population of Connecticut was 622,700, of which 492,708 was native and 129,992 foreign. From the eighth State in order of population in 1790, it had fallen to twenty-eighth in 1880. Of this population, 112,915 were at work in the 4,488 factories of the State, the capital of these being $120,480,275, the annual wages $43,501,518; value of materials $102,183,341, and that of the finished product $185,697,211. The manufacture of firearms, clocks, India-rubber goods, wagons and carriages, hardware, britannia and table ware, cutlery, cotton and woolen goods, machinery, and sewing-machines were the leading industries; but patent industries, in which Connecticut leads all the States, are the most numerous sources of her prosperity. The assessed valuation of the State was $228,791,267 for real estate, and $98,386,118 for personal property, these of course representing a much larger real value. With 1.24% of the population of the United States, its people held 3.24% of the national registered bond-debt. There were in 1885 eighty-four savings-banks, with 256,097 depositors, and deposits amounting to $92,481,525; ten stock fire-insurance companies, with assets of $24,040,193; seventeen mutual fire-insurance companies, with assets of $1,195,297; and nine life-insurance companies, with gross receipts of $110,839,326 and liabilities of $99,321,018. There were twenty-two railroads, with a length of 974 miles, and a total value of about $90,000,000. Their general management has been excellent: in 1884 they carried 16,957,574 passengers, of whom but one was fatally injured.

Agriculture still occupied about 45,000 persons, with a capital of about $125,000,000 invested in 30,598 farms, containing 1,642,188 acres of improved and 811,353 acres of unimproved land. The average size of the farms had decreased from 106 acres in 1850, 99 acres in 1860, and 93 acres in 1870, to 80 acres in 1880.

The commonwealth government still remains a comparatively simple one. The annual revenues and expenditures are about a million and a half. About one third of this is drawn from the towns by taxation, another third from taxes on railroad companies, and the bulk of the remainder from taxes on mutual fire-insurance companies and savings-banks. The total debt, December 1, 1885, was $4,271,000; and the permanent school fund, $2,028,124. The principal items of expenditure, outside of interest on the debt, were about $200,000 each for judicial expenses, common schools, and humane institutions, and about $100,000 each for legislative expenses and the militia.

Before closing this brief summary of the material progress of the commonwealth during the century, a still briefer space may fairly be given to its political history during the same period. At the beginning of the century, as has been said already, Connecticut was a steadily Federalist State, and it continued so until the election of 1818, or as long as the Federal party existed. In presidential elections it has been the steadiest in its general opposition to the national Democratic party. It has cast its electoral vote for Federal, Whig, or Republican candidates at every election except five: 1820, 1836, 1852, 1876, and 1884. But the popular majorities have always been very slight; and the feeling of the minority party that it had "a fighting chance" in the State has been kept up by its share of success in the frequently recurring State elections. The pluralities have usually been exceedingly small. In the election of 1884 the Democratic vote was 67,182 and the Republican 65,898, so that the Democratic plurality, which decided the State's electoral vote, was but 1,284, and there was a scattering vote besides of 4,179, or over thrice the deciding plurality.

The completeness of town supremacy over local concerns gave rise to two incidents in the political history of the State, which those who treat of it would willingly pass over in silence, if that were possible. At the very outset of the anti-slavery struggle in 1831 the free negroes of the United States determined to establish a college for their young men, with a mechanical department. New Haven was fixed upon as the location, partly by reason of its academic atmosphere, and partly by reason of the State's advantages for mechanical education. The announcement raised a storm of opposition in New Haven. The city officers and voters, in public meeting, denounced the project, and directed every means to be taken to defeat it. Such action was at once fatal to the proposed college, and it came to nothing. Early in 1833, Prudence Crandall, a young Quaker girl of Windham county, wrote to Garrison that she proposed to turn her girls' school at Canterbury into a school for colored children. The change was carried out during the year, and raised a more angry local storm than that which had been met in New Haven. A town meeting declared the school a nuisance; the pupils were insulted on the streets; the vagrant act was invoked against them without success; and at last the leaders of the opposition went to the general assembly, and obtained the passage of an act forbidding the introduction into the State of negroes from another State, for purposes of instruction, without the written consent of the selectmen of the town. Under the act Miss Crandall was arrested, and by the advice of her friends went to jail for a night. Trial after trial failed to convict her; and "boycotting," as it is now called, was brought into play in its most aggravated forms. Even her church took part, and excluded her from attendance with her pupils. Finally, all other means having failed, her house was broken open at midnight by a mob, the inmates were turned out of doors, and the house and its contents were ruined. Miss Crandall then gave up her enterprise.

One would not care to be retained for the defense in the consideration of the Crandall episode; he can only wonder that Connecticut men could have been guilty of the persecutions which were inflicted upon a girl whose pictured countenance is almost a sufficient plea for her. But there are some points which should be brought to the reader's attention as essential to a just judgment. The commonwealth of Connecticut was a most unfortunate place for such an experiment, simply because of its peculiar local constitution. On the one hand, it was a great responsibility upon a little Windham county town to assume the burden of an odium which far larger places would not have ventured to take up at the time. Towns in other States might shirk responsibility by pleading that such an establishment was the work of a superior power; in a Connecticut town it must be taken as the act and deed of the town itself. On the other hand, the universal feeling in the State, that a town should have the amplest liberty of control in its local affairs, made it easy for the town's controlling influence to get from the general assembly the act recognizing its selectmen's right to decide on this question, — an act whose form was so closely in accord with the general tenor of the Connecticut system that legislators must have felt it difficult to find objections to it, even if they disliked its new principle. Popular passion had thus a strong impelling force and a temptingly clear field before it, and the opportunity thus afforded may do something to explain the whole affair. At least, the second consideration should do something to exonerate the people of the commonwealth at large.

With the exception of these unpleasant features, the political history of the commonwealth has been uneventful, and the only friction yet noticeable is in some points in which the old forms of local government have seemed to become too narrow for the commonwealth's growth. Most of the dissatisfaction has come from the constitution of the general assembly. The representation of the political units of the State in it has always been somewhat peculiar, owing to the survival of the original elements. The lower house has never been considered a popular body: it is the historical representative of the towns, with all their original feeling of town equality. A majority of the lower house need not represent anything approaching a popular majority. The senate was intended to represent the popular majority, but the twenty-four districts from which its members are selected have offered too tempting a prize for gerrymandering to be resisted. In other States, it is the apportionment of the lower house which is usually subjected to this process; in Connecticut, it is the senate. The party which finds itself in a majority on the popular vote, and yet in a minority in the lower house, is apt to charge injustice there also. And yet the historical student, however much he may regret unequal apportionment in the senate, cannot but regret any attempt to disturb the ancient apportionment in the lower house. It is one of the few remnants of the original constitution of the commonwealth, and speaks too plainly the history of Connecticut to be willingly abandoned.

CHAPTER XIX.

CONNECTICUT IN THE WAR FOR THE UNION.

Now that the heat and passion of the war for the Union have so far died away, it must be admitted that the hasty rush into hostilities was largely due to the prevalent belief in the seceding States that the North and West would not fight. The belief rested on different grounds as to the two sections. The West would not fight because it was in her interest to secure peaceable use of the Mississippi, and thus mutual interest was to guard the South from an enemy for whom it had considerable respect. The manufacturing regions of the North would not fight because they dared not; and if they should attempt to fight, the South would ask no better or safer amusement than a conflict with them. History should have taught all men more wisdom: the Flemish artisan had long ago shown the world how his craft could fight upon occasion, and the Northern mechanics only repeated and emphasized the lesson. The aversion to war as an abstract principle was strongest among such as the typical Connecticut workman. He could see no use in it; it was not in the line of his training or ambitions; it interfered seriously with all that he longed to do in the world. All this really made him a more dangerous enemy, for when he was forced into warlike occupation he went to work at it with a peculiar determination to finish the matter and get rid of it as soon as possible. But the average Southerner's opinion was undoubtedly voiced by Governor Hammond of South Carolina, when he said that the "manual laborers and operatives of the North" were "essentially slaves," "the mudsills of society," the difference being that "our slaves are hired for life and are well compensated; yours are hired by the day and not cared for." Above others, he would probably have been amused by the notion of an actual regiment of Connecticut mechanics and tin-peddlers as a possible element in the decision of the great question.

It is a fair instance of the commonwealth's indifference to military glory that her militia system was so completely out of gear in 1861 that she was unable to provide even the single regiment of militia assigned to her in the first call of President Lincoln. Up to the last moment her people were intensely busy with the machinery and mechanical industries which had given them so large a place in the material development of the country.

A remarkable feature of the war was the group of "war governors" who directed the energies of their States during the struggle, and stand out above the mass of those who have occupied the office. To this group Connecticut made a notable contribution in the person of her war governor, William A. Buckingham, of Norwich, one of the class of manufacturers and business men who have so often served the commonwealth. January 17, 1861, he issued his proclamation to the militia of the State, warning them that their services might be needed at any moment, and urging them to be "ready to render such service as any exigency might demand." The ranks of the militia were not filled as they should have been; but the prudent governor, on his personal responsibility, ordered the quartermaster to buy equipments for 5,000 men. They did good service just when they were most needed.

In the spring of 1861, Governor Buckingham was reëlected by a vote of 43,012 to 41,003 for James C. Loomis. April 16, he called for a regiment of volunteers, as there was not even a regiment of organized militia to fill President Lincoln's call on the commonwealth. The step was unauthorized by law, but the governor relied on the general assembly to validate it at the coming session. In this he represented the people exactly, for they had caught fire at the capture of Sumter. More than five times the State's quota volunteered, — fifty-four companies instead of ten. But the curious feature of the case, as illustrating the survival underneath of the primitive constitution of the commonwealth, is the way in which the work was done. The commonwealth was met by an emergency utterly unprovided for by law; the legislature was not in session, and the governor was the only available representative of commonwealth power. All this apparent chaos did not disturb the people in the least. They fell back at once upon the resources of their town system, as they would have done in 1637. Town meetings all over the State met and exercised their reserved powers to tide over the crisis. Money was voted to support the families of volunteers, and to insure a prompt response to the governor's call. By tens and fifteens and twenty-fives, the little towns poured in their contributions of men; the cities and large towns sent larger numbers, and added larger contributions of money; and soon the governor was justified in going to Washington and inducing the administration to accept three regiments from Connecticut instead of one.

When the legislature met in May, it ratified the governor's acts, and appropriated $2,000,000 for military expenses. Extra pay, to the amount of $30 a year, was voted to each enlisted man during the war, besides support for families of volunteers, six dollars per month for the wife and two dollars per month for each child under fourteen. The support was to continue until the expiration of the term of enlistment, even though the soldier should die before that time. Beyond such general acts as these, it may be said with considerable accuracy that the commonwealth organization did little, and had little to do, for the conduct of the war: the war was managed, as far as Connecticut was concerned, by the towns, just as in the American Revolution. Many of them are still staggering under the load of debt which bears witness to their unselfish devotion to the cause.

All through the war, the votes of the two great parties remained about as close as in 1861. The minority contained a "peace party," and its proceedings, raising of peace flags, etc., were a constant exasperation to the people. The legislature met it in a fashion quite characteristic of Connecticut. It voted that any such flag was a "nuisance," to be abated by any constable or justice of the peace of a town, or by the sheriff of the county. Even here, however, unofficial representatives of the towns were usually first to abate the nuisance, as the town committees of safety had done nearly a century before.

The first Connecticut regiment did not reach Washington until May 13. To compensate for the delay, it came perfectly prepared, even to 50,000 rounds of ammunition, and rations and forage for twenty days. The second and third regiments followed within a day or two, all in the same condition of complete preparation. The three took part in the battle of Bull Run. They led the advance, opened the battle, were not demoralized,

and covered the retreat, — a pretty fair record for
"mudsills" in their first battle. To illustrate the
business habits which the Connecticut men carried
into war-making, it is worth while to note that,
when they marched back into their quarters near
Washington, they not only brought their own
camp equipage in perfect condition, but the camp
equipage of three other regiments, and two pieces
of artillery, which they had found abandoned and
had thoughtfully taken possession of on the way.
The three regiments were three-months' men, but
their members reënlisted almost to a man; and
the high character of these first Connecticut representatives
in the field may be estimated from
the fact that more than five hundred of them became
commissioned officers during the war.

Call after call was made for troops, and the old
commonwealth kept her quota more than full.
She had in the service at various times twenty-eight
regiments of infantry, two regiments and
three batteries of artillery, and one regiment and
a squadron of cavalry, numbering 54,882 volunteers
of all terms of service, or, if the terms are
all reduced to a three-years' average, 48,181
three-years' men, 6,698 more than her quota. For
a State with but about 80,000 voters, and about
50,000 able-bodied men on her militia rolls in
1861, the percentage of volunteers is very high;
indeed, not more than one or two States excelled
it. There were 97 officers and 1,094 men killed

in action, 48 officers and 663 men who died from wounds, 63 officers and 3,246 men who died from disease, and 21 officers and 389 men who were reported missing.

The men who filled the Connecticut rolls were to an unusual degree typical of the best elements of the commonwealth's history. Many of the names show that their possessors were of foreign blood or birth, but the mass of them are those which have been familiar to the State since its colonial foundation. It was peculiarly appropriate that almost the first victim should have been Theodore Winthrop of New Haven, for he drew his blood from Connecticut's first governor, John Winthrop. To one who has followed the history of the State with any close attention, the rolls of her regiments are productive of a curious sensation. He finds the same names which he has seen again and again in the town histories; he can almost tell from the recurring names on the rolls the town from which each company was enlisted; and it sometimes seems as if the dead soldiers of the Pequot or King Philip's war had sprung to life again to answer the cry of a new country. And yet the alien names, whose owners made up so large a part of the State's military history, are as fair a reason for satisfaction, for they are a standing proof that Connecticut's catholic spirit of hospitality has been met by a loyal adoption of the institutions and spirit of the old commonwealth.

Any attempt to enumerate the contributions of Connecticut to the military and naval service of the United States must be embarrassing. It would seem unfair to omit the names, like those of Grant and Sherman, of men who drew their blood from Connecticut, and their powers for good from the institutions of her founders; and yet such a list would stretch out far beyond the space which could possibly be given to it. But even though the attention is confined to the commonwealth's more direct contributions, the list is long enough to be embarrassing. To the navy, Connecticut contributed its secretary, Gideon Welles, rear admirals Andrew H. Foote of New Haven, and F. H. Gregory of Norwalk, and commodores John Rogers and C. R. P. Rogers of New London, and R. B. Hitchcock. In the army, Winthrop has been mentioned already. Among the Connecticut major-generals were Alfred H. Terry of New Haven, Darius N. Couch of Norwalk, John Sedgwick of Cornwall Hollow, J. K. F. Mansfield of Middletown, Jos. A. Mower of New London, J. R. Hawley of Hartford, H. W. Birge of Norwich, and R. O. Tyler of Hartford; and among the brigadier-generals, Nathaniel Lyon of Eastford, G. A. Stedman of Hartford, O. S. Ferry of Norwalk, Daniel Tyler and Edward Harland of Norwich, and A. von Steinwehr of Wallingford. So large a contribution of distinguished officers is doubly remarkable as coming from so small a

State, and from a State which did not enter the conflict out of any diseased passion for military glory, but simply out of the national necessity of the case. If we should attempt to pass below the higher grades of officers, the list of Connecticut men who fought their way into command of regiments or companies, in the service of their own or other States, would be almost endless. Commonwealth and towns have marked their gratitude to their representatives in the war. They have shown that a commonwealth's aversion to war is entirely compatible with the most unyielding stubbornness when it is forced upon her, and that the eminence of her sons in the arts of peace can never again be taken as a safe indication that they are easy victims for attack. It was with no small pride that the people of Connecticut watched the close of the war, as one of her children held Lee's army in an iron grasp on the James, while another was moving up irresistibly from the far South, sweeping up the remaining forces of the Confederacy into a great net, from which there was no escape. And the military historian of the commonwealth may well be permitted to close this chapter for her : —

"The first great martyrs of the war — Ellsworth, Winthrop, Ward, and Lyon — were of Connecticut stock. A Connecticut general, with Connecticut regiments, opened the battle of Bull Run and closed it; and a Connecticut regiment was marshaled in front of the farm-house at Appomattox when Lee surrendered to a soldier of Connecticut blood. A Connecticut flag first displaced the palmetto upon the soil of South Carolina; a Connecticut flag was first planted in Mississippi; a Connecticut flag was first unfurled before New Orleans. Upon the reclaimed walls of Pulaski, Donelson, Macon, Jackson, St. Philip, Morgan, Wagner, Sumter, Fisher, our State left its ineffaceable mark. The sons of Connecticut followed the illustrious grandson of Connecticut as he swung his army with amazing momentum from the fastnesses of Tennessee to the Confederacy's vital centre. At Antietam, Gettysburg, and in all the fierce campaigns of Virginia, our soldiers won crimson glories; and at Port Hudson they were the very first and readiest. . . . On the banks of every river of the South, and in the battle-smoke of every contested ridge and mountain-peak, the sons of Connecticut have stood and patiently struggled. In every ransomed State we have a holy acre on which the storm has left its emerald waves, — three thousand indistinguishable hillocks on lonely lake and stream, in field and tangled thicket."

If the writer of the foregoing paragraph had repeated the stately dirge of the general court of two hundred years ago, it would have been but a just connection between the spirit of the fathers and of their children: "The bitter cold, the tarled swamp, the tedious march, the strong fort, the numerous and stubborn enemy they contended with, for their God, king, and country, be their trophies over death. . . . Our mourners, over all the colony, witness for our men that they were not unfaithful in that day."

CHAPTER XX.

CONCLUSION.

ONE can hardly study the history of the commonwealth of Connecticut without receiving a stronger sense of the impression which institutions can make upon a people. Of course, the institutions of the commonwealth of 1639 were but the embodiment of the natures of the people who framed them; they were made as they were because their people could not live comfortably under any others. But the original people, few as they were in number and feeble in resources, were acting for a multitude whom none of them could have numbered. Indirect as the connection may seem, there is not an individual in the commonwealth, or indeed in the United States, who does not owe something to the will of Thomas Hooker and his people that democracy should be the rule of their commonwealth.

Some one has said that nothing in our national system has been permanently good or successful unless it was originally drawn from the State systems. The idea is very far from fanciful, and in it is one of the claims of Connecticut to a place among the commonwealths which have strongly influenced the national development of the United States. The facts that the Massachusetts Court of Assistants, in 1630–34, was determined to ignore the towns in the new government, that the towns found it difficult to compel recognition without a conflict with the church, and that there was a wilderness to the southwest, were not particularly important in themselves; but in them was the germ of the American Senate and House of Representatives, and of the principles on which the American commonwealths were at last united into one federal system. The judicial position given by circumstances to the Connecticut delegates in the convention of 1787 would have been of no value whatever if the delegates had not had something in their hands to offer for the convention's consideration, and that something the institutions of Connecticut had been brooding over for a hundred and fifty years. There was probably not a public man in Connecticut in 1787 who was not prepared to accept the peculiar federative idea of the constitution, if it should be presented to him; his commonwealth democracy had prepared him for it. The selection of their ablest representatives to go to Philadelphia was only a step in the evolution of those who were competent to suggest the idea, not simply to accept it. They were but the medium of communication; behind them was the history of the commonwealth for a century and a half, and behind that the primitive democracy.

It would be difficult to find anything new to say of the virtues and force of the Puritan of 1630-60, who, as Macaulay puts it, " brought to civil and military affairs a coolness of judgment and an immutability of purpose which some writers have thought inconsistent with religious zeal, but which were in fact the necessary effects of it." Nowhere is this combination of coolness of judgment and firmness of purpose more notable than in the early history of Connecticut. And yet it had its drawbacks. Such an ecclesiastical system as theirs is always spoken of as if it were an intrusion of religion into civil affairs. In fact, it is really objectionable in that it always turns out to be just the opposite, — an intrusion of civil affairs into religion. Even in founding a democracy, the makers of Connecticut made it one in which He whose kingdom is not of this world would have been quite out of place. The perfection of a machine is in its power to correct its own errors. After all, the crowning testimony to the perfection of the political machine which was set going on the banks of the Connecticut is that it did not allow religion and democracy to corrupt one another permanently, that it eliminated the evils of their junction as they appeared, and that it severed the unnatural bond of union just as soon as it could be done.

Finally, the Connecticut system was one which developed high individual energy and capacity, though in later times, when the spread of democracy among all the American commonwealths has given all men the same privileges, it has shown itself most prominently in the development of the Connecticut mechanic. Government never was, to the Connecticut man, an institution against which he was to lean for rest; or which he was to use for the purpose of evading the consequences of his own heedlessness; or which was to swallow up his personality. It was to him a thing of special purpose, to be restricted to its narrowest effective limits, and to be worked, like any other machine, to its highest capacity within its proper limits. He saw in government of any sort his creature, not his maker. If his fellows saw in him the capacity to act as a part of the governmental machine, he would sink his own personality in it; but the act was voluntary, a sacrifice for the sake of the commonwealth, not an involuntary absorption into a higher personality. In these later days, when the individual is withering at a rate faster than seems to be altogether convenient, when it is believed that democracy and individualism are no longer quite convertible terms, there may be a useful lesson in the record of the commonwealth of Connecticut, — unbroken success so far as she has followed out her fundamental principle, embarrassment and danger only so far as she has allowed it to be infringed.

APPENDIX.

THE CONSTITUTION OF 1639.

(Abbreviations only are modernized.)

FORASMUCH as it hath pleased the Allmighty God by the wise disposition of his diuyne providence so to Order and dispose of things that we the Inhabitants and Residents of Windsor, Harteford and Wethersfield are now cohabiting and dwelling in and vppon the River of Conectecotte and the Lands thereunto adioyneing; And well knowing where a people are gathered together the word of God requires that to mayntayne the peace and vnion of such a people there should be an orderly and decent Gouerment established according to God, to order and dispose of the affayres of the people at all seasons as occation shall require; doe therefore assotiate and conioyne our selues to be as one Publike State or Commonwelth; and doe, for our selues and our Successors and such as shall be adioyned to vs att any tyme hereafter, enter into Combination and Confederation togather, to mayntayne and presearue the liberty and purity of the gospell of our Lord Jesus which we now professe, as also the disciplyne of the Churches, which according to the truth of the said gospell is now practised amongst vs; As also in our Ciuell Affaires to be guided and gouerned according to such Lawes, Rules, Orders and decrees as shall be made, ordered & decreed, as followeth:—

1. It is Ordered, sentenced and decreed, that there shall be yerely two generall Assemblies or Courts, the first on the second thursday in Aprill, the other the second thursday in September, following; the first shall be called the Courte of Election, wherein shall be yerely Chosen from tyme to tyme soe many Magestrats and other publike Officers as shall be found requisitte; Whereof one to be chosen Gouernour for the yeare ensueing and vntill another be chosen, and noe other Magestrate to be chosen for more than one yeare; provided alwayes there be sixe chosen besids the Gouernour; which being chosen and sworn according to an Oath recorded for that purpose shall haue power to administer justice according to the Lawes here established, and for want thereof according to the rule of the word of God; which choise shall be made by all that are admitted freemen and haue taken the Oath of Fidellity, and doe cohabitte within this Jurisdiction, (hauing beene admitted Inhabitants by the major part of the Towne wherein they liue) [1] or the mayor parte of such as shall be then present.

2. It is Ordered, sentensed and decreed, that the Election of the aforesaid Magestrats shall be on this manner: euery person present and quallified for choyse shall bring in (to the persons deputed to receaue them) one single paper with the name of him written in yt whom he desires to haue Gouernour, and he that hath

---

[1] Inserted at a later period.

the greatest number of papers shall be Gouernour for that yeare. And the rest of the Magestrats or publike Officers to be chosen in this manner: The Secretary for the tyme being shall first read the names of all that are to be put to choise and then shall seuerally nominate them distinctly, and euery one that would haue the person nominated to be chosen shall bring in one single paper written vppon, and he that would not haue him chosen shall bring in a blanke; and euery one that hath more written papers than blanks shall be a Magestrat for that yeare; which papers shall be receaued and told by one or more that shall be then chosen by the court and sworne to be faythfull therein; but in case there should not be sixe chosen as aforesaid, besids the Gouernor, out of those which are nominated, then he or they which haue the most written papers shall be a Magestrate or Magestrats for the ensueing yeare, to make vp the foresaid number.

3. It is Ordered, sentenced and decreed, that the Secretary shall not nominate any person, nor shall any person be chosen newly into the Magestracy which was not propownded in some Generall Courte before, to be nominated the next Election; and to that end yt shall be lawfull for ech of the Townes aforesaid by their deputyes to nominate any two whom they conceaue fitte to be putte to Election; and the Courte may ad so many more as they iudge requisitt.

4. It is Ordered, sentenced and decreed that noe person be chosen Gouernor aboue once in two yeares, and that the Gouernor be alwayes a member of some approved congregation, and formerly of the Magestracy within this Jurisdiction; and all the Magestrats Free-

men of this Commonwelth : and that no Magestrate or other publike officer shall execute any parte of his or their Office before they are seuerally sworne, which shall be done in the face of the Courte if they be present, and in case of absence by some deputed for that purpose.

5. It is Ordered, sentenced and decreed, that to the aforesaid Courte of Election the seuerall Townes shall send their deputyes, and when the Elections are ended they may proceed in any publike searuice as at other Courts. Also the other Generall Courte in September shall be for makeing of lawes, and any other publike occation which conserns the good of the Commonwelth.

6. It is Ordered, sentenced and decreed, that the Gouernor shall, either by himselfe or by the secretary, send out summons to the Constables of euery Towne for the cauleing of these two standing Courts, one month at lest before their seuerall tymes : And also if the Gouernor and the gretest parte of the Magestrats see cause vppon any spetiall occation to call a generall Courte, they may giue order to the secretary soe to doe within fowerteene dayes warneing : and if vrgent necesslty so require, vppon a shorter notice, glueing sufficient grownds for yt to the deputyes when they meete, or els be questioned for the same ; And if the Gouernor and Mayor parte of Magestrats shall ether neglect or refuse to call the two Generall standing Courts or ether of them, as also at other tymes when the occations of the Commonwelth require, the Freemen thereof, or the Mayor parte of them, shall petition to them soe to doe : if then yt be ether denyed or neglected the said Freemen or the Mayor parte of them shall haue power to giue order to the

APPENDIX. 393

Constables of the seuerall Townes to doe the same, and so may meete togather, and chuse to themselues a Moderator, and may proceed to do any Acte of power, which any other Generall Courte may.

7. It is Ordered, sentenced and decreed that after there are warrants giuen out for any of the said Generall Courts, the Constable or Constables of ech Towne shall forthwith give notice distinctly to the inhabitants of the same, in some Publike Assembly or by goeing or sending from howse to howse, that at a place and tyme by him or them lymited and sett, they meet and assemble themselues togather to elect and chuse certen deputyes to be att the Generall Courte then following to agitate the afayres of the commonwelth; which said Deputyes shall be chosen by all that are admitted Inhabitants in the seuerall Townes and haue taken the oath of fidellity; prouided that non be chosen a Depnty for any Generall Courte which is not a Freeman of this Commonwelth. .

The foresaid deputyes shall be chosen in manner following: euery person that is present and quallified as before expressed, shall bring the names of such, written in seuerall papers, as they desire to haue chosen for that Imployment, and these 3 or 4, more or lesse, being the number agreed on to be chosen for that tyme, that haue greatest number of papers written for them shall be deputyes for that Courte; whose names shall be endorsed on the backe side of the warrant and returned into the Courte, with the Constable or Constables hand vnto the same.

8. It is Ordered, sentenced and decreed, that Wyndsor, Hartford and Wethersfield shall haue power, ech

Towne, to send fower of their freemen as their deputyes to euery Generall Courte; and whatsoeuer other Townes shall be hereafter added to this Jurisdiction, they shall send so many deputyes as the Courte shall judge meete, a resonable proportion to the number of freemen that are in the said Townes being to be attended therein; which deputyes shall haue the power of the whole Towne to giue their voats and alowance to all such lawes and orders as may be for the publike good, and unto which the said Townes are to be bownd.

9. It is Ordered and decreed, that the deputyes thus chosen shall haue power and liberty to appoynt a tyme and a place of meeting togather before any Generall Courte to aduise and consult of all such things as may concerne the good of the publike, as also to examine their owne Elections, whether according to the order, and if they or the gretest parte of them find any such election to be illegall they may seclud such for present from their meeting, and returne the same and their resons to the Courte; and if yt proue true, the Courte may fyne the party or partyes so intruding and the Towne, if they see cause, and giue out a warrant to goe to a newe election in a legall way, ether in parte or in whole. Also the said deputyes shall haue power to fyne any that shall be disorderly at their meetings, or for not comming in due tyme or place according to appoyntment; and they may returne the said fynes into the Courte if yt be refused to be paid, and the Tresurer to take notice of yt, and to estreete or levy the same as he does other fynes.

10. It is Ordered, sentenced and decreed, that euery Generall Courte, except such as through neglect of the

Gouernor and the greatest parte of Magestrats the Freemen themselves doe call, shall consist of the Gouernor, or some one chosen to moderate the Court, and 4 other Magestrats at lest, with the mayor parte of the deputyes of the seuerall Townes legally chosen; and in case the Freemen or mayor parte of them, through neglect or refusall of the Gouernor and mayor parte of the magestrats, shall call a Courte, yt shall consist of the mayor parte of Freemen that are present or their deputyes, with a Moderator chosen by them: In which said Generall Courts shall consist the supreme power of the Commonwelth, and they only shall haue power to make lawes or repeale them, to graunt leuyes, to admitt of Freemen, dispose of lands vndisposed of, to seuerall Townes or persons, and also shall haue power to call ether Courte or Magestrate or any other person whatsoeuer into question for any misdemeanour, and may for just causes displace or deale otherwise according to the nature of the offence; and also may deale in any other matter that concerns the good of this commonwelth, excepte election of Magestrats, which shall be done by the whole boddy of Freemen.

In which Courte the Gouernour or Moderator shall haue power to order the Courte to giue liberty of spech, and silence vnceasonable and disorderly speakeings, to put all things to voate, and in case the voate be equall to haue the casting voice. But non of these Courts shall be adiorned or dissolued without the conseut of the maior parte of the Court.

11. It is ordered, sentenced and decreed, that when any Generall Courte vppon the occatious of the Commonwelth haue agreed vppon any summe or summes of

mony to be leuyed vppon the seuerall Townes within this Jurisdiction, that a Committee be chosen to sett out and appoynt what shall be the proportion of euery Towne to pay of the said leuy, provided the Committees be made vp of an equall number out of each Towne.

14th January, 1638, the 11 Orders abouesaid are voted.

[Until 1752, the legal year in England began March 25 (Lady Day), not January 1. All the days between January 1 and March 25 of the year which we now call 1639 were therefore then a part of the year 1638; so that the date of the Constitution is given by its own terms as 1638, instead of 1639. The whole document may be found in *Connecticut Public Records*, I. 20–25.]

BIBLIOGRAPHY.

1. The general histories of the United States: BANCROFT, HILDRETH, BRYANT and GAY, SCHOULER, MCMASTER, PITKIN, HOLMES, et als.

2. PALFREY'S History of New England; SAVAGE'S Winthrop's History of New England; BRADFORD'S New England Chronology; HUBBARD'S General History of New England; OLIVER'S Puritan Commonwealth, chapter ii, (Episcopalian view); BACKUS'S History of New England (Baptist view); CHURCH'S History of King Philip's War; DRAKE'S French and Indian War in New England; Mass. Hist. Soc. Publications, particularly GARDENER'S Relation of the Pequot Wars, and VINCENT'S True Relation; MATHER'S Magnalia Christi; BACON'S Genesis of the New England Churches; FELT'S Ecclesiastical History of New England.

3. DOYLE'S American Colonies; LODGE'S English Colonies in America; FORCE'S Colonial Tracts.

4. HUTCHINSON'S History of Massachusetts; ARNOLD'S History of Rhode Island; BARTLETT'S Records of Rhode Island; HALL'S History of Vermont; BRODHEAD'S History of New York; O'CALLAGHAN'S History of New Netherlands; 2 O'CALLAGHAN'S Documentary History of New York (Leisler Administration); HAZARD'S Pennsylvania Archives; SHEAFER'S Historical Map of Pennsylvania; REGENTS' Report on the Boundaries of the State of New York; BOWEN'S Boundary Disputes of Connecticut; PRIME'S History of Long Island; THOMPSON'S History of Long Island; WOOD'S First Settlement of Long Island Towns.

5. The general histories of Connecticut: TRUMBULL, DWIGHT, HOLLISTER, and CARPENTER and ARTHUR; ATWATER'S History

of New Haven; LEVERMORE's Republic of New Haven; LAMBERT's History of New Haven Colony; Colonial Records of Connecticut, edited by J. H. TRUMBULL and C. J. HOADLY; Colonial Records of New Haven, edited by HOADLY; BARBER's Connecticut Historical Collections.

6. Connecticut Historical Society Proceedings, particularly HOOKER's Letter to Winthrop, BULKELEY's People's Right to Election, HOADLY's Public Seal of Connecticut, The Hartford Church Controversy, and Correspondence of Silas Deane; New Haven Historical Society Papers, particularly BACON's Civil Government in New Haven, TROWBRIDGE's History of the Long Wharf, BRONSON's Connecticut Currency, WHITAKER's Early History of Southold, GOODRICH's Invasion of New Haven, DEXTER's Memoranda on the Regicides, TROWBRIDGE's Ancient Houses in New Haven, BEARDSLEY's Mohegan Land Controversy, E. C. BALDWIN's Branford Annals, S. E. BALDWIN's New York Boundary Line, BRONSON's Early Government of Connecticut, and DEXTER's Early Relations between New Netherland and New England; Connecticut Valley Historical Society Papers, particularly the Review of PETERS's History; PERCIVAL's Geology of Connecticut. See also the Introduction to PALFREY; DE FOREST's Indians of Connecticut; 2 HAZARD's State Papers (New England Commissioners); BRODHEAD's Government of Sir Edmund Andros.

7. J. H. TRUMBULL's Notes on the Constitutions of Connecticut, and True Blue Laws; PETERS's General History of Connecticut; HINMAN's Code of 1650, and Antiquities of Connecticut; FOWLER's Local Law in Connecticut; BACON's Contributions to the Ecclesiastical History of Connecticut; BEARDSLEY's History of the Episcopal Church in Connecticut; JOHNSTON's Genesis of a New England State (Connecticut).

8. MINER's History of Wyoming; H. M. HOYT's Brief of the Wyoming Title, with the very complete bibliography at page 101, the volume being the fairest and best account of the controversy that I have found.

9. PHELPS's History of the Newgate of Connecticut; ELLIOT's Debates; President DWIGHT's Travels in New England and New York; WOOD's Administration of John Adams; GOODRICH's Recollections of a Life-Time; DWIGHT's History of the

APPENDIX. 899

Hartford Convention; ADAMS's New England Federalism (Gould's letter); J. H. TRUMBULL's Defence of Stonington; BUSHNELL's Historical Estimate of Connecticut (in his Work and Play); BISHOP's History of American Manufactures; An Historical and Industrial Review of Connecticut (1884); E. E. HALE's Brown Univ. Address; EVEREST's Poets of Connecticut; FRENCH's Art and Artists in Connecticut; CROFFUT and MORRIS's History of Connecticut during the Recent War.

10. STUART's Hartford in the Olden Time; TRUMBULL's History of Hartford County (the first volume has been used most largely); WALKER's 250th Anniversary of the First Church of Hartford; STILES's History of Ancient Windsor, and Supplement; HALL's History of Norwalk; CAULKINS's History of New London, and History of Norwich; HUNTINGTON's History of Stamford; MEAD's History of Greenwich; GARDINER's Notes on East Hampton (N. Y. Hist. Soc. Pub., 1869); HOLLAND's History of Western Massachusetts; MORRIS's Early History of Springfield, Mass.; COTHREN's History of Ancient Woodbury; CHAPIN's History of Glastenbury; LARNED's History of Windham County; KILBOURNE's Biographical History of Litchfield County; WOODRUFF's History of Litchfield; BRONSON's History of Waterbury; ROY's History of Norfolk; DAVIS's History of Wallingford and Meriden; TAINTOR's Records of Colchester; PHELPS's History of Simsbury, Granby, and Canton; BOYD's Annals of Winchester; ANDREWS's History of New Britain; FOWLER's History of Durham; TODD's History of Redding; SHARPE's History of Seymour; ORCUTT's History of Wolcott, and History of Torrington; DEXTER's New Haven in 1784, and Town Names in Connecticut.

11. KINGSLEY's Historical Discourse, New Haven, 1838; BACON's Historical Discourses, New Haven, 1838; WOOLSEY's Historical Discourse, Yale College, 1850; Litchfield County Centennial Addresses, 1851; FIELD's Centennial Address, Middletown, 1853; GILMAN's Historical Address, Norwich, 1859; W. L. KINGSLEY's Yale College: A Sketch of its History.

12. ALLEN's Biographical Dictionary; SPARKS's Library of American Biography; WINTHROP's Life and Letters of Winthrop (senior); Mass. Hist. Soc. Coll., ser. 5, vol. 8 (Winthrop Papers); New York Hist. Soc. Coll., ser. 2, vol. ii.; MOORE's

Memoir of Eaton; STILES's History of the Regicides; WARREN's Three Judges; STUART's Life of Jonathan Trumbull; BEARDSLEY's Life of William Samuel Johnson; HUMPHREYS's Life of Putnam; CUTLER's Life of Putnam; WOLCOTT Memorial; HOLMES's Life of President Stiles; SPRAGUE's Life of President Dwight; WESTCOTT's Life of John Fitch; GOODWIN's Genealogical Notes; FLANDERS' or VAN SANTVOORD's Lives of the Chief Justices (for Ellsworth); LOSSING's or SANDERSON's Lives of the Signers (for Sherman, Huntington, Williams, and Wolcott); WARD's Life of Percival; PIERCE's Life of Goodyear; HOWE's Eminent Mechanics; HOPPIN's Life of A. H. Foote; STOWE's Men of Our Time (for W. A. Buckingham).

THE GOVERNORS OF CONNECTICUT.

These were chosen annually until 1876, and thereafter for two years. Until John Winthrop's second election, immediate reëlection was forbidden.

1639–40, John Haynes.
1640–41, Edward Hopkins.
1641–42, John Haynes.
1642–43, George Wyllys.
1643–44, John Haynes.
1644–45, Edward Hopkins.
1645–46, John Haynes.
1646–47, Edward Hopkins.
1647–48, John Haynes.
1648–49, Edward Hopkins.
1649–50, John Haynes.
1650–51, Edward Hopkins.
1651–52, John Haynes.
1652–53, Edward Hopkins.
1653–54, John Haynes.
1654–55, Edward Hopkins.
1655–56, Thomas Welles.
1656–57, John Webster.
1657–58, John Winthrop.
1658–59, Thomas Welles.
1659–76, John Winthrop.
1676–83, William Leete.
1683–87, Robert Treat.
1687–89, (Andros.)
1689–98, Robert Treat.
1698–1707, Fitz John Winthrop.
1707–24, Gurdon Saltonstall.
1724–41, Joseph Talcott.
1741–50, Jonathan Law.
1750–54, Roger Wolcott.
1754–66, Thomas Fitch.
1766–69, William Pitkin.
1769–84, Jonathan Trumbull.
1784–86, Matthew Griswold.
1786–96, Samuel Huntington.
1796–98, Oliver Wolcott.
1798–1809, Jonathan Trumbull.
1809–11, John Treadwell.
1811–13, Roger Griswold.
1813–17, John Cotton Smith.
1817–27, Oliver Wolcott.
1827–31, Gideon Tomlinson.
1831–33, John S. Peters.
1833–34, H. W. Edwards.

CONNECTICUT.

1834–35, Samuel A. Foote.
1835–38, H. W. Edwards.
1838–42, W. W. Ellsworth.
1842–44, C. F. Cleveland.
1844–46, Roger S. Baldwin.
1846–49, Clark Bissell.
1849–50, Joseph Trumbull.
1850–54, Thomas H. Seymour.
1854–55, Henry Dutton.
1855–57, W. T. Minor.
1857–58, A. H. Holley.
1858–66, W. A. Buckingham.
1866–67, Joseph R. Hawley.
1867–69, James E. English.
1869–70, Marshall Jewell.
1870–71, James E. English.
1871–73, Marshall Jewell.
1873–76, Charles R. Ingersoll.
1876–79, R. D. Hubbard.
1879–81, Charles B. Andrews.
1881–83, H. B. Bigelow.
1883–85, Thomas M. Waller.
1885–87, Henry B. Harrison.
1887–89, Phineas T. Lounsbury.

INDEX.

ABERCROMBIE, Gen. James, 261.
Adams, Prof. H. B., 135.
Agawam, 56.
Agriculture, 3, 330, 338, 342, 357, 368.
Albany, N. Y., 251, 259, 276.
Allen, Ethan, 272, 283.
Allen, Ira, 272.
Allyn, John, 81, 160, 202, 266.
Alsop, Richard, 340.
Andrew, Samuel, 340.
Andrews, William, 92.
Andros, Sir Edmund, 125; at Saybrook, 194, 195; in New York, 197; in Connecticut, 199; at Hartford, 200; supports Rhode Island, 213; downfall, 203.
Annapolis Convention, 318.
Ansonia, 358.
Argal, Captain, 146.
Arnold, Benedict, 40, 292, 303; at New London, 312, 314.
Aspinwall, Dr. William, 342.
Assistants, in Massachusetts, 65 foll., 386; in Connecticut, 172, 190, 269.
Atherton Company, 211, 214.

BACON, Dr. Leonard, 98.
Ballot, the, 77.
Bangs, Dr. Nathan, 356.
Banks, 338, 368.
Baptism, 225.
Baptists, the, 236.
Barbadoes, 267.
"Battle of the Kegs," 297.
Beach, Rev. John, 302.
Beach, Dr. John W., 356.
Belcher, Gov. Jonathan, 300.
Bellows' Falls, 299.
Berkeley, Bishop, 242.
Berlin, 357, 358.
Birge, Gen. H. W., 381.
Birmingham, 361.
Blake, Admiral, 155.
Block Island, 31.
Blok, Adrian, 7.
"Blue Laws," 105.

Blue-lights, 350.
Boundaries: disputes, 114; with the Dutch, 148; under the charter, 168, 173, 273; with New York, 193, 205, 207; with Massachusetts, 207, 209, 271; with Rhode Island, 209 foll.
Boroughs, 337.
Boston, 84, 116, 203, 266, 288, 292.
Boteler, Lady Alice, 112, 117.
Brainard, J. G. C., 340.
Brandt, 278.
Branford, admission to New Haven, 106; settlement, 138; meeting at, 239.
Brass, 361 foll.
Bridgeport, 337, 359.
Bromfield, Major, 313.
Brooke, Lord, 8, 110, 168.
Brotherton tribe, the, 54, 55.
Brownell, Bishop, 355.
Buckingham, Gov. Wm. A., 376.
Buildings, 124.
Bull, Captain Thomas, 194, 195, 251.
Bull Run, 378-9, 382.
Bunker Hill, 292.
Bushnell, David, 296.
Butler, John, 278.

CABOTS, the, 7, 11, 145.
Capital city, 174, 270, 354.
Cambridge, Mass., 60.
Cambridge platform, the, 226.
Canonchet, 28, 53.
Canterbury, 370.
Carlisle Grant, the, 8.
Carthagena expedition, the, 256.
Cassasinamon, 51.
Cemeteries, 340.
Charter, the, 170 foll., 199, 201, 202, 204, 347, 356.
Charter Oak, the, 25, 123, 200, 204.
Chase, Bishop, 351.
Chauncey, Nathanael, 240.
Cheevers, Ezekiel, 92.
Cheneys, the, 342.
Cheshire, 355.

Chipmans, the, 272.
Chittenden, Gov. Thomas, 272.
Choate, Rufus, 209.
Church and commonwealth, 77, 221, 224, 228, 232, 233, 347, 354-355, 387.
Church and town, 6, 59, 220, 224, 229, 236, 268.
Church of England, the, 235, 236, 242; in the Revolution, 302; after the Revolution, 346; in 1818, 352.
Cincinnati, the Society of the, 317.
Cities, 337, 338.
Clap, Pres. Thomas, 243.
Clocks, 359 foll.
Coal, 345, 358.
Colt, Samuel, 363.
Commerce, 339.
Common lands, 95, 97.
Confederation, articles of, 315.
Congregational Church, the, 60, 222, 230, 345; see Establishment, the.
Congress, 320 foll.
Congressmen, election of, 333.
Connecticut River, the, 2, 7, 8, 17, 23, 272, 358; imposts, 115, 143, 153.
Connecticut, position and boundaries, 1; area, 2; products, 3; harbors, 4; granted to Plymouth Company, 7; title, 8, 11; commonwealth of, 12; settlement, 20; constitution, 63; seal, 73; motto, 74; territorial claims, 102; social conditions, 128; colonial policy, 129, 289; regicides in, 165; charter, 166 foll., 285; the Andros episode, 199; in 1680, 265; population, 270; final territory, 281; in the Revolution, 294, 310; becomes a State, 304; influence in forming the constitution, 320 foll., 386; industrial development, 328 foll.; politics, 345, 369 foll.; in the war of 1812, 349 foll.; in the war for the Union, 374 foll.
Constables, 78, 79, 135, 174, 180, 181, 210, 268, 335.
Constitution of the United States, the, 319 foll.
Constitution of 1639, adopted, 63; origin, 73; provisions, 74 and Appendix; democratic nature, 79.
Constitution of 1818, 337, 353, 357.
Convention of 1787, the, 319 foll., 386.
Copper, 3, 300.
Cornbury, Edward Hyde, Lord, 253.
Corporation Act, the, 367.
Cotton, John, 17, 65, 69.
Cotton-gin, the, 363.
Couch, Gen. D. N., 381.
Council, the, 269, 332.
Counties, 189, 190.
Country pay, 249.

Courts, 57, 190, 354; in New Haven, 93, 104.
Covenant, owning the, 227.
Crandall, Prudence, 370.
Cromwell, Oliver, 154, 155, 164.
"Cuba," the, 299.
Cummings, Dr. Joseph, 356.
Cutler, Rev. Timothy, 242.

DAGGETT, Rev. Naphtali, 244.
Danbury, 303.
Darley, Henry, 110.
Dartmouth College, 55.
Davenport, Rev. John, 82, 92, 221; his "fundamental orders," 90; removal to Boston, 160; dealings with the regicides, 164; on the union with Connecticut, 175 foll.; proposal of a college, 239.
Day, Pres. Jeremiah, 245.
Deane, Silas, 291.
Debt, 369.
Decatur, Commodore Stephen, 350.
Delaware Company, formed, 146; failure, 147.
Democracy in Massachusetts, 64, 132; in Connecticut, 63, 70, 77, 79, 141, 205, 220, 226, 261, 318, 356, 366, 385-387.
Democratic party, 345-48, 352, 353, 369.
Deputies, 76, 80, 172, 268.
Derby, 267, 343, 361.
Dissenters, 231, 234, 238, 346, 347, 352.
Dixon, Jeremiah, 92.
Dongan, Gov. Thomas, 199, 205.
Dorchester, 17, 24.
Dudley, Joseph, 190, 218, 253.
Dummer, Fort, 271.
Dutch, the, in Connecticut, 7, 14, 16, 21, 23, 30, 51; fort at Hartford, 122, 148, 154; intercourse with New England, 144; treaty of Hartford, 148; conquered, 188, 193, 260.
Dutch West India Company, the, 145, 147.
Dwight, Pres. Timothy, 232.
Dwight, Pres. Timothy, 245.
Dwight, Theodore, 340.

EAST Hampton, L. I., 135, 138.
Eaton, Rev. Samuel, 88.
Eaton, Theophilus, 84, 92, 138; house, 89; "magistrate," 93; governor, 103; death, 158; family, 159.
Ecclesiastical affairs, 220 foll., 387.
Edwards, Pierpont, 338.
Edwards, Rev. Jonathan, 232.
Election laws, 77, 332, 354.
Election sermon, 334.
Eliot, John, 19, 54.
Eliot, Dr. Samuel, 355.
Ellsworth, Col. E. E., 381.

INDEX. 405

Ellsworth, Oliver, 319, 325, 327.
Endicott, John, 32.
Episcopal Church (see Church of England).
Establishment, the, 231, 234, 237, 345, 347.

FAIRFIELD, 20, 44, 135, 308.
Farmington, 135.
Feake, Robert, 150.
Federal party, 345–346, 350, 352.
Feldspar, 4.
Fenwick, George, 8, 110; comes to Saybrook, 112; commissioner, 113; sells Saybrook, 115; death, 117.
Ferry, Gen. O. S., 381.
Financial affairs, 248 foll.
Fire-arms, 363–364.
"Fire Lands," 282, 309.
Fish, 5.
Fisher's Island, 140, 207.
Fitch, Gov. Thomas, 287.
Fitch, John, 126.
Fitch, Rev. James, 54, 113, 218.
Five Nations, the, 27.
Fletcher, Gov. Benjamin, 195, 204.
Foote, Admiral A. H., 381.
"Forty Fort," 277.
Foss, Dr. Cyrus, 356.
Franklin, Benjamin, 259, 286, 325.
Free burgesses, 91, 103.
Free planters, 86, 91, 92, 103, 177.
French in Connecticut, the, 312.
French wars, 250 foll.
Fugill, Thomas, 92.

GALLOP, John, 31.
Gardiner, Lyon, 33, 112.
Garret, Hermon, 51.
Garrison, W. L., 370.
General Assembly, 269, 290, 354, 373.
General Court, 34, 57, 58; powers, 75; organization, 78; (see General Assembly.)
General election, 333.
George, battle of Lake, 259.
Gilbert, Matthew, 92.
Goddard, Calvin, 351.
Goffe, William, 163 foll.
Gold, 4.
Gold, Nathan, 80.
Goodrich, Chauncey, 351.
Goodrich, Elizur, 346.
Goodwin, Dr. D. R., 355.
Goodwin, William, 123, 228.
Goodyear, Charles, 364.
Goodyear, Stephen, 102, 103.
Gookin, Daniel, 54.
Gorges grant, 8.
Governor, election of, 76, 77; reëlection, 77; in New Haven, 93, 104.
Granby coppers, 3, 300.

Grant, Gen. U. S., 381.
Greenfield Hill, 44.
Green's Farms, 308.
Greenwich, 150.
Gregory, Commodore F. H., 381.
Griswold, Fort, 312, 313.
Griswold, Gov. Roger, 349.
Groton, 37, 52.
Guilford, 43; origin, 83; people, 84; purchase, 87; settlement, 88; organization, 93.

HADDAM, 267.
Hadley, Mass., 164, 228.
Hale, Captain Nathan, 295.
Hale, Rev. E. E., 367.
Halfway Covenant, the, 227.
Hamilton grant, the, 8, 9, 215, 216.
Hammond, Gov. James H., 375.
Hampshire grants, the, 272.
Hardware, 357.
Harland, Gen. Edward, 381.
Hartford, 6, 7, 11, 15, 22, 34, 56; democracy in, 73; town clerks, 81; early topography, 120; treaty of, 148; made the capital, 174; church, 223, 224; city, 337, 338, 340, 341; manufactures, 358 foll.
Hartford wits, the, 340, 341.
Hartford Convention, the, 350–352.
Harvard College, 239.
Hasselring, Sir Arthur, 110.
Havana, 263.
Hawley, Gen. J. R., 381.
Haynes, John, 18, 21, 80, 123; death, 158.
Haynes, Rev. Joseph, 228.
Hazard, Samuel, 276.
Hempstead, L. I., 139.
Hillhouse, James, 282, 351.
Hillhouse, William, 82.
Hinsdale, Theodore, 367.
Hitchcock, Commodore R. B., 381.
Holland, 145, 154, 193.
Holmes, William, 15.
Hooker, Rev. Thomas, 18, 209; letter to Winthrop, 58, 70; democracy, 69, 73; sermon of 1638, 72; house, 123; death, 158; influence, 221, 321, 322, 365, 385.
Hopkins, Edward, 80, 114, 123; death, 158.
Hopkins grammar schools, 158.
Hopkins, Lemuel, 340.
Hopkinson, Francis, 297.
Horse brand, 269.
Horse Neck, 306.
Howe, George, Lord, 261.
Howe, John J., 360.
Hudson, Henry, 145.
Hull, Captain Isaac, 339.
Humphreys, David, 340, 343.

Humphreysville, 343.
Huntington, Gov. Samuel, 326.
Huntington, L. I., 107, 135, 138.
Hutchinson, Gov. Thomas, 66.
Hutchinson, Mrs. Anne, 51, 84.

INDIAN tribes, 26.
Industrial development, 328 foll.
Ingersoll, Jared, 286.
Ingersoll, Jared, 352.
Insurance, 338, 368.
Interlopers, 339.
Iowa, 11.
Iron, 3, 343–345, 358.

JACKSON, Dr. Abner, 355.
Jefferson, Thomas, 80, 345, 346.
Jerome, Chauncey, 359.
Jesup, Col. T. S., 351.
Johnson, Sir William, 259.
Johnson, William S., 319, 327.
Judges' Cave, the, 164.
Jury, trial by, 189.

KERFOOT, Dr. J. B., 355.
Kieft, Gov. William, 146.
Killingworth, 240.
King Philip's war, 196.
King's Province, 211.
Kingston, Pa., 277.
Kingston, R. I., 212, 213.
Knight, Mrs., 249.
Knox, Gen. Henry, 318.

LABOR Bureau, Connecticut, 365.
Land, 75, 96; in New Hampshire, 94; individual ownership of, 96.
Laud, 83, 108.
Law, Gov. Jonathan, 81, 342.
Lawrence, Henry, 110.
Lead, 3.
Ledyard, 52.
Ledyard, Col. William, 312, 313.
Lee, Gen. Charles, 294.
Leete, Gov. William, 102, 162, 183, 189.
Leffingwell, Thomas, 113.
Legal tender, 254, 257, 258.
Legislature, 57(see General Assembly).
Leisler, 251.
Lexington, 291.
Liberty, Sons of, 97.
Limestone, 4.
Limited Liability, 367.
London Company, 7.
Long Island, 2, 137, 148, 168; becomes a part of New York, 188, 194; in the Revolution, 311.
Long Wharf, the, 339.
Loomis, James C., 376.
Loudoun, the Earl of, 261.
Louisburg, 258, 262.
Ludlow, Roger, 18, 19, 56, 80, 154.

Luzerne county, 284.
Lyman, General Phineas, 260, 262.
Lyme, 267.
Lynn, Mass., 137.
Lyon, General Nathaniel, 381.

McFINGAL, 288.
Macaulay, 387.
Mackintosh, Sir James, 106.
Madison, James, 325.
Magistrates, 70, 76, 77; mode of election, 78; in New Haven, 93.
Malbon, Richard, 92.
Manchester, 342.
Mansfield, 342.
Mansfield, Gen. J. K. F., 381.
Manufactures, 343, 345, 352, 357 foll.
Marble, 4.
Mason, John, 34, 113, 172, 216.
Massachusetts Bay, 14, 17, 18, 61; democracy in, 64, 65; charter, 65, 67, 131, 198; laws, 69; relations with Connecticut, 129; relations to the New England union, 142–152; boundary disputes, 207, 271; in the Revolution, 288.
Maverick, Rev. John, 18, 19.
Mayflower, the, 63.
Mechanics, 357 foll., 361 foll., 374 foll., 388.
Meigs, Col. Return J., 304.
Meriden, 337, 358.
Methodist Church, 237, 352.
Miantonomoh, 28, 36, 47, 48, 50.
Middletown, 2, 135, 136, 337, 355.
Milborn, 252.
Milford, 83, 240; origin, 83; people, 84; purchase, 87; settlement, 88; organization, 93; burgesses, 103.
Militia, 375.
Mohawks, 27.
Mohegan, 29.
Mohegans, 53, 216.
Momaugin, 87.
Money, 248.
Monk, Gen., 163.
Mononotto, 43, 46.
Montowese, 87.
Montreal, 253.
Montville, 54.
Mower, Gen. Jos. A., 381.
Mules, 331.

NAILS, 3.
Narragansett Bay, 14, 173, 210.
Narragansett Indians, 28, 32, 46, 51, 53, 212.
Naugatuck River, 358.
Navigation Act, 155.
Neptune, the, 339.
New Amsterdam, 14; becomes New York city, 188.

INDEX. 407

Newark, N. J., 107, 138.
New Britain, 358.
New Connecticut, 273.
New England, 1.
New England union, 102, 114, 116, 143; difficulties with the Dutch, 147, 152; nullification by Massachusetts, 157; failure, 132, 157.
Newgate, 301.
New Hampshire, 271.
New Haven, 2, 5, 10, 26, 61; origin, 83; people, 84; settlement, 86; purchase, 87; early topography, 88; covenant, 89; constitution, 90; legislation, 98; name, 101; confederation, 102; organization, 103; enters New England Union, 104; the Delaware venture, 146; phantom ship, 155; proposal to migrate, 156; the regicides, 163; proclaims Charles II., 167; included in Connecticut charter, 173; resists, 175; weakness, 175 foll.; yields, 188, 189; Yale at, 241; British at, 244, 308; capital, 270; city, 337–340; embargo, 346; convention, 348; manufactures, 358; proposed negro college, 370.
"New lights," 233, 236.
New London, 5, 40, 135, 140, 337, 349; Arnold's raid, 312.
Newman, Robert, 92.
New Milford, 357.
New tenor, 256.
Newtown (Cambridge), 17.
New York, 193, 197, 205, 207, 282; boundary, 272; in the Revolution, 293, 303, 306; in the confederation, 316, 318.
New York city, 127, 188.
Northampton, Mass., 232.
Norwalk, 135, 136, 223, 309.
Norwich, 48, 113, 135, 141, 217, 337, 358.
"Notions," 357.
Nullification, the first, 157.

Occom, Samson, 55.
Ohio, 127.
Oldham, John, 17, 31.
Old tenor, 256.
Olin, Dr. Stephen, 356.
Owning the covenant, 227.

Palmer, Nathan, 307.
Paper currency, 250 foll.
Parsons, J. C., 127.
Patents, 362, 368.
Patrick, Capt., 36, 42, 45, 150.
Pawcatuck River, the, 210, 213.
Peace party, the, 378.
Peage, 248.
Peddlers, 357.

Peekskill, N. Y., 306.
"Pelham," 350.
Penn, William, 274.
Pennamites and Yankees, 283.
Pennsylvania, 127, 273, 274, 284 (see Wyoming).
Pequot country, the, 3, 59, 139, 209.
Pequot Hill, 37.
Pequot war, the, 34 foll.
Pequots, the, 16, 28, 32, 42, 46, 52, 209.
Percival, J. G., 340.
Peters, Gov. John S., 310.
Peters, Rev. Samuel, 105; his "History," 298; his "natural" history, 299; returns to Connecticut, 310; death, 310.
Peters, Rev. Thomas, 113.
Philadelphia, 274.
Philip's war, King, 196.
Phillips, Rev. George, 18, 19.
Phillips, Wendell, 19.
Pierson, Rev. Abraham, 54, 107, 138.
Pierson, Rev. Abraham, 240.
Pillars, the seven, 90, 92.
Pins, 361.
Pitkin, Gov. William, 287.
Pitt, William, 261.
Plainfield, 267, 269.
Plymouth Company, the, 6, 7, 8, 137, 215.
Plymouth colony, the, 14, 16; democracy, 63.
Pomfret, 261, 307.
Population, 270, 329, 330, 367.
Ponderson, John, 92.
Porter, Pres. Noah, 245.
Port Royal, 253.
Presbyterianism, 230, 232.
Prices, regulation of, 100.
Prison-ships, 298.
Probate courts, 75, 336.
Proclamation money, 258.
Proprietors, 97.
Prudden, Rev. Peter, 88.
Puritans, the, 387.
Putnam, Gen. Israel, 261, 263, 292, 306, 307.
Pynchon, Dr. I. R., 355.
Pynchon, William, 18.

Quakers, the, 175, 236.
Quebec, 253, 262.
Quinnipiack, 85.
Quo warranto, 199.

Railroads, 368.
Randolph, Edward, 198, 211.
Randolph, John, 331.
Raslères, De, 14.
Rates, 137.
Reading, 302, 306.
Regicides, the, 163 foll.

Republican party, the, 369.
Reserve, the Western, 127, 282, 315.
Revolver, the, 363.
Rhode Island, 209 foll., 317.
Richmond grant, the, 8.
Ridgefield, 304.
Rivington, James, 293.
Roads, 125.
Rogers, Commodore C. R. P., 351.
Rogers, Commodore John, 351.
Rossiter, Bray, 178.
Rossiter, John, 178.
Roxbury, 18.
Ruyter, Admiral de, 155.

SACHEM'S Head, 44.
Saffery, 207.
Salem, Mass., 261.
Salisbury, 344.
Saltonstall, Gov. Gurdon, 80.
Saltonstall, Sir Richard, 110.
Sandemanians, the, 346.
Sassacus, 29, 30, 32, 46.
Saugatuck, 303.
Say and Sele grant, the, 8, 9, 23, 109, 168.
Saybrook, 2, 23, 33, 135, 240, 349; name, 112; sold to Connecticut, 115; Commencement at, 242.
Saybrook platform, the, 231 foll., 237.
Schenectady, N. Y., 251.
Schools, 101, 267, 282, 328, 369.
Seabury, Bishop, 238.
Sears, Isaac, 293.
Sedgwick, Gen. John, 381.
Selden, John, 79.
Selectmen, 76, 238, 332, 335, 354.
Senate, 77, 354; of the United States, 326.
Sequin, 33.
Sharp's rifle, 364.
Sheep, 342, 343.
Sherman, Gen. W. T., 381.
Sherman, Roger, 319, 324, 327, 357.
Sherman, Roger Minot, 351.
Sigourney, Mrs. L. H., 340.
Silk, 342.
Silver, 4.
Simsbury, 3, 267, 300.
Six Nations, the, 27.
Slaves, 267.
Slitting-mill, 344.
Smith, Dr. A. W., 356.
Smith, Dr. G. W., 355.
Smith, Gov. John Cotton, 356.
Smith, Nathaniel, 351.
Society, church and, 60.
Somers, John, 204.
"Sons of Liberty," 97, 286.
Southampton, L. I., 135, 138, 223.
Southerton, 210.
South Norwalk, 337.

Southold, L. I., purchased, 88; admission to New Haven, 106, 138; feeling in, 179.
"Sow business," the, 68.
Specie, 250.
Spencer, Gen. Joseph, 292.
Springfield, founded, 20, 25, 56; becomes a Massachusetts town, 58, 143, 208.
Stamford, purchased, 87; feeling in, 179.
Stamp Act, the, 285 foll.
"Stand-up Law," the, 353.
State prison, the, 300.
State sovereignty, 304, 305, 315, 316, 323.
Stedman, Gen. G. A., 381.
Steinwehr, Gen. A. von, 381.
Stiles, Pres. Ezra, 245, 334, 342, 346.
Stirling grant, the, 137.
Stone, Capt., 30.
Stone, Rev. Samuel, 18, 19, 35, 123, 228.
Stonington, 37, 210, 293, 297, 349.
Story, Judge, 66.
Stoughton, William, 42.
Stratford, 135, 235, 237.
Strong, Rev. Nathan, 341.
Stuyvesant, Gov. Peter, 147, 151, 185.
Suffrage, 60, 75, 173, 174, 224, 226, 332, 353, 354; in New Haven, 91, 226; in Massachusetts, 66.
Susquehanna Company, the, 275, 283.
Swamp fight, the, 196, 212.
Swift, Zephaniah, 351.

TALCOTT, John, 57.
Talcott, Joseph, 80.
Tatobam, 29.
Taxation, 78; in kind, 100, 249, 369; lists, 136, 137, 267, 368; church, 224, 229, 231, 237, 354; and paper currency, 254 foll.
Tennant, Rev. Gilbert, 232.
Terry, Eli, 359.
Terry, Gen. A. H., 381.
Thames River, the, 5, 35.
Ticonderoga, 262, 291.
Tinware, 357.
Toleration party, the, 352-53.
Tories, 97, 298, 300, 302, 309, 310, 346.
Totten, Dr. Silas, 355.
Town-system, the, 6, 12, 58, 61, 75, 79, 134, 135, 192, 268, 290, 305; in Massachusetts, 66, 67; in New Haven, 84, 102, 177; in Vermont, 272; in Pennsylvania, 278.
"Town-born," 339.
Township, the, 220, 268.
Tracy, Uriah, 331.
Treadwell, John, 351.
Treat, Gov. Robert, 196, 199-201.

INDEX. 409

Treby, 204.
Trinity College, 355.
Trumbull, Benjamin, 288.
Trumbull, Fort, 312.
Trumbull, Gov. Jonathan, 286, 294.
Trumbull, Gov. Jonathan, 81, 287.
Trumbull, J. H., 71, 288.
Trumbull, John, 287.
Trumbull, John, 288, 340.
Trumbull, H. C., 288.
Trumbull, Lyman, 288.
Tryon, Gov. William, 303, 307, 309.
Turner, Nathaniel, 92, 94.
Tyler, Gen. Daniel, 381.
Tyler, Gen. R. O., 381.

Uncas, 29, 35, 46, 53, 217.
Underhill, Captain John, 38.
Union, the American, 62, 263.
Union, the New England, 102, 114, 116, 143; difficulties with the Dutch, 147, 152; nullification by Massachusetts, 157; failure, 132, 157.
United colonies, the, 49.
Utica, N. Y., 274.

Van Corlear, John, 15.
Vane, Gov. Harry, 32, 33.
Van Tromp, Admiral, 155.
Van Twiller, Gov. Walter, 15.
Vermont, 127, 136, 271, 273, 291.
Vernon, Admiral, 256.
Virginia, 280, 315, 320, 323.

Wadsworth, Captain Joseph, 195, 201.
Walker, Admiral Hovenden, 253.
Wallingford, 267.
Wampum, 248.
Ward, 204.
Warham, Rev. John, 18, 19.
Wars, 250 foll.
Warwick grant, 8, 9, 109, 115, 118.
Warwick Neck, 214.
Washington College, 355.
Washington, George, 294, 295, 311, 317, 343.
Waterbury, 267, 337, 358, 359.
Water power, 360.
Watertown, 17.
Webb, Gen., 261.
Webster, Gov. John, 228.
Wells, Thomas, 80.
Welles, Gideon, 381.
Wentworth, Gov. Benning, 272.
Wentworth, Strafford, Earl of, 108, 115.
Wesleyan University, 355.
Westchester, 186.
Western Reserve, the, 127, 282, 315.
West Haven, 308.
Westmoreland, 277, 279.
West Point, N. Y., 306.

Wethersfield, 11, 21, 22, 33, 56, 312; dissensions in, 93, 134, 164, 223; commencement at, 242; State prison, 301.
Whalley, Edward, 163 foll.
"Whapperknocker," the, 299.
Wharf, the Long, 339.
Wheaton, Dr., 355.
Wheelock, Ebenezer, 55.
Whitfield, Rev. Henry, 88.
Whitefield, Rev. Henry, 232, 234.
Whiting, John, 81.
Whiting, Joseph, 81.
Whiting, Nathan, 260.
Whiting, Rev. Joseph, 228.
Whitney, Eli, 363.
Whitneyville, 363.
Wickford, R. I., 185, 210.
Wigglesworth, Rev. Michael, 228.
William and Mary, 208, 251.
Williams, Dr. John, 355.
Williams, Rev. Elisha, 242.
Williams, Roger, 32.
Wilson, James, 320.
Winchester Arms Co., 364.
Windham, 299.
Windsor, 11, 15, 22, 25, 56.
Winslow, Gov. Edward, 14.
Winthrop, Fitz John, 160, 202, 204, 252.
Winthrop, Jr., John, 8, 23, 77, 80, 110, 343; at Pequot, 140; governor, 160; sent to England, 166; obtains a charter, 177 foll., 210.
Winthrop, Sr., John, 14, 58, 110; letter to Hooker, 66.
Winthrop, Theodore, 380.
Winthrop, Wait, 202.
Wolcott, Henry, 158.
Wolcott, Jr., Henry, 71.
Wolcott, Oliver, 294.
Wolcott, Oliver, 352.
Wolfe, Gen. James, 261.
Wood, John, 245.
Woodbury, 267.
Woodward, 207.
Wool, 342, 343.
Woolsey, Pres. T. D., 245.
Wooster, Gen. David, 292, 303, 304.
Wyllys, George, 81.
Wyllys, Hezekiah, 81.
Wyllys, Samuel, 81.
Wyllys Family, the, 123, 161, 201.
Wyoming, migration to, 127; settlement, 275 foll.; massacre, 278; failure, 279.

Yale College, 101, 238 foll.; University, 247.
Yale, David, 158.
Yale, Elihu, 241.
"Yankee Notions," 357.

American Commonwealths.

EDITED BY
HORACE E. SCUDDER.

A series of volumes narrating the history of such States of the Union as have exerted a positive influence in the shaping of the national government, or have a striking political, social, or economical history.

The commonwealth has always been a positive force in American history, and it is believed that no better time could be found for a statement of the life inherent in the States than when the unity of the nation has been assured; and it is hoped by this means to throw new light upon the development of the country, and to give a fresh point of view for the study of American history.

This series is under the editorial care of Mr. Horace E. Scudder, who is well known both as a student of American history and as a writer.

The aim of the Editor will be to secure trustworthy and graphic narratives, which shall have substantial value as historical monographs and at the same time do full justice to the picturesque elements of the subjects. The volumes are uniform in size and general style with the series of "American Statesmen" and "American Men of Letters," and are furnished with maps, indexes, and such brief critical apparatus as add to the thoroughness of the work.

Speaking of the series, the *Boston Journal* says: "It is clear that this series will occupy an entirely new place in our historical literature. Written by competent and aptly chosen authors, from fresh materials, in convenient form, and with a due regard to proportion and proper emphasis, they promise to supply most satisfactorily a positive want."

PRESS NOTICES.

"VIRGINIA."

Mr. Cooke has made a fascinating volume — one which it will be very difficult to surpass either in method or interest. . . . True historic insight appears through all these pages, and an earnest desire to do all parties and religions perfect justice. The story of the settlement of Virginia is told in full. . . . It is made as interesting as a romance. — *The Critic* (New York).

No more acceptable writer could have been selected to tell the story of Virginia's history. — *Educational Journal of Virginia* (Richmond, Va.).

"OREGON."

The long and interesting story of the struggle of five nations for the possession of Oregon is told in the graphic and reliable narrative of William Barrows. . . . A more fascinating record has seldom been written. . . . Careful research and pictorial skill of narrative commend this book of antecedent history to all interested in the rapid march and wonderful development of our American civilization upon the Pacific coast. — *Springfield Republican.*

There is so much that is new and informing embodied in this little volume that we commend it with enthusiasm. It is written with great ability. — *Magazine of American History* (New York).

"MARYLAND."

With great care and labor he has sought out and studied original documents. By the aid of these he is able to give his work a value and interest that would have been impossible had he followed slavishly the commonly accepted authorities on his subject. His investigation in regard to toleration in Maryland is particularly noticeable. — *New York Evening Post.*

A substantial contribution to the history of America. — *Magazine of American History.*

"KENTUCKY."

Professor Shaler has made use of much valuable existing material, and by a patient, discriminating, and judicious choice has given us a complete and impartial record of the various stages through which this State has passed from its first settlement to the present time. No one will read this story of the building of one of the great commonwealths of this Union without feelings of deep interest, and that the author has done his work well and impartially will be the general verdict. — *Christian at Work* (New York).

A capital example of what a short State history should be. — *Hartford Courant.*

"KANSAS."

In all respects one of the very best of the series. . . . His work exhibits diligent research, discrimination in the selection of materials, and skill in combining his chosen stuff into a narration that has unity, and order, and lucidity. It is an excellent presentation of the important aspects and vital principles of the Kansas struggle. — *Hartford Courant.*

"MICHIGAN."

An ably written and charmingly interesting volume. . . . For variety of incident, for transitions in experience, for importance of events, and for brilliancy and ability in the service of the leading actors, the history of Michigan offers rare attractions; and the writer of it has brought to his task the most excellent gifts and powers as a vigorous, impartial, and thoroughly accomplished historian. — *Christian Register* (Boston).

"CALIFORNIA."

Mr. Royce has made an admirable study. He has established his view and fortified his position with a wealth of illustration from incident and reminiscence. The story is made altogether entertaining. . . . Of the country and its productions, of pioneer life and character, of social and political questions, of business and industrial enterprises, he has given us full and intelligent accounts. — *Boston Transcript.*

It is the most truthful and graphic description that has been written of this wonderful history which has from time to time been written in scraps and sketches. — *Chicago Inter-Ocean.*

HOUGHTON, MIFFLIN & CO., Publishers,
Boston and New York.

NOW READY.

Virginia. A History of the People. By JOHN ESTEN COOKE, author of "The Virginia Comedians," "Life of Stonewall Jackson," "Life of General Robert E. Lee," etc.

Oregon. The Struggle for Possession. By WILLIAM BARROWS, D. D.

Maryland. By WILLIAM HAND BROWNE, Associate of Johns Hopkins University.

Kentucky. By NATHANIEL SOUTHGATE SHALER, S. D., Professor of Palæontology, Harvard University, recently Director of the Kentucky State Survey.

Michigan. By Hon. T. M. COOLEY, LL. D.

Kansas. By LEVERETT W. SPRING, Professor of English Literature in the University of Kansas.

California. By JOSIAH ROYCE, Instructor in Philosophy in Harvard University.

New York. By Hon. ELLIS H. ROBERTS. 2 vols.

Connecticut. By ALEXANDER JOHNSTON, author of a "Handbook of American Politics," Professor of Jurisprudence and Political Economy in the College of New Jersey.

IN PREPARATION.

Tennessee. By JAMES PHELAN, Ph. D. (Leipsic).

Pennsylvania. By Hon. WAYNE MCVEAGH, late Attorney-General of the United States.

Missouri. By LUCIEN CARR, M. A., Assistant Curator of the Peabody Museum of Archæology.

Ohio. By Hon. RUFUS KING.

New Jersey. By AUSTIN SCOTT, Ph. D. Professor of History in Rutgers College.

Others to be announced hereafter. Each volume, with Maps, 16mo, gilt top, $1.25.

American Statesmen.

A Series of Biographies of Men conspicuous in the Political History of the United States.

EDITED BY

JOHN T. MORSE, Jr.

The object of this series is not merely to give a number of unconnected narratives of men in American political life, but to produce books which shall, when taken together, indicate the lines of political thought and development in American history.

The volumes now ready are as follows. —

John Quincy Adams. By JOHN T. MORSE, JR.
Alexander Hamilton. By HENRY CABOT LODGE.
John C. Calhoun. By DR. H. VON HOLST.
Andrew Jackson. By PROF. W. G. SUMNER.
John Randolph. By HENRY ADAMS.
James Monroe. By PRES. DANIEL C. GILMAN.
Thomas Jefferson. By JOHN T. MORSE, JR.
Daniel Webster. By HENRY CABOT LODGE.
Albert Gallatin. By JOHN AUSTIN STEVENS.
James Madison. By SYDNEY HOWARD GAY.
John Adams. By JOHN T. MORSE, JR.
John Marshall. By A. B. MAGRUDER.
Samuel Adams. By JAMES K. HOSMER.
Thomas H. Benton. By THEODORE ROOSEVELT.
Henry Clay. By Hon. CARL SCHURZ. 2 vols.

IN PRESS.

Patrick Henry. By MOSES COIT TYLER.

IN PREPARATION.

George Washington. By HENRY CABOT LODGE. 2 vols.
Martin Van Buren. By HON. WM. DORSHEIMER.

Others to be announced hereafter. Each volume, 16mo, gilt top, $1.25.

ESTIMATES OF THE PRESS.

"JOHN QUINCY ADAMS."

That Mr. Morse's conclusions will in the main be those of posterity we have very little doubt, and he has set an admirable example to his coadjutors in respect of interesting narrative, just proportion, and judicial candor. — *New York Evening Post.*

Mr. Morse has written closely, compactly, intelligently, fearlessly, honestly. — *New York Times.*

"ALEXANDER HAMILTON."

The biography of Mr. Lodge is calm and dignified throughout. He has the virtue — rare indeed among biographers — of impartiality. He has done his work with conscientious care, and the biography of Hamilton is a book which cannot have too many readers. It is more than a biography; it is a study in the science of government. — *St. Paul Pioneer-Press.*

"JOHN C. CALHOUN."

Nothing can exceed the skill with which the political career of the great South Carolinian is portrayed in these pages. The work is superior to any other number of the series thus far, and we do not think it can be surpassed by any of those that are to come. The whole discussion in relation to Calhoun's position is eminently philosophical and just. — *The Dial* (Chicago).

"ANDREW JACKSON."

Prof. Sumner has, . . . all in all, made the justest long estimate of Jackson that has had itself put between the covers of a book. — *New York Times.*

One of the most masterly monographs that we have ever had the pleasure of reading. It is calm and clear. — *Providence Journal.*

"JOHN RANDOLPH."

The book has been to me intensely interesting. . . . It is rich in new facts and side lights, and is worthy of its place in the already brilliant series of monographs on American Statesmen. — Prof. MOSES COIT TYLER.

Remarkably interesting. . . . The biography has all the elements of popularity, and cannot fail to be widely read. — *Hartford Courant.*

"JAMES MONROE."

In clearness of style, and in all points of literary workmanship, from cover to cover, the volume is well-nigh perfect. There is also a calmness of judgment, a correctness of taste, and an absence of partisanship which are too frequently wanting in biographies, and especially in political biographies. — *American Literary Churchman* (Baltimore).

The most readable of all the lives that have ever been written of the great jurist. — *San Francisco Bulletin.*

"THOMAS JEFFERSON."

The book is exceedingly interesting and readable. The attention of the reader is strongly seized at once, and he is carried along in spite of himself, sometimes protesting, sometimes doubting, yet unable to lay the book down. — *Chicago Standard.*

The requirements of political biography have rarely been met so satisfactorily as in this memoir of Jefferson. — *Boston Journal.*

"DANIEL WEBSTER."

It will be read by students of history; it will be invaluable as a work of reference; it will be an authority as regards matters of fact and criticism; it hits the key-note of Webster's durable and ever-growing fame; it is adequate, calm, impartial; it is admirable. — *Philadelphia Press.*

The task has been achieved ably, admirably, and faithfully. — *Boston Transcript.*

"ALBERT GALLATIN."

It is one of the most carefully prepared of these very valuable volumes, . . . abounding in information not so readily accessible as is that pertaining to men more often treated by the biographer. . . . The whole work covers a ground which the political student cannot afford to neglect. — *Boston Correspondent Hartford Courant.*

Frank, simple, and straightforward. — *New York Tribune.*

"JAMES MADISON."

The execution of the work deserves the highest praise. It is very readable, in a bright and vigorous style, and is marked by unity and consecutiveness of plan. — *The Nation* (New York).

An able book. . . . Mr. Gay writes with an eye single to truth. — *The Critic* (New York).

"JOHN ADAMS."

A good piece of literary work. . . . It covers the ground thoroughly, and gives just the sort of simple and succinct account that is wanted. — *Evening Post* (New York).

A model of condensation and selection, as well as of graphic portraiture and clear and interesting historical narrative. — *Christian Intelligencer* (New York).

"JOHN MARSHALL."

Well done, with simplicity, clearness, precision, and judgment, and in a spirit of moderation and equity. A valuable addition to the series. — *New York Tribune.*

"SAMUEL ADAMS."

Thoroughly appreciative and sympathetic, yet fair and critical. . . . This biography is a piece of good work — a clear and simple presentation of a noble man and pure patriot; it is written in a spirit of candor and humanity. — *Worcester Spy.*

A brilliant and enthusiastic book, which it will do every American much good to read. — *The Beacon* (Boston).

⁎ *For sale by all booksellers. Sent, post-paid, on receipt of price by the Publishers,*

HOUGHTON, MIFFLIN & COMPANY,

BOSTON AND NEW YORK.

www.ingramcontent.com/pod-product-compliance
Lightning Source LLC
Chambersburg PA
CBHW020542300426
44111CB00008B/758